WAYS OF MANKIND

WAYS OF MANKIND

THE BEACON PRESS · BOSTON

WAYS OF MANKIND

THIRTEEN DRAMAS OF PEOPLES OF THE WORLD AND HOW THEY LIVE, BY

Lister Sinclair

Len Peterson

Eugene S. Hallman

George Salverson

EDITED AND WITH COMMENTARY BY

Walter Goldschmidt

ILLUSTRATED BY

Arminta Neal

THE BEACON PRESS • BOSTON

LP record albums of the original radio programs of *Ways of Mankind* are available on order to schools, institutions, and others from the National Association of Educational Broadcasters, University of Illinois, Urbana, Illinois.

Library of Congress catalog card number: 54–8422

Copyright 1954

THE NATIONAL ASSOCIATION

OF EDUCATIONAL BROADCASTERS

Printed in U.S.A.

CONTENTS

⇛⇛⇛

WAYS OF MANKIND

INTRODUCTION

The world is both storybook and museum. And of the many wonders of the world, the greatest is man himself and the many ways of life that he has developed in the half-million years of his existence on six continents and a myriad of islands.

The world is a storybook because its tales are many and its drama varied. The infinite diversity of human thoughts and actions, the wonderful devices which have been the product of man's ingenuity, and the even more imaginative stories he has invented about his world—all give to the story of man the dimensions of fiction. It is fitting that we use the form of the play to describe these many ways of mankind.

But the world is also a museum. The world is real, man's behavior is real; they are a proper subject for the scholar and the scientist. Therefore, it is proper also that these dramas be the stories of the real world. They come out of the works of students of society who have made the world their laboratory, and human social behavior the artifacts they study.

In all drama there is unity and diversity; so too with ours. For the most important lesson that studies of man provide is the lesson that human societies share certain essential forms, despite their many specific differences. Common threads run through the diverse fabrics of each society. We will return again and again to this idea because it is the most important one our studies have to make. And we must never lose sight of the fact that we—you and I and the members of our own society—share this unity.

All of us, everywhere in the world, have grown up surrounded by parents, by the more remote kin of aunts, uncles, and grandparents, by neighbors and friends. All these people share a basic set of ideas, a way of seeing things and speaking about them, a way of doing things and of feeling about them. As we grow up we come to share these thoughts and feelings, these customs and understandings. For reasons that are clear and simple, this fact of growing up into an already existing society is true for all human beings, in al places, and at all times. In terms of anthropology, this can be said more shortly: All men live in societies and acquire the behavior of the societies in which they live. For man by his very nature is committed to living with his fellows; he lives by learning and learns the ways his companions teach him. These ways are called culture.

The culture we acquire is like the air we breathe: we take it for granted. In a sense, we cannot see our own culture, because it is too much a part of us. Since it is everywhere, it is nowhere. We confuse culture with all mankind—for our own culture is to us the very nature of mankind. So too with other peoples living in other cultures. Primitive peoples often translate the name they give themselves as "man," in contrast to their name for neighboring tribes or "non-man"—barbarians.

It is both natural and proper that we should feel that our culture is somehow right, that it is the best in the world. It is natural for the reason already mentioned: we grow up to know it as the ways of the world. And it is quite *proper* that we have this feeling—for a healthy society requires its members to feel committed to its assumptions; it demands of them loyalties that are deep and continuous. Societies are made of people, but people form societies only when they share a common culture and share it both with sentiment and with conviction. Loyalties are as necessary as they are inevitable.

The need for commitment has its reverse side: it makes for disrespect of others, for prejudice, discrimination, and blindness. In the modern world, this is unfortunate. For the vision of the present is the vision of a single world living in peace and harmony, not under unified rule of a single power or through the adoption of a single cultural system, but rather through learning mutual respect for the different ways of peoples in other parts of the world. We need, each of us, to cherish our own culture for ourselves, while still recognizing that other peoples may find other ways of life more satisfying.

To achieve this mutual respect we must have understanding—mere tolerance won't do. It is for just this reason that the scholars who study the behavior of human beings and the manner of life of the exotic peoples in foreign parts have taken on a special importance in recent years. But it is not enough for this understanding to be the possession of specialists and scholars. To be useful, it must be shared by all. For the understanding of other peoples must be the work of all of us or it bears no fruit; it must underlie policy in actions that determine or influence international relations. And this, in turn, means that people must want policies based upon such understanding.

This is the broad and bold aim of this book—to present real understanding of major issues in human behavior in a form that people can enjoy and comprehend.

1. CULTURE

Cultures are many, though man is one. Each people has its own set of solutions to the universal imperatives of human social life. The manner in which they meet these challenges is their culture.

Culture may be thought of as a force affecting all human behavior. To understand any act of any person, you must see it in the setting of the culture to which he belongs. Our capacity for culture, as we have seen, rests on our biological heritage. But culture itself is not merely a response to biological needs. The range of cultural responses is great, and the particular cultural forms of any particular society derive from its historical and environmental backgrounds. The culture of any one people is a unique set of solutions to general biological and social needs.

Culture is the pattern of learned behavior shared by the members of a society. It includes not only the way of making things and doing things, but the pattern of relationships among people, the attitudes they foster, the beliefs and ideas they have, and even the feelings with which they respond. Culture is not merely customs—though customs are a part of culture. For culture is the patterned whole of responses, the more or less consistent unity that links the many diverse elements of living into a way of life.

Since culture is learned, it is acquired by each person as he grows up. Some of his culture he learns by unconscious imitation, some by deliberate copying, and some he is conscientiously taught. An infant begins to experience his culture from the moment of birth: Is he wrapped in soft cloth or tied to a cradle board? Is he handled by an impersonal nurse in spotless uniform or is he secluded in a special hut with his mother? Are scientific formulas prepared for him, or is there a shaman's incantation? Henceforward the infant, the child, the youth, even the old man is normally surrounded by people who share his culture, and this culture is communicated or reinforced by every experience. Culture is the learned behavior he shares with his society.

If culture is learned it must pass from one generation to the next; it stands to reason that it continues through time. Our own culture is a product of centuries of development. Some features can be traced back to ancient Greece and Rome; some, we are certain, had their origins in the later Stone Age. Of course, cultures do not remain the same from one time to another. New techniques are learned from neighbors; new things are invented; new styles, new needs, and new situations arise. So cultures change. This is indeed the advantage of cultural behavior over instinctive behavior—the relative ease with which it can change to meet new conditions or to master new environments.

Culture not only changes but also accumulates. Throughout the centuries that man has been capable of culture, he has discovered new things, invented new devices, found new answers. To be sure, he has often lost knowledge no longer useful because conditions have changed, or techniques have become obsolete through the invention of better techniques. For instance, the chipping of flint is practically a lost art, since flint tools are little used in modern life. But, on the whole, this accumulation means added mastery of the environment, more control by man over his fate. And when man conceives of writing and records his knowledge, when it is preserved in books and always available, then there is no end to the knowledge that can be accumulated. For it no longer depends upon human memories.

The cultures that have been built for centuries on the knowledge of writing have outdistanced those in the more remote parts of the globe. Before the era of exploration, the knowledge of inventions developed in the centers of civilization in the Near East, in southern Asia, in Europe, and in Middle America did not spread through all parts of the world. Crucial inventions and discoveries, such as farming and herding, the use of metals and writing, failed to reach South Africa, Australia, the polar regions, and elsewhere. Some peoples could not use the new techniques for environmental reasons, others because the routes were too long or blocked.

Our culture is in the direct line of descent from the sources of many of these inventions—which were not all made by Europeans. Ours is a complex culture, with a great total store of knowledge. But we must not confuse complexity with superiority, or greater mastery over environment with moral virtue. All cultures, even the poorest known to the anthropologists, are extremely complex and contain far more than can be set forth in detail.

We can best understand the complexity of cultures by thinking of the many faces a culture must have. In the first place, all cultures have a vast store of technical knowledge. Think of our engineering, and agriculture, and medicine, and the host of other specialities. All people have stores of such technical knowledge, each worked out in minute detail: the feathering of an arrow, just where certain fruits will be ripe in the valley, how best to stalk the elk, the gathering of grasses and roots for basketry, the construction of a house. On and on run the details—yet this is only one department of culture.

Language is a second important aspect. Probably no dictionary is as long as our own English dictionary; but they are all extensive. Each language has its own complexities of grammar and syntax, with its proper usages for particular occasions—such as polite forms and current slang.

From language, we may turn to the realm of ideas. All peoples have systematic beliefs about the origin of the world, about the beginning of man and the reasons for his way of life; all people have notions of right and wrong, of propriety and impropriety. Every culture has so large a mythology that it is doubtful if all the stories known to all the members of a single tribe of primitive people have ever been recorded by any anthropologist.

These suggest another department, the arts. All cultures find esthetic enjoyment in song, dance, and decoration. The intricacy and variety of songs, dances, and bodily decoration for almost any tribe could fill large volumes. There are not only techniques to be learned but also canons of taste—for each culture has its own way of defining the beautiful.

In every culture, also, the relations among individuals are defined. *Status* and *role* are universal—but each culture has its own way of viewing status, and its own definition of the proper role for each status. Authority is always allocated—but not necessarily to the same persons, or for the same reasons, or with the same delineation of powers. Groups are everywhere defined—but here they may be a matter of age, there a matter of birth, and again a matter of some special criterion.

Even feelings are influenced by one's culture. Some are obvious, such as our own dislike of the idea of eating grubs or dogs, which other people find delicious. But others are not so obvious—our attitudes toward our sisters; our feelings about failure or competition; our spine-tingling sensations roused by words like *nation* or *mother*. These are culturally established: that is, we do not inherit such sentiments, but we *acquire* them as part of our cultural behavior. The fact that such sentiments are derived from culture makes them no less real, no less important; let there be no mistake on this score. The cultural world is a real world; the feeling of revulsion we have toward the eating of grubs, or the fear found among some people when they see a whirlwind, is a real revulsion, a real fear. They move men as firmly as the revulsion toward poison or the fear of a forest fire. Men act in terms of the beliefs and feelings they acquire through their culture. They will die readily in battles fought by cultural directive.

All cultures are complex, covering a wide arc of human behavior and touching upon every human act. But culture is not a mere hodgepodge of knowledge and ideas and things and feelings. It is an integrated whole, a patterned fabric. The various parts are in harmony with one another. To see the harmony among the various parts of culture one must look at one particular culture.

"Stand-in for a Murderer" tells of the Tlingit Indians, who dwelt in the rich fiord region of southeast Alaska and had a rich culture to match. Social life revolved about two interrelated factors: the clan organization and the emphasis upon wealth and status.

Clans were large groups of people who felt themselves to be related by descent through a common ancestor and thus a common relation to a mythical "totem" animal. The clans dwelt in large plank houses, many families to a house, and owned and shared the fishing and gathering places. Clan membership followed from the mother's side, so that boys inherited from their uncles—their mothers' brothers. Clans regulated marriage, initiation ceremonies, funeral ceremonies. The clan thus was a family unit with common residence, common property, common ceremonies, all encompassed by a feeling of religious unity. In many ways each clan was a unit unto itself; the relations among clans rested less on government than on custom, with some resort to clan feuds. Some clans were more powerful than others.

The rich resources of the area made it possible to accumulate many goods, and the

Tlingit set great store by property. They jealously guarded their lands, but they also had many forms of wealth—great ceremonial copper shields, elaborate hand-woven blankets, stored foods, and property associated with crests, titles, and special ceremonial privileges. The property resided with the clans but was held by individual persons, so that a man's station depended on the property he inherited. Though clans were family units, the members had widely different positions of prestige, and they jealously guarded their prerogatives. Status was elaborately calibrated, and any gathering was dominated by protocol. Moreover, the Tlingit personality was dominated by pride, and any slight might result in reprisal. The relation of pride to wealth was direct: a person suffering an insult would fling money before his tormentor to wipe out the shame.

The relative positions of individuals rested on wealth, and ceremonies among clans took the form of great feasts, or potlatches. These were lavish displays of the hosts' generosity; not only was food consumed in great quantities, but much was wasted, and the feast concluded with the giving of elaborate gifts and the destruction of much wealth. Such performances demonstrated the power and prestige of the clan; its leaders hoped to shame their guests by giving more than could be returned. Even if these feasts left the clan destitute of food and treasures, they re-established its prestige and reaffirmed its rights to the land. The acts were preserved in memory by the carving of elaborate totem poles that symbolized the privileges and rights.

The pattern of Tlingit culture was exuberant, with property as the goad to action, with the display of wealth as the symbol of virtue, with pride and arrogance as the dominant personality motifs. These reappear in every facet of Tlingit social life. It is in this context, and in the context of clan unity and clan loyalty, that it was possible for a Tlingit Indian to act as stand-in for a murderer.

Stand-in for a Murderer

LEN PETERSON

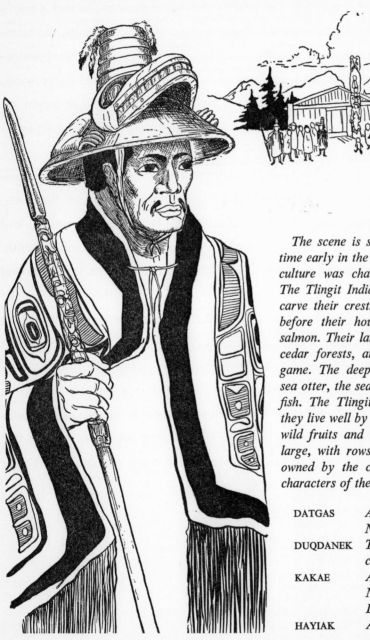

The scene is set in southeast Alaska, some time early in the nineteenth century, before the culture was changed by modern civilization. The Tlingit Indians are one of the tribes who carve their crests on giant totem poles to set before their houses. Their rivers teem with salmon. Their lands are covered with pine and cedar forests, and these are filled with wild game. The deep fiords are the home of the sea otter, the seal, the salmon, and many other fish. The Tlingit Indians' country is rich, and they live well by hunting, fishing, and gathering wild fruits and vegetables. Their villages are large, with rows of great plank houses, each owned by the clan that lives within it. The characters of the story are:

DATGAS   *A young nobleman of the Nanyaayi clan.*

DUQDANEK   *The old chief of the Nanyaayi clan.*

KAKAE   *A young nobleman of the Nanyaayi, higher in rank than Datgas.*

HAYIAK   *Another Nanyaayi noble.*

➤➤➤-➤➤

HAIMAS   *A young noble of the Kanhaades clan.*

TSAGUEDI   *Chief of the Kanhaades clan.*

DATGAS

I go to my glory and my death. I go willingly, my chief.

DUQDANEK

Keep before you, Datgas, only the honor of your clan, the Nanyaayi.

DATGAS

And the shame to my clan if I do not go forth to mock battle to be killed.

KAKAE

You die a great warrior, Datgas.

DATGAS

And there will be an end to the humiliation the Kanhaades feel for the killing of their warrior Haimas by our noble Kakae. I die for Kakae's deed.

DUQDANEK

Outside, the Kanhaades and the Nanyaayi are drawn up, waiting still.

DATGAS

I go; bearing high the honor of the Nanyaayi!

[MUSIC]

DATGAS

(*Chanting.*) Floating down from the Stikine, he thinks about the lives of the Nanyaayi children. I am very glad you took pity on me. Now I am going up to the ghost world. Yaiiia—aia—

(*The battle begins with clash of spear against shield.*)

NARRATOR

Datgas made a show of attacking. He was quick, strong, and brave. Always in battle he had felt most alive and worthy of his ancestors and his clan. His adversary now, though a great chief and honorable brave, was not so quick and strong. Again and again Datgas might have thrust his spear or knife through the aging chief's defense. Datgas easily parried Tsaguedi's thrusts—until he recalled his duty

to his clan. He fought carelessly then, and Tsaguedi thrust his spear home—into the heart of Datgas the warrior.

[MUSIC]

ANTHROPOLOGIST

This scene takes place in front of the cedar-plank houses of the Tlingit Indians of southeast Alaska. Datgas, a skillful warrior, sacrifices his life in mock combat with a rival chieftain. To us this seems a foolish, an insane act. To Datgas and his people, it was neither. Many things that people of foreign lands do seem strange to us, because we don't understand the whys and wherefores of the acts. Such behavior is understood by the anthropologist in terms of the culture.

Let us try to understand the action of Datgas in terms of the Tlingit culture. Consider first a sense of property:

[MUSIC]

NARRATOR

Spring slipped down the mountains into the valleys of southeast Alaska and quickly turned into summer. Every day the snowline moved noticeably farther up the mountainsides. The Nanyaayi clan of the Tlingit Indians gathered along the Stikine River. The time of the salmon run was at hand. Last year it had not been good, but this year when it came it was bountiful indeed.

With spear and gaff they pulled the large, firm, tasty fish from the foaming torrent. The first salmon they caught was treated with the same respect they paid to a chief. A feast was given in its honor to win its forgiveness and good will. Then fishing went on. Some of the salmon was cooked, but most of it was split and hung from the rafters of the huts to dry. The Nanyaayi were happy. They would have food for a long time to come. (*Pause.*) But then like a storm cloud some news brought by one of their warriors, Datgas, moved a shadow across the vista ahead.

[MUSIC]

DATGAS
The Kanhaades are here.

KAKAE
Where?

DATGAS
Down the river at the cataracts.

KAKAE
How many?

DATGAS
It is a large band, Kakae, much larger than ours.

KAKAE
Do they come to fight, Datgas?

DATGAS
They have their women and babies with them. They are building huts and setting their Raven crests out front. They have even raised a totem pole.

DUQDANEK
They have come to stay. They have come to take our fishing waters.

HAYIAK
Are their hunting grounds and fishing waters not already vast?

DUQDANEK
The salmon do not fill their rivers as they do the Stikine.

KAKAE
We shall attack them and drive them away! Call the head men. Gather in my sweatroom for a council of war.

DUQDANEK
We are outnumbered, Datgas says.

KAKAE
Bravery and fierceness are better than numbers, Duqdanek. Attack without warning, attack them at night.

DUQDANEK
The Kanhaades is a large and scattered clan.

HAYIAK
Yes, if we ambush those down the Stikine from here and kill them all, that will not end it—only begin it.

DATGAS
Did they not force us to leave our old hunting ground? Do we let them drive us on again?

DUQDANEK
Long ago that was. In peace we have lived many seasons. We are of the same great Tlingit nation, many of their women are our wives—

KAKAE
A cause for war—

HAYIAK
You are young, Kakae, and wish for trophies. But not this time. You are noble and brave; enough trophies will come your way.

DUQDANEK
We shall hold a potlatch, a feast, for the Kanhaades.

HAYIAK
And shame them into leaving our fishing grounds.

DUQDANEK
Gather all your wealth, Hayiak, Kakae, and Datgas. The Kanhaades have given many great potlatches, but this will surpass any of them. Their hosts they will dare not insult further by remaining on our fishing grounds. We shall shame them with great gifts, shame them, shame them. In dark humiliation they will withdraw.

[MUSIC]

ANTHROPOLOGIST
But what's this? Protection of property by giving it away? Defeating an enemy by giving him a feast? Yes, this is in the pattern of Tlingit culture—and probably the most economic military tactic in the world. For honor comes to those who can outgive their rivals, who can make the greater display of generosity —a game perhaps not unknown to hostesses in our culture. But here among the Tlingit it is a dominant cultural motif: the famous potlatch ceremony, the rival gift-giving. Let's see how it works out.

[MUSIC]

CHANT

There is a rich man coming. Keep silent. When it is ended, they always say, "It is all gone." There is a rich man coming. Keep silent. When it is ended, they always say, "It is all gone."

NARRATOR

The potlatch was arranged. The Kanhaades accepted the invitation of the Nanyaayi, and came wearing their ceremonial costumes and carrying their valuable emblems engraved on copper shields, emblems inherited and emblems won. The Nanyaayi greeted them wearing their finest costumes. Food was piled in great stacks, deer meat, berries, salmon, trout, and wooden boxes full of candlefish oil. There were songs, storytelling, speeches, and much exchanging of gifts. Fur blankets, slaves, cedar-log canoes, and copper shields changed hands, each clan trying to outdo the other in generosity. Gifts were destroyed in the great fires to add to the ostentation. And slaves were killed—to the accompaniment of a chant.

[DRUMS]

CHANT

The words of people are now backing down
    on me, the words of worthless people.
The words of people are now backing down
    on me, the words of worthless people.
(*A voice cries out in great pain and the chant increases in intensity*.)
The words of people are now backing down
    on me, the words of worthless people!
The words of worthless people! . . . The words
    of worthless people, the words of worthless
    people, the words of worthless people. . .

DUQDANEK

(*Watching the scene of the potlatch ceremony with Hayiak.*)
Hayiak, we have given away more than the Kanhaades.

HAYIAK

Yes, Duqdanek, we have shamed them. They have nothing more of value to give away or destroy.

DUQDANEK

They look over at us with sullen eyes.

HAYIAK

They will slink away.

DUQDANEK

Look! Kakae comes out with still another copper shield.

HAYIAK

It is not needed. They are already beaten.

DUQDANEK

Kakae must win grandly; that is Kakae in everything.

HAYIAK

But who is he giving it to? To one of their lesser nobles, Haimas. What is that for?

DUQDANEK

Haimas is small, but his talk has been big. Kakae would shut him up forever.

[DRUMS]

KAKAE

(*At the scene of the potlatch, taunting Haimas with a chant.*)
Haimas only made a pretense with cedar bark.
He made it into copper plates.
Will you come back here?

Do you think we never have feasts, the Nanyaayi?

HAYIAK

That has made Haimas very angry. He is not going to attack Kakae?

DUQDANEK

No, he is going to answer with a song.

HAIMAS

Kakae!

[DRUMS]

HAIMAS

(*Chanting in reply.*) Kakae, I hate what you say, I hate to have you talk to me—because you have spots all over your face.

DUQDANEK

Oh, grave insult.

HAIMAS

And you look like a slave!

KAKAE

Haimas, I am Kakae, one of the noblest of the Nanyaayi, and for what you have just said, you die!

HAYIAK

Kakae has unsheathed his knife. (*The crowd reacts in fear.*) He has stabbed Haimas! (*The crowd reacts in anger; a voice is heard above the noise.*)

VOICE

Haimas is dead!

HAYIAK

Now there will be a war.

[MUSIC]

ANTHROPOLOGIST

The enemy was vanquished with gifts. But now another element in Tlingit culture intervenes, for in Tlingit culture wealth and property are measures of status, and status is jealously guarded, and in such a culture there are excesses of pride that endanger the peace and safety. The Tlingit and their neighbors are deeply concerned with face, they are resentful, suspicious, and hostile. Such personality traits seem to the Tlingit to be the very nature of man.

Another aspect of Tlingit culture comes to the fore—the strength of clan organization and clan loyalty.

[MUSIC]

DUQDANEK

(*The crowd is still angry.*) I must prevent a battle. If I can get between them with my sacred Grizzly Bear emblem—
(*The murmuring grows louder as Duqdanek rushes to reach them.*)
No, no, do not fight, do not fight, Nanyaayi and Kanhaades! There will be retribution! No, no, do not make war! Honor the Grizzly Bear crest and the Wolf crest of the Nanyaayi, and the Raven crest of the Kanhaades! There will be justice!

[MUSIC]

TSAGUEDI

We honor the Grizzly Bear crest and the Raven crest. If there is justice, we shall not make war.

DUQDANEK

Tsaguedi of the Kanhaades, never have the Nanyaayi failed in justice.

TSAGUEDI

Duqdanek of the Nanyaayi, Haimas who has been killed belonged to the council of chiefs; he was the son of a great chief, Dexhintadeuxe, slain fighting against the Kwakiutl. Haimas was a brave warrior. And the feasts he has given have raised his prestige high.

DUQDANEK

But he is not the equal of Kakae who killed him.

TSAGUEDI

And so we do not ask for the death of Kakae. But the warrior from your clan who is to die must be the equal of Haimas in bravery, wealth, and prestige.

DUQDANEK

The warrior chosen will not dishonor your warrior Haimas. At least he will be the equal of the dead Haimas. We would not dishonor our clan by sacrificing less than you have lost.

>>>->>>

TSAGUEDI

We are the people who feel higher than all others in the world.

DUQDANEK

We are the people who feel higher than all others in the world.

[MUSIC]

NARRATOR

The head men of the Nanyaayi clan and the head men of the Kanhaades clan met to choose the warrior who was to die for the murder of Haimas. Several warriors were selected by the Nanyaayi chiefs, but in the eyes of the Kanhaades chiefs they were not of the rank of the slain warrior. Several warriors suggested by the Kanhaades chiefs were, according to the Nanyaayi chiefs, of far too high rank to be sacrificed for the slaying of a minor noble. The haggling went on for a full day, and not until sundown did they settle on a warrior acceptable to both clans.

[MUSIC]

DUQDANEK

I shall go to him then and inform him and tell him to prepare.

TSAGUEDI

His death will bring honor to himself, and to the slain Haimas, and to our two clans.

[MUSIC]

DUQDANEK

So that justice and honor be done to Haimas of the Kanhaades, killed while a guest of our potlatch, you are to die—Datgas.

DATGAS

I am to die, my chief.

DUQDANEK

You are to be slain in combat, you are to die a great warrior, Datgas.

DATGAS

I am to die a great warrior, my chief.

DUQDANEK

Prepare for the battle, Datgas.

DATGAS

I shall prepare.

KAKAE

Datgas!

DATGAS

Kakae, who slew Haimas, speak!

KAKAE

We have weathered together many storms on the open water, Datgas, and together have hunted along many trails. Back to back we have fought off the Haida, the Kwakiutl, and our Raven clans. But now I have forced you into a battle alone—to die for your clan.

DATGAS

The great Kakae could not die to make good the death of the lowly Haimas. I know that one day you will die in a manner equal to your noble rank, Kakae.

KAKAE

In songs of the Nanyaayi, and in stories, the name of Datgas will be remembered and handed down.

DATGAS

I shall prepare for the combat.

DUQDANEK

The time is yours to choose.

DATGAS

My fasting begins at this hour. I shall want a while to bid farewell to my brothers and my wife and young ones. I shall speak to the Wolf and the Grizzly Bear. And then I shall be ready.

[MUSIC]

NARRATOR

The day of the execution. Datgas drew on his ceremonial garments, his Grizzly Bear cloak, and his bear headpiece with eyes and ears of abalone shell. And he stepped forth from his house. His clan were assembled on either side. Across the clearing were the Kanhaades.

DATGAS

(*Delivering an oration.*) Long ago during the flood the Nanyaayi climbed the mountain Sekuqleca on the Stikine River, and a grizzly bear and a mountain goat followed them. When my people stopped, the bear and the goat stopped, and when they moved again the bear and the goat followed. At last they killed the bear and kept its skin with the claws and the teeth. So we claim the grizzly bear for our own. In the time we have had the bearskin we have given away many slaves and many furs. It is for this reason we give great names to our children. All Tlingit speak of the Nanyaayi as the chief ones owning the grizzly bear.

[DRUMS]

DATGAS

(*Chanting.*) Come here, you bear, the highest bear of all bears.

Come here, you bear, the highest bear of all bears.

Come here, you bear, the highest bear of all bears.

[MUSIC]

NARRATOR

Datgas went on at considerable length, as was the custom among the Tlingit Indians, telling of the deeds of his clan and his ancestors and ending with his own history. Then he looked over at the Kanhaades. One of their number in ceremonial robes and with painted face had moved out from the others, a shell-tipped spear in one hand, a knife in the other. This was the man who was to slay him in mock combat—in mock but glorious combat. But before he had come far, Datgas scowled and raised his arm.

DATGAS

Stop! Come no farther! Who is this you send to fight with me? Kaogu! Kaogu, who has fought in but three battles, and in one of which he ran! What emblems can he show me? How much did he pay for his bride? Was it ten blankets and one old canoe? Kaogu! At the only feast he ever gave he was mercilessly shamed! Send me a warrior,

a chief—worthy to do battle with me, worthy to claim the death of Datgas!

[MUSIC]

NARRATOR

Shaking and pale with anger and humiliation, Datgas turned and strode back into his house. The Nanyaayi were proud of their warrior Datgas. This moment would go down in their legends. Datgas was aware of his greatness and he would accept death at the hands of no warrior less noble and brave than himself. So it was to be. So it had always been ordered. The Nanyaayi standing there felt they had taken on new prestige, felt more closely bound together as a clan. They waited with staring black eyes for the Kanhaades to rectify their blunder. The Kanhaades chiefs gathered in council. And Datgas brooded in his house. He had come out to die, but death had come to him in a miserable guise and he he had refused it. Now he must prepare again.

[MUSIC]

DATGAS

I have faced death many times; I can face it once more. But I was prepared to meet it as a friend. Now I cannot. But still I shall go out again—to keep our two clans at peace and maintain the high honor of my clan. Do we not say there is no greater act for a Tlingit Indian? But I shall miss many things.

DUQDANEK

Datgas! Datgas!

DATGAS

My chief, Duqdanek!

DUQDANEK

The greatest chief among the Kanhaades has come forward.

DATGAS

To offer another poor warrior to slay me in combat?

DUQDANEK

No, Datgas.

DATGAS

Or is it a slave they offer now? Tell them I shall defend myself and strike back! If they do not send a warrior worthy of me I shall kill him and fling money after him to pay for his corpse!

DUQDANEK

Datgas, their greatest chief, Tsaguedi himself, has come forward to join with you in combat. He invited you to come. The highest honor, he says, is due you.

DATGAS

Tsaguedi will fight me?

DUQDANEK

He is confident you are worthy.

DATGAS

I shall go to meet him!

DUQDANEK

Kakae, place the Grizzly Bear cloak on Datgas once more. Hayiak, hand him his spear.

DATGAS

And my knife. The battle of Datgas and Tsaguedi. I go to my glory and my death.

[MUSIC]

NARRATOR

Datgas moved forward with a lithe, brave step to meet Tsaguedi, his adversary and executioner.

[DRUMS]

DATGAS

Floating down from the Stikine,
He thinks about the lives of the Nanyaayi children.
I am very glad you took pity on me.
Now I am going up to the ghost world.
Yaiiia—aia—

(*The battle begins with clash of spear against shield.*)

NARRATOR

And so, as we already know, Datgas died. With pomp and circumstance, with head held high, he died in a mock battle with a man of high honor whom he might easily have slain.

[MUSIC]

TSAGUEDI

I have seen no braver death on the field of battle than his death at my hands this day.

DUQDANEK

Hayiak, have his body laid out in state—the body of a noble and brave warrior.

KAKAE

I brought shame to the Nanyaayi clan; he removed it. I shall raise a totem pole in his honor. The great carver Oyai of the Canyon tribe shall carve it. It will tell of the greatness of Datgas.

DUQDANEK

His soul has gone to Kiwa-Kawa, the highest heaven.

[MUSIC]

ANTHROPOLOGIST

And so Datgas' soul went to the highest heaven, and we learn that Datgas' brave act was inspired by religion as well as by clan loyalty and personal pride. In the Tlingit religion, death in battle was a sacred death that had its reward in afterlife, but Datgas' sacrifice was considered even more sacred. The clan will enshrine this deed as the sacred symbol on its totem pole as inspiration for its future generations.

[DRUMS]

NARRATOR

The affair ended with a peace dance. The two clans gathered once again facing each other at some distance.

TSAGUEDI

Men of the Nanyaayi, come exchange with me!

DUQDANEK

Men of the Kanhaades, come exchange with me!

NARRATOR

Four men of noble rank from each clan offered themselves as hostages. Messengers, very warlike in manner, crossed over to their respective enemies and brought back the hostages. Now the mood of the ritual changed. The peaceful spirit took over. The hostages were transformed into deer, gentle, peaceful, harmless deer. Four days they fasted in the houses of the chiefs. Then their fingers were tied together, and they were allowed to eat—but only with their left hand, the peaceful hand that fights poorly. They ate from stone slabs; the peace was to be lasting. The Kanhaades had been humbled at the potlatch held in their honor and were withdrawing from the fishing grounds of the Nanyaayi along the Stikine River. Also, the Nanyaayi had atoned for the killing of the Kanhaades warrior, Haimas.

[DRUMS]

HAYIAK

(*Chanting.*) My masters, I am feeling very lonely away.

I am singing inside.

I am crying about myself.

NARRATOR

The hostages then put on the ceremonial robes of the hummingbird, the salmon-trap, or the robin, representative of peace, and addressed the clans.

TSAGUEDI

I nod my head toward you.

DUQDANEK

The deer has now gone in among my clan. We feel no anger.

NARRATOR

The hostages danced the dance of peace. Eagle down, the supreme token of peace, was placed on their heads, and they were released to their clans. So peace was publicly proclaimed. The ritual ended.

ANTHROPOLOGIST

And so, with the completion of the ritual, we learn that an act that seems foolhardy and suicidal actually has deep and rational motivation within the framework of the culture. Through this we learn the true meaning of the concept of culture, and the great importance that culture has in formulating human behavior.

2. LANGUAGE

>>>->>>

Language is necessary for culture; yet it is a part of culture. We cannot conceive of the development of technology, art, religion, and social relations without an elaborate means of communication. We can see this clearly if we remember that culture is learned behavior—and if we try to imagine how it would be to learn most of the things we know without having them explained to us. How language began or whether it came before other elements in culture is only a matter of speculation; but because language is so important we are sure it must have existed very early in human history.

Man is the only animal with speech. It is his truly distinctive feature. We know the parrot imitates the sounds of human speech, but this is not language. Scientists have made many efforts to teach apes to speak, but never successfully. One spent six months trying to teach an orangutan to talk, and she seemed to have learned "cup" for water and "papa" for her teacher. Then she died—presumably not from the mental exertion. Two young psychologists had a chimpanzee live with them and grow up with their baby. The chimp learned everything faster than the baby did—except speech. Apes have the physical equipment to make sounds: larynx, tongue, palate. Apparently they lack the mental ability to use language. It is doubtful if the reason given by one anthropologist—that they have nothing to say—is the true one.

Many animals communicate with one another. We know of crows and their keeping watch; we know about mating calls. Gibbons, the small agile apes of southeast Asia, have a "vocabulary" of different calls that mean certain things, such as "danger," "get away," and the like. But there is all the difference in the world between these calls and true language. Animals can express only immediate states of mind.

Language, on the other hand, is the re-creation of experience in sound. It can not only communicate the subjective feeling of the speaker, but also describe objectively. Above all, it is not bound to the immediate, but can call forth events from the past, discuss occurrences that are far away, imagine the future. Through language we can learn about experiences that we *will* probably never have, such as an arctic exploration; and experiences that we *can* never have (somebody else's dream). Language expresses also the relationship between things in time and space; it allows for the expression of the conditional as well as the actual, the potential as well as the real. With language we can relate cause to effect, action to actor, event to circumstance. All these things can be done in all languages, even though they are done differently.

Words are the symbols for reality. They classify the events of our environment, and all of them generalize and divide the infinite variety that the real world presents. "Boy" is as much a generalization as "love," and even the name of a person assumes a unity that growth and change of mood cannot destroy. Though we may say that "he is beside himself with rage," we still see him as the same person and call him by the same name. In English we think in terms of "parts of speech": nouns are the names of things; verbs are the names of actions; adjectives and adverbs are attributes of things and actions. Though the same word may be both noun and verb, we treat one as the name of a thing, the other as the name of an action. The importance of this distinction is so great that we are compelled always to distinguish between them, but if we reflect upon verbs and nouns we begin to see that our notion is arbitrary—a grammatical convention. A wave of the hand or an ocean wave is a noun, but both are action rather than thing. Modern physics gives reason to consider such a solid thing as stone to be molecular action, while we readily talk about electricity as a thing. And in English each act must have an actor. There must be an agent responsible, and our language requires that we provide one even when it is unnecessary. We say, "It is raining"—though "rains" is more what we mean.

Other languages do not make these same distinctions. Words do not necessarily divide into nouns and verbs. The act and actor may be part of the same word, and the actor less important than the action. To speakers of such a language, the world is seen with different eyes. Trees and boys and love still exist, of course. But language expresses the relationships between things in time and space, and these relationships are differently perceived. "The world in which different societies live are distinct worlds, not merely the same world with different labels attached." That is the way the linguist and anthropologist

➽➽➽➽➽➽➽➽➽➽➽➽➽➽➽➽➽➽➽➽➽➽➽➽➽➽➽➽➽➽➽➽➽➽➽➽➽➽➽

Edward Sapir expressed the fact that the language a people speak imposes a classification of things and events, and projects a whole logic upon the world.

This idea may be shocking, because everyone has started to learn his language before his earliest memory. But it is this fact of the early learning of language that makes the influence of language understandable. Before we learn to speak we have had few experiences—we have used our senses, we have felt pain and pleasure, we have distinguished a few persons in our environment, we have learned to crawl or perhaps to walk a little. But most of the things we later do we first experience in words. Our mothers usually express in words the things that are happening to us. The world in large measure comes to us in words—particularly the doing of things or the seeing of relations. Our habits tend to follow these words, our thoughts to follow our grammar.

Of course, all of us think that the way we speak of the world is the way it really is. And in the cultural sense, that is the way it is to each speaker. But the real world is far too complex to be recorded in ordinary spoken language; indeed the ability to speak means the ability to agree upon certain important generalizations, and to overlook the many individual differences among things. Since every tree is ultimately unique, we could have no botany if a separate word were used for each tree. It cannot be otherwise.

Language, then, is part of culture, as well as being crucial to it. We learn our language as part of the pattern of our cultural behavior—just as we learn to like certain foods, to make certain tools, to believe in certain gods. But because we learn other parts of our culture through the language we speak, language inevitably becomes the lens through which we see our culture and the whole world. Language pervades every other aspect of culture. Since language sets the world view of its speakers, we must learn to appreciate the differences that different languages imply if we are to understand the peoples of the world. We must also learn to appreciate the effects of our own language upon our own thought if ultimately we are to get beyond the limitations our culture imposes upon us, and understand the world as seen by other cultures or the world of scientific reality.

A Word in Your Ear

LISTER SINCLAIR

Two narrators take us to scenes that show the relationship between language and culture. One of them is "Here," who likes to point out things about our own language; the other is "There," who finds his examples in distant lands. The other characters are self-explanatory.

HERE

Watch your language! Remember whom you're speaking to! To the ladies, speak Italian; to the gentlemen, French; to the birds, English; to the dogs, German; and Spanish should be spoken only to God!

[MUSIC]

HERE

All people have language with which to express their feelings.

THERE

But language is not the same as expressing your feelings. Some people think animals have language because they can often express their feelings; as when in the arctic wilderness, we hear the wolf. (*An arctic wolf howls in the distance.*)

HERE

But there is all the difference in the world between that wolf and this. (*A human "wolf-whistle" is heard.*)

THERE

The four-legged wolf howl expresses its feelings there and then, and so does the wolf-whistle. But the whistler can back up his expression with language.

HUMAN

How about taking in a show on Saturday night?

HERE

And that is a communication about another time and another place. It is true language, not just expression of feeling. And all human beings have language—from the Eskimo by the Arctic Ocean, warm in his kayak with his suit of furs, to the Patagonian by the Antarctic Ocean, shivering in his canoe with a fire in it, because he wears almost no clothes at all. From one extreme to the other, all people have language.

[MUSIC]

THERE

What's more, all these languages are adequate. They all do the job—communication. Their variety, both of sound and structure, is incredible, but each stands relatively unchanging with its own traditions and flavor. For instance, the Persian speaks.

PERSIAN

In Paradise, the serpent spoke Arabic, the most persuasive of all languages; Adam and Eve spoke Persian, the most poetic of all languages; and the angel Gabriel spoke Turkish, the most threatening of all languages.

HERE

On the other hand, in the Highlands of Scotland, the tradition goes that Scots Gaelic was the language spoken by Adam and Eve in Paradise.

THERE

As for English, many other peoples think it sounds like the twittering of birds, rapid, shrill, and mysterious. To the Navaho, whose speech is precise in the exact intonation of every syllable, English is just a lot of slop. And to anyone who speaks a language rich in vowels, such as Italian or Japanese, English, with its clustering clots of consonant strengths, is enough to give a crocodile the lockjaw.

HERE

For we often think that whatever we speak

ourselves is the proper thing—that what the other fellow speaks is scarcely more than a string of grunts.

WIFE

I see by the paper there are over fifteen hundred different languages spoken in the world today.

HUSBAND

(*Engrossed in the sports section*.) Oh.

WIFE

And it says there are more families of languages among the American Indians than in the whole of the Old World.

HUSBAND

Uh.

WIFE

Well, everyone knows Indians don't talk properly. They just grunt.

HUSBAND

Uh-uh.

WIFE

You aren't listening. (*Pause*.) Are you?

HUSBAND

(*Now puts down his paper*.) Hmmm?

WIFE

Are you listening?

HUSBAND

(*With the false enthusiasm of one who hasn't been*.) M-hm!

WIFE

I say Indians don't talk properly. They just grunt.

HUSBAND

Huh?

WIFE

Grunt!

HUSBAND

Uh!

WIFE

What do you think?

HUSBAND

U-u-u-u-u-u-uh—language is language, and grunts are grunts.

[MUSIC]

HERE

One man's speech is another man's jargon, but all people have language, and these languages are highly diverse in form. But always we begin by speaking as we think, and end by thinking as we speak. Our language is an expression of our culture, shaped by the way we are brought up: and on the other hand, the way we are brought up is shaped by our language.

THERE

For, as we know from our own language, English, language reflects place, time, age, sex, and circumstance. And this is true of other languages.

HERE

Language reflects place.

THERE

As everybody knows, very often the most foreign thing about a foreign country is the foreign language.

HERE

And English-speakers can't visit one another's country without meeting the great Transatlantic Rift.

AMERICAN

Lookit, Jack, when you get off the streetcar, get off the pavement, get on the sidewalk, go two blocks, turn right, there's a drugstore on the corner, take the elevator down to the gar*age*. You can't miss it.

ENGLISH

All right, chum. You mean, when I get off the tram, get off the road, get *on* the pavement, take the second turning to the right, there's a chemist's shop on the corner, take the lift down to the *gar*age. What do you mean, I can't miss it?

THERE

Language then, is a function of place.

[MUSIC]

HERE

And language is a function of time. Listen to the Lord's Prayer as it sounded nearly six hundred years ago.

WICLIF

Oure Fadir that art in heuenes, halwid be thi name; thi kyngdom cumme to; be thi wille don as in heuen and in erthe; gif to vs this day oure breed ouer other substaunce; and forgeve to vs oure dettis, as we forgeve to oure dettours; and leede vs nat in to temptacioun, but delyuere vs fro yuel. Amen.

THERE

Then, quite soon after the Norman Conquest, English had a tang of French to it. But let's jump back beyond 1066 and listen to English in its hard Teutonic infancy as Anglo-Saxon —the Lord's Prayer in the year 1000 A.D.

ANGLO-SAXON

Faeder ure thu the eart on heofonum; si thin name gehalgod. To-becume thin rice. Gewurthe thin wille on eorthan swa swa on heofonum. Urne gedaeghwamlican hlaf syle us to daeg. And forgyf us ure gyltas swa swa we forgyfath urum gyltendum. And ne gelaed thu us on costnunge ac alys us of yfele. Sothlice.

HERE

Language then is a function of time. And even modern English still keeps the record of that Norman Conquest. The Saxons became the servants, and looked after the beasts while they were alive, and their names are still the Saxon ones.

SAXON

Ox. Calf. Sheep. Swine.

THERE

Compare the German: Ochs. Kalb. Schaf. Schwein.

HERE

But when they were killed, their meat was served up to the Norman master; and on the table those animals' names are still the Norman ones.

NORMAN

Beef. Veal. Mutton. Pork.

THERE

Compare the French: Bœuf. Veau. Mouton. Porc. Language reflects culture.

[MUSIC]

HERE

Language is a function of age. We don't expect a child to talk like a college professor.

INFANT

Simple harmonic motion can therefore be represented graphically by a sine or cosine curve.

THERE

Nor do we expect a college professor to talk like a child.

PROFESSOR

What's the matter? said the doctor.

What's the matter? said the nurse.

What's the matter? said the lady with the alligator purse.

[MUSIC]

THERE

Language is also a function of sex. Among the Carayahi Indians of Brazil, the women and the men speak different languages. For example, the word for girl is *yadokoma* in the women's language, but *yadoma* in the men's. The men and women speak a slightly different language.

HERE

And in English? Here's a traveler chewing his cigar in the smoking room of the Santa Fe Chief. But he's speaking the women's language.

SALESMAN

I don't want to be catty, but, my dear, it was

Διότι τόσον ἠγάπησεν Ибо таку возлюбим

Ϧui aut facit 生。 ... Our father wh

simply too terrible. I really thought I should have died. I just wanted to sink right through the floor. My gracious me, I thought, if Bert and Charlie aren't wearing that same cunning Homburg hat.

HERE

Unfortunately, in our society the men's language is taboo to women—that is to say, they are supposed not to know it. So I'm afraid we daren't give you an example of a lady speaking the men's language. Sailors present.

[MUSIC]

THERE

Language is a function of occasion. There is a time for one kind of speech, and a time for another. Sir James Frazer tells us that in Siam there is a special language to be used when discussing the Siamese King. The hairs of his head, the soles of his feet, the breath of his body, indeed every single detail of his person, both outward and inward, have particular names. When he eats or drinks or walks, a special word indicates that these acts are being performed by the sovereign, and such words cannot possibly be applied to the acts of any other person whatever.

HERE

We do not perhaps carry things quite as far as that, but nonetheless a fellow may be greeted casually when he comes into the office.

AMIABLE

Hi, Charlie boy, how's the kid? What've you got to say for yourself?

HERE

But a few minutes later, when the board meeting convenes, he is addressed more formally.

AMIABLE

And now, Charles, we trust you have overcome the hardships of your journey. Would you be so good as to present your report regarding market conditions in the west.

THERE

The Chinese are famous for their elaborate forms of greeting. But other languages are far more complicated. For example, the Nootka Indians of Vancouver Island not only distinguish, by their choice of words, the sex of a person speaking, the sex of the person spoken to, and whether the speaker is more or less important than the person spoken to; but also, on top of this, have a special way of talking to a man who is left-handed, and a special way of talking to a man who is circumcised.

HERE

English cannot go this far. But, even so, language must be suitable to the occasion. Queen Victoria certainly knew this when she expressed her dislike of Gladstone.

QUEEN VICTORIA

Mr. Gladstone always addresses me as if I were a Public Meeting.

HERE

And imagine a politician proposing in the language he uses on the platform.

POLITICIAN

Unaccustomed as I am to private proposals, I kneel before you today, unwilling—nay, reluctant—to assume the burdens of matrimonial office, but nonetheless prepared to bow to your opinion, and dedicate myself unselfishly if I receive an unmistakable draft.

[MUSIC]

(*The Wedding March.*)

THERE

Language, therefore, by reflecting place, time, age, sex, and circumstance, is a function of society. Language reflects culture.

HERE

The easiest way to see this is through vocabulary. The Eskimos have no word for coconut, and the Samoans have no word for snow.

ESKIMO

And neither do the Eskimos.

HERE
I beg your pardon?

ESKIMO
We Eskimos have no word for snow. Ask me the word for snow, and I ask you: What kind of snow? Snow is to us Eskimos too important to be dismissed with one word. We have many words telling us, for instance, when it fell, and describing its exact condition to us. For the knowledge is vital, and our lives may depend on it.

THERE
Since language reflects society, whatever is important in society has many words in the language. The Arabs have a thousand words for sword. And the Siberian Chuckchee, who live on the shores of the Arctic Ocean, have thirty or so words describing the skins of the caribou. Here is just one of them:

CHUCKCHEE
Cechenyaqilhm.

THERE
This Chuckchee word means that the underleg of the caribou skin is greyish, and that it is light grey on the groins, but that the prevailing body color is brown. And there are innumerable similar examples. The Yurok Indians of California place a high value on woodpecker scalps and obsidian blades. And besides the ordinary set of numerals (1, 2, 3, and so forth) they have two extra sets—one for counting woodpecker scalps, and another one for counting obsidian blades.

HERE
English is full of relics of vocabulary that remind us that other days thought other things important. There was a time when English-speaking men lived very much by hunting. They had special words for congregations of animals: a flock of sheep and a herd of cattle, but a pride of lions, a skulk of foxes, and a gaggle of geese.

They also had special words for the carving of each of the animals and birds of the chase when they arrived on the table ready to eat. Nowadays if we have a pile of game birds we want carved, the cook will say:

COOK
Hey, mac!

MAC
Yeah?

COOK
Cut up them birds, will you?

HERE
For nowadays one game bird is much like another: out of season.

THERE
But to the Elizabethans, game birds were the very meat of life, and their carving required a special and ornate vocabulary.

COOK
You, sirrah!

MAC
Anon?

COOK
Dismember that heron, unbrace that mallard, allay that pheasant, wing that partridge, display that quail, unjoint that bittern, thigh that woodcock, lift that swan, and rear that goose. As for that curlew—

MAC
Aye, sir?

COOK
Unlatch it!

[MUSIC]
("*Come to the Cookhouse Door.*")

HERE
A noble handful that has been replaced by other rich treasures of vocabulary as *our* language (like all other languages) has changed to reflect our culture.

ESKIMO
As we Eskimos found out when I was sent down to study your culture. Your language is like ours, very often. Our Eskimo language, like many other North American Indian languages, is polysynthetic.

HERE

How's that—polysynthetic?

ESKIMO

Not an Eskimo word but an English word—polysynthetic. One word means a whole phrase, one word has in it the compressed wreckage of a phrase. Thus suppose we wish to say in Eskimo: "When they were about to go out they would take the boot-stretcher using it to thrash the dogs because they usually stay in the entrance passage."

That is twenty-six words in English. In Eskimo it is six words: *Anilerunik:* ("when they were about to go out"). *Kammiut* ("the boot-stretcher"). *Tingussaat* ("they would take it"). *Anaataralongo* ("using it to thrash with"). *Qimmit* ("the dogs"). *Torsooneetaommata* ("because they usually stay in the entrance passage").

HERE

But where does English contain words that are the compressed wreckage of a phrase, as you put it?

ESKIMO

In English, not exactly like Eskimo, but nearly like. The other day I saw a newspaper headline: "UNRRA DP'S LAUD UNESCO." Back to my dictionary I go. There I find the word *laud*—nothing else. The other words are missing. Then it is explained to me. These other words are not normal English; they are instead the compressed wreckage of phrases. Four words, "UNRRA DP'S LAUD UNESCO," means: "United Nations Relief and Rehabilitation Agency Displaced Persons Laud the United Nations Educational, Scientific, and Cultural Organization."

ESKIMO

Seventeen words compressed into four. Well, that's about average for Eskimo!

[MUSIC]

THERE

Again, language reflects culture. As modern life sets up more elaborate agencies and organizations, modern language adapts itself, and forms words and builds polysynthetic forms almost like the Eskimo. Other languages besides English have been doing this. German, for example. *Gestapo* stands for *Geheime Staats Polizei* ("secret state police"). *Flak* is the compressed wreckage of *Flugzeugsabwehrkanone* ("anti-aircraft cannon.")

HERE

As we think, so we speak; as we speak, so we think. As we are taught reading, writing, and arithmetic, as we are taught our manners and the way things are done in the world we live in, so we are taught our language. And as we learn our language from our mother's lips, we also learn the customs and attitudes of our society. For language reflects these customs and attitudes—that is, language reflects culture.

THERE

(*A child wails and misbehaves.*) Over here, for instance, is a child misbehaving; and here comes its mother. She's going to tell it to behave properly. But let us notice carefully what word she uses.

MOTHER

John, be *good!* (*The child subsides.*)

HERE

Be good. The English-speaking child that misbehaves is bad, or naughty, or wicked. So is the Italian-speaking child, or the Greek-speaking one.

THERE

But listen to what the French mother says to her child.

FRENCH MOTHER

Jean, sois sage!

THERE

Sois sage: be wise. The French-speaking child that misbehaves is not bad, it is foolish, it is imprudent, it is injudicious.

HERE

In the Scandinavian countries, things are different again.

SWEDISH MOTHER

Jan, var snell!

NORWEGIAN MOTHER
Jan, ble snil!
HERE
Both mean the same thing: be friendly, be
kind. So the misbehaving Scandinavian child
is unfriendly, unkind, uncooperative.
THERE
Things are very different in Germany.
GERMAN MOTHER
Hans, sei artig!
THERE
Be in line! The misbehaving German child is
not conforming, it is out of step, out of line.
A mother of the Hopi Indians of the south-
west United States has the same idea, only in
a more gentle spirit.
HOPI MOTHER
No, no, no, no—that is not the Hopi way.
THERE
Hopi is the right thing, the proper way to do
things, the way the affairs of the tribe, and
indeed of the Universe, are managed. The
Hopi child that misbehaves is not bad, or
imprudent or unfriendly, or, quite, out of
line. He is not on the Hopi way; he is not
marching in step with the Hopi view of destiny
and of life.
HERE
So, even in the words a mother says to her
misbehaving child, we can detect again how
language reflects culture.
MOTHER
Johnny, be good!
FRENCH MOTHER
Jean, sois sage: be wise!
SWEDISH MOTHER
Jan, var snell: be friendly!
GERMAN MOTHER
Hans, sei artig: get back in line!
HOPI MOTHER
No, no, no, no: that is not the Hopi way!
              [MUSIC: "*Rock-a-bye Baby.*"]
THERE
East of New Guinea, in the southern Pacific,
lie the Trobriand Islands. The people who live

there are great mariners, lively and active.
But they take no interest in things changing.
If a thing changes, then it becomes something
else, and they call it something else.
HERE
Just as we do not introduce an old gentleman
with a long white beard as the bouncing baby
boy Jim Jones.
JIM
(*A very old man.*) Very pleased to make your
acquaintance.
THERE
(*Confidentially to* HERE.) Buster here isn't any
more a bouncing baby boy than I am.
JIM
Ah, but you see, once upon a time I was, in
the long, long ago.
HERE
(*Dismissing him briskly.*) But he isn't now. In
fact, we don't think of him as a kind of modi-
fied infant, but as something else—an old
gentleman, a different kind of animal.
THERE
Now the Trobriand Islanders think like this
all the time. They raise a yam crop, and a
first-rate yam has a special name.
TROBRIAND ISLANDER
Taytu.
THERE
But an overripe yam is not overripe taytu;
it's different. It is:
TROBRIAND ISLANDER
Yowana.
THERE
And a yowana with underground shoots isn't
yowana any more, but . . .
TROBRIAND ISLANDER
Silisata.
THERE
Though with new tubers on the underground
shoots, it isn't silisata of any kind, but now:
TROBRIAND ISLANDER
Gadena.
THERE
Among the Trobriand Islanders, in short, the

name of a thing alone is all you need say about it.

HERE

How different with us. Consider the case of a fellow being shown a new baby. (*A baby starts to cry*.) It is red-faced, boiled-looking, dribbling, cross-eyed, and squalling. The fond parents are watching you like hawks. You have to say something. But what?

FELLOW

How intelligent-looking?

HERE

But it looks like a moron!

FELLOW

How beautiful?

HERE

Just look at the ugly little beast!

FELLOW

How small and tiny?

HERE

For that, they'll kill you. He's three thirty-seconds of an ounce overweight: he's a giant!

FELLOW

How exactly like his father?

HERE

Say that, and he'll punch you right on the nose. There's nothing you can say. All you can do is shuffle around from one foot to the other and look as foolish as the baby.

THERE

But in the Trobriand Islands, the whole thing's simple. Show a Trobriand Islander the same messy, bellowing brat, and he says:

TROBRIAND ISLANDER

How baby!

THERE

How baby—which nobody can deny, and everyone's happy!

HERE

Yet our language is like the Trobriand in some ways, just as our society is like theirs in some ways. They place a high value on yams, and have an elaborate yam vocabulary. We place a high value on other things, and have an even more complicated and exact vocabulary to describe the special objects of *our* interest. Just look here. (*The traffic noises of a busy street*.) Standing on a downtown street corner, we have a Trobriand Islander, who has come to study our society. He's talking to a guy and writing down the answers.

TROBRIAND ISLANDER

What is the name of that thing on wheels going by now—the green one?

GUY

That's a Plymouth.

TROBRIAND ISLANDER

Plymouth. There is another green one, also a Plymouth.

GUY

No, it's green, but it ain't a Plymouth. That's a Studebaker. Studie has a kind of turret in the middle.

TROBRIAND ISLANDER

Then here is a great big Studebaker.

GUY

No, the big one with the kind of turret, that's a Cadillac.

TROBRIAND ISLANDER

Here is another big one. This is a Cadillac?

GUY

No, no—look at the back! That's a Lincoln.

HERE

And so it goes on of course. That Trobriand Islander will be there for a week. And then we'll break it to him that there's a difference between one year's model and the next. A week! He'll be there for a year.

THERE

But when he goes home, he'll talk to his friends just as our travelers come home and talk to us.

TROBRIAND ISLANDER

They are a very peculiar people attaching fantastic importance to little differences among their automobiles, so that a certain kind of small automobile is called a Plymouth; but with a turret in the middle, it is not a Plymouth with a turret, but a Studebaker. Quite a different word. And a big thing like a sort of Studebaker with other differences here and there is not a big Studebaker, but a different word again, a Cadillac. And so it goes on. They are a very peculiar people.

[MUSIC]

THERE

Now we come to the most striking and interesting example of language reflecting culture—the wonderful and varied language of the Navaho Indians.

[MUSIC]
(*Navaho "Night Way."*)

THERE

The Navaho Indians live in the great red desert of the southwest United States, not very far from the Grand Canyon, in Arizona. Their nomadic life is filled with uncertainties, and they seek security and balance in ritual and ceremony, by which they find their place in the natural harmony of the universe, and health and a sense of belonging.

HERE

Now life on this vast, unconsidering mountain desert is very much influenced by forces the Navaho do not command—the long drought, the sudden torrential rain, the sweep of epidemic disease.

THERE

And the Navaho view of the Universe seems to be connected with what they have learned from the country that is their home.

HERE

We try to control nature.

NAVAHO

We seek to understand it, and our place within it.

HERE

To us, the world is made up of beings and things that act on other beings and things.

NAVAHO

To us Navaho, the world is one of actions and events associated with things, among which our own acts are only a few among many.

HERE

Our own outlook is centered on things. Our language is centered on nouns, which are the names of things. The first words our children learn might well be the names of things.

MOTHER

Man. Ball. Boat. Bird.

NAVAHO

Our Navaho outlook is focused on actions and events, our language on verbs. The first words our children learn may well be those expressive of actions.

NAVAHO MOTHER

Standing. Rolling. Sailing. Flying.

HERE

Navaho words, like those of Eskimo, are often polysynthetic, the compressed wreckage of phrases. Take a single word.

NAVAHO

Ná sh'ááh

HERE

And it means: "I am causing a round object to turn over, to turn upside down."

THERE

Navaho has many words for what we speak of as moving—a word for a round object moving, a fabric moving, and many more. And pronouns and adverbs are only parts of the verb, for the verb is central in Navaho speech just as actions are central in Navaho thinking.

HERE

We have a few verbs that are perhaps similar. The word *shrug* must carry with it the idea of *shoulder;* you can't shrug your stomach.

THERE

In English we say, "John is dying," just as we say, "John is walking," or "John is working"—for we speak even of death as though it were an act performed. But the Navaho, translated, says something like:

NAVAHO

Dying is taking place with John.

HERE

We are active toward nature; we think of our world as full of objects doing things to other objects; our language is centered on nouns, the names of things.

NAVAHO

We Navaho see ourselves as part of nature, in harmony with it; our world is one of actions to which we, and other things, are linked. Our language centers on the verb, expressive of acting.

THERE

Finally, here is an editorial in a Navaho newspaper. The writer is angry. He wants to know why a school is not built at Kayenta, though other places have schools. But he expresses his indignation in the Navaho way.

NAVAHO

The school at Kayenta, in vain we are hoping for it. Many children here have no school to attend. To one who comes here to see, there are 300 or more children who are in this state, who have no school. Therefore let a school become a reality here at Kayenta. Long ago this matter was brought up. Why is this so, please?

[MUSIC]

THERE

So the Navaho treats his events as if they merely occurred, where we would try to put the blame on somebody.

HERE

And this is so much a part of English language, just as it is of English thoughts, that even translating the Navaho puts back into the speech some of the nouns that the Navaho didn't use.

THERE

Language, then, reflects thought, and formulates our way of thinking.

3. TECHNOLOGY

Man is the only species—except, perhaps, certain bacteria—that lives in all parts of the globe. He has conquered the Arctic as well as the jungle, the desert as well as the green valley and the grassy plain. Man has reached every significant part of the earth not covered with ice or water, and has even moved out onto some of these. He has done this rapidly and without major changes in bodily structure or physiology. He has been able to do this because he has culture. He can learn new ways of meeting situations and lose old ones within a short space of time, and not merely by biological selectivity. Man shapes the environment to his own ends, whereas other animals are shaped to the demands of their environment.

Technology is the aspect of culture that is responsible for this adaptability. Technology is the stored knowledge of how to do things. It includes the practical knowledge for wresting a livelihood from the jungle, the desert, or the soil. It includes the knowledge of how to prepare and preserve the food man gets. It includes the fabrication of clothes and the building of houses to give him protection against the inclemency of the weather. It includes the manufacture of weapons of the chase and warfare for protection and aggression. It includes also the tools with which he makes all these other things, and many, many more.

Man is not the only animal to make things: bees, beavers, and many birds alter the environment to suit their needs. They do so by instinct. Apes, at least in captivity, use sticks and stones as instruments to aid them in securing food. But in both cases something is lacking to distinguish their behavior from human technical accomplishments. The bee and the beaver pass their "knowledge" of building from one generation to the next, but they cannot adapt it to widely differing situations. The apes' behavior is apparently an adaptive one, providing insights to meet immediate needs. But there is no transmission of these insights from parent to offspring; there is no continuity and no opportunity to accumulate

>>>->>>

knowledge. There are only the repetitive acts of individual genius (if we may apply this word to apes).

The capacity to make things and the transmission of this knowledge are older than man. Archeological records associate this ability—and hence culture—with some of the extinct forms of manlike creatures. We owe to them, presumably, those first efforts which gave us stone tools and fire. Since that time, man has developed museumsful of technical accomplishments—some humble but eternally useful, such as string (known to all living primitives), some more noble, such as the wheel, the plow, the smelting of iron, and the herding of flocks. The hands were freed from doing duty in supporting the body; the fingers lengthened into flexible grasping instruments with the thumb in opposition. This was accomplished in some pre-human stage, apparently as a result of living in trees. Whatever the source, the hands are remarkably versatile and can be used both for picking up a needle and heaving a rock—the basic all-purpose tool. They hang from long arms by three flexible joints to add to their maneuverability.

To aid our hands we have eyes, which are also versatile. The human eye is equipped for color, and with a focusing device for range, and with a "shutter" to adjust for differences in light, and with an extremely fine-grained retina for accuracy in detail. Other animals have eyes that do one thing or another better than ours, but none have eyes that do so many things so well. And on top of this, we have stereoscopic vision, a gift shared by very few animals. Stereoscopic vision operates like the range finder on a modern camera to give a sharp appreciation of depth. This was a necessary aid if the full utility of the hand was to be realized. (Try threading a needle or lighting a cigarette with one eye closed—and you will soon discover the importance of focusing both eyes on your work.)

Man is able to discriminate and to record in his memory those little differences between objects that distinguish food from poison, safety from danger. It is doubtful if he differs in this from most higher animals, except in the fact that he uses all his senses— sight, hearing, smell, taste, and feel—rather than concentrating on one or two.

More important yet is the human capacity for reasoning from cause to effect. Perhaps it is just because he can make things that man is in the habit of thinking that certain acts have certain consequences—of applying the principle "if this, then that." (If I feather the arrow it will fly straight. If I heat the metal, it will become malleable.) The application of these principles of relationship are necessary for invention. According to some psychologists, necessary too is insight: the ability to construct in the mind certain relationships that are not found in nature. From time to time apes have been observed doing just that; men, however, do it as a regular thing.

But by far the most important endowment man has is the ability to store and transmit knowledge. Fire-making did not have to be reinvented after its first discoverer died. This talent rests, of course, in speech, and its subsidiary (and much later) invention: writing.

Man is a creator, and it is natural that he should everywhere believe in some creator god. But just how creative man is, is a question that has long vexed scholars. All we can do is set certain limits. We know, on the one hand, that man has been sufficiently inventive to enable him to survive in all environments capable of supporting human life. From desert to ice cap, man has been able to meet his minimum needs. We know, too, that many inventions have been made more than once—planting of crops, herding of animals, working of metals, writing. On the other hand, we know also that inventions are not easily come by. Man has been known to make do with inadequate techniques and to fail for centuries on end to find better methods. Though man invents in response to needs, he does not always find the adequate response. And if we were suddenly deprived of the many gadgets of our civilization—and of the memory of them—we would not immediately re-invent them.

For man's technical knowledge has been a slow accumulation. It was at least half a million years ago that some manlike creature discovered the use of fire and of shaped stones to increase his effectiveness. It has been ten thousand years since man first thought of planting shoots or seeds to assure a future crop, or to husband flocks for his continued use. The use of iron came much later, while gunpowder, steam energy, electricity, and atomic energy are developments of recent history.

We must remember that invention builds upon invention. There cannot be atomic energy without radiation labs, radiation labs without steel, steel without controlled furnaces. The product of man's ingenuity is cumulative, and grows with increased tempo as more things beget yet more things.

➢➢➢-➢➢

Modern technology, of which we are so justly proud, is the product of this technologic accumulation. It is not the creation of any single people, for each race has contributed to it; and, indeed, its beginnings must be attributed to species who inhabited the earth before us. It is this accumulated technical knowledge that makes man the superior animal that he is— that makes this single species able to live in both tropics and Arctic. It is important to remember that we owe the beginnings of this knowledge to lesser animals than man, and ennobling to know that all branches of the human species have contributed to it.

Ours is a technologic culture, for we have specialized in this aspect of life. We tend to look upon cultures that get by with more primitive methods not only as primitive but also as inferior. But we should remember what we owe to others in the development of our technology. Ralph Linton has caught the spirit of this debt in the following passage:

"Our solid American citizen awakens in a bed built on a pattern which originated in the Near East but which was modified in Northern Europe before it was transmitted to America. He throws back covers made from cotton, domesticated in India, or linen, domesticated in the Near East, or wool from sheep, also domesticated in the Near East, or silk, the use of which was discovered in China. All of these materials have been spun and woven by processes invented in the Near East. He slips into his moccasins, invented by the Indians of the Eastern woodlands, and goes to the bathroom, whose fixtures are a mixture of European and American inventions, both of recent date. He takes off his pajamas, a garment invented in India, and washes with soap invented by the ancient Gauls. He then shaves, a masochistic rite which seems to have been derived from either Sumer or ancient Egypt.

"Returning to the bedroom, he removes his clothes from a chair of southern European type and proceeds to dress. He puts on garments whose form originally derived from the skin clothing of the nomads of the Asiatic steppes, puts on shoes made from skins tanned by a process invented in ancient Egypt and cut to a pattern derived from the classical civilizations of the Mediterranean, and ties around his neck a strip of bright-colored cloth which is a vestigial survival of the shoulder shawls worn by the seventeenth-century Croatians. Before going out for breakfast he glances through the window, made of glass invented in Egypt, and if it is raining puts on overshoes made of rubber discovered by the

Central American Indians and takes an umbrella, invented in southeastern Asia. Upon his head he puts a hat made of felt, a material invented in the Asiatic steppes.

"On his way to breakfast he stops to buy a paper, paying for it with coins, an ancient Lydian invention. At the restaurant a whole new series of borrowed elements confronts him. His plate is made of a form of pottery invented in China. His knife is of steel, an alloy first made in southern India, his fork a medieval Italian invention, and his spoon a derivative of a Roman original. He begins breakfast with an orange, from the eastern Mediterranean, a canteloupe from Persia, or perhaps a piece of African watermelon. With this he has coffee, an Abyssinian plant, with cream and sugar. Both the domestication of cows and the idea of milking them originated in the Near East, while sugar was first made in India. After his fruit and first coffee he goes on to waffles, cakes made by a Scandinavian technique from wheat domesticated in Asia Minor. Over these he pours maple syrup, invented by the Indians of the Eastern woodlands. As a side dish he may have the egg of a species of bird domesticated in Indo-China, or thin strips of the flesh of an animal domesticated in Eastern Asia which have been salted and smoked by a process developed in northern Europe.

"When our friend has finished eating he settles back to smoke, an American Indian habit, consuming a plant domesticated in Brazil in either a pipe, derived from the Indians of Virginia, or a cigarette, derived from Mexico. If he is hardy enough he may even attempt a cigar, transmitted to us from the Antilles by way of Spain. While smoking he reads the news of the day, imprinted in characters invented by the ancient Semites upon a material invented in China by a process invented in Germany. As he absorbs the accounts of foreign troubles he will, if he is a good conservative citizen, thank a Hebrew deity in an Indo-European language that he is 100 per cent American." *

* Ralph Linton, *The Study of Man* (1936), pp. 326–327.

Survival

EUGENE S. HALLMAN

>>>->>>

We are on an arctic flight with:

NELSON *A mining engineer on his first trip to the Arctic.*

CARTER *An elderly doctor on an emergency call to an arctic village.*

ARVIK *An Eskimo returning from two years in the service.*

STEVENS *The pilot.*

NELSON

It began one February day on a bush plane flying to Pelly Bay. There were three of us in the cabin—a Dr. Carter, myself, and a young Eskimo named Arvik. I had never been into the far north until the company sent me up to examine a property.

CARTER

(*Talking over the noise of the motor.*) And in spite of what this young man has told you, Nelson—the Arctic is a nasty, brutal place.

ARVIK

To the white man, Dr. Carter. Not to my people.

CARTER

You've been away, Arvik. Your two years in the army will make it look different.

ARVIK

That may be so, Dr. Carter.

NELSON

Tell me, haven't the big new developments made a change—the mines, the new defense centers?

CARTER

Ah, yes! But that's different. The white man's Arctic is something else altogether. It's insulated, tied by a long umbilical cord to the outside. The aim is to make the Arctic as much like New York or Montreal as you can—without women.

NELSON

(*Laughing.*) And the natives on the outside looking in.

CARTER

As always.

ARVIK

We have our life. Away from the trading posts and the camps, many live in the old way.

NELSON

Hunting? Fishing?

ARVIK

Yes.

CARTER

And lending your wives. Mind you, Nelson— I'm not an old arctic hand. Can't be when I'm only up here on emergency cases. But the life I see in the native camps—well, it's no life for a human being. Ignorant, brutal, stultifying.

ARVIK

The land is hard—but I will be glad to see my people again.

CARTER

Ever seen a dog tied to a stake and killed with a whip, Nelson?

NELSON

No.

CARTER

I have. Whenever I dream of getting lost up here, you know what I see? A great, long umbilical cord and a husky dog creeping up on it. (*The engine coughs, then conks out.*)

ARVIK

Listen!

CARTER

Wonder what's up. Are we landing?

NELSON

Doesn't sound like—

STEVENS
(*Coming through the inter-com.*) Fasten your belts! Get your belts on fast! I've got to make a wheels-up landing. The escape door's on your left under the red light. Hurry!

NELSON
Good lord!

ARVIK
Roll a blanket in front of your face. If we crash it will save your head.

NELSON
At least the ice looks smooth.

ARVIK
No. It will be rough along the shore.

STEVENS
Coming in! Coming in! Get ready!

CARTER
Oh, lord, I hope he makes it.

NELSON
Hold on! Hold on! Here we go!
    (*There is a grating of the aircraft on the ice, a jolting crash. Then dead silence.*)

CARTER
Any bones I can set? (*Arvik and Nelson can't help but laugh.*)

NELSON
That wasn't as bad as I expected.

STEVENS
(*Opening the pilot's door and calling urgently.*) Let's get out of here! Quick!

CARTER
But, Captain Stevens, it's a little—

STEVENS
Get out! The left tank has split. There might be a fire. Grab what you can—blankets, clothes, parachutes, anything! But get out fast!

NELSON
We jumped out into the blinding midday sun and ran. From a hundred yards away we lay in snow—afraid to watch and afraid not to. Great clouds of vapor hissed away from our mouths. I could feel the cold creeping into my body, spreading down from my armpits

and out from my groin. And then a red curl of flame reached the gasoline. A great explosion and a sudden redness!

STEVENS
No, no, no, no!

CARTER
Easy, Stevens, easy.

NELSON
Put this blanket around him, Carter.

STEVENS
I couldn't even call base. Didn't have time, didn't have time.

NELSON
A part of my mind kept repeating an old army phrase: Take stock of equipment. Equipment. I could feel the matches in my pocket and the chocolate bar I had bought at the PX in Churchill. Cigarettes. My pen and pencil. And otherwise just clothes—and a batch of magnetometer maps in my bag. I don't know what the others were thinking. We just lay there in our parkas, watching Arvik poking about in the smoking, twisted pieces of the plane.

ARVIK
Who wishes to hunt the shore for wood?

NELSON
It's just rock and snow. There isn't any wood.

ARVIK
Along the shore the driftwood will be there. Frozen, lying under the snow. There is always wood on this coast.

CARTER
I'll go.

ARVIK
Take Captain Stevens along with you, Doctor. Look for small drifts above the ice. Kick them. If you find wood, here is a bar from the plane's wing to pry it loose.

CARTER
Okay, okay.

ARVIK
Do not touch it with your skin—it will stick.

STEVENS
What are you going to do?

ARVIK
Mr. Nelson and I will make a snow house.

CARTER
Just like that?

ARVIK
There is nothing else. We cannot live in the open.

NELSON
Call me Jim when you feel like it.

ARVIK
Jim?

NELSON
Yeah, sure. Jim.

ARVIK
There are pieces of metal by the plane, Jim. They can make us two snow knives. Maybe

they will build us a house before the sun goes.

NELSON
(*He and Arvik are hacking and slicing at the frozen snow.*) How long have we got, Arvik?

ARVIK
Enough. We were lucky to find the right snow so quickly.

NELSON
I was lucky. You knew where to look.

ARVIK
There are many kinds of snow—one good for the sled, one good for water, one good for building. Many, many kinds.

NELSON
Am I cutting it right now?

ARVIK
No, no, Jim, the block will break. Here: you slide the steel back and forth, deeper into the drift, a little longer to save time. Now, underneath. Yes, yes. That is a better one.

NELSON
I do one, you do ten. And *my* wrist aches.

ARVIK
It is not used to this. It is cold. Put your hands inside your pants while I place the blocks.

NELSON
I didn't know these things were built in a spiral.

ARVIK
What is a spiral?

NELSON
You're making one.

ARVIK
Oh?

NELSON
Sure. You built the bottom row in a circle—then sliced it off in a sort of climbing curve.

ARVIK
Is that wrong to you?

NELSON
No, no. It's smart engineering. All you have to do is build around till you get to the top—one continuous row.

ARVIK
We have always done it like this. How are your hands now?

NELSON
I guess they're alive. They sting enough.

ARVIK
Good. Hand me the blocks that are cut.

NELSON
In just over an hour Arvik built us an igloo, using the snow the cold had frozen—to keep

out the cold. Without knowing geometry he constructed a perfect half-sphere, knowing the right shape to offer the wind the least resistance known to aerodynamics. The final block in the peak of the igloo was the same as the keystone any stonemason knows. And the door faced south to the sun.

(*Pause*.)

Carter and Stevens came back with one bleached timber between them. Soon Arvik had taken the wood into our igloo. After he had thawed an end, he started chipping and whittling at one end, singing monotonously.

CARTER
For heaven's sake, can't you stop that whistling?

ARVIK
It is a song I learned in the Army, Dr. Carter.

Perhaps it does not suit the work of chipping wood for a fire.

CARTER
Uh.

NELSON
Getting anywhere, Arvik?

ARVIK
The wood is still frozen. Where I have thawed it between my hands it is wet. The center will be dry enough for a fire—if I can split it with the stone knife. (*Pause*.)

CARTER
What time is it, Stevens?

STEVENS
Six o'clock, by my luminous dial.

CARTER
They won't come now, will they?

STEVENS
No. There won't be any planes over.

CARTER
If it hadn't been for that blasted oil line of yours, Stevens—

STEVENS
It was a fluke, I tell you. Nobody can call those things.

CARTER
I know, I know, I know.

NELSON
The umbilical cord has broken, Carter.

CARTER
Eh? What do you mean?

NELSON
What you were saying a minute before the crash. Our life line's been cut. The umbilical cord isn't going to bring us the gimmicks to get out of this one.

ARVIK
Give me a match now. I have the wood ready.

NELSON
Here's two. That leaves forty-one to go, Arvik. Don't waste them. (*The precious match is scratched.*)

CARTER
Keep your fingers crossed.

ARVIK
Come, little chip of wood. Come, make a flame for us. Now I will fan you softly, softly.

NELSON
It's beginning to glow.

STEVENS
Blow on it. (*Stevens leans forward and blows.*) Blow on it, Arvik.

ARVIK
Stop! Stop it, Stevens!

STEVENS
I was just—

ARVIK
Now it is gone. You cannot blow a fire to life, Captain. Your breath is wet in this cold. A flame must be fanned with your mitt or a stick.

STEVENS
I'm sorry. I didn't know.

ARVIK
I will try again when it dries.

STEVENS
The mistakes you can make!

NELSON
Forget it, Stevens. Reminds me of a thing I read during the war: If you get lost in the jungle, remember the natives can teach you a lot. They've got the know-how of centuries right in their heads. They know *how* to live *where* they live. You don't.

STEVENS
Well, did you?

NELSON
Get lost, you mean?

STEVENS
Yeah.

NELSON
Twice. I read the survival manual from cover to cover. But I sure watched the natives.

CARTER
Tell me, how do they start fires?

NELSON
They were pretty smart about fires. In the jungle they use a piece of string and three sticks of wood.

STEVENS
How does it work?

NELSON
They use a wooden bow, perhaps a couple of feet long. By looping the string around a stick they can make it twirl every time the bow is moved back and forth.

STEVENS
Like a drill?

NELSON
That's right. You place one end of the drill in a notch in the wood you're trying to light, and saw like mad with the bow. Bow spins drill. Drill rubs wood. Fire burns wood.

STEVENS
Nothing to it, eh?

NELSON
I left out the hard part.

STEVENS
What's that?

NELSON
Cutting the notch you're drilling in. It's got to be shaped like a keyhole. Your drill works in the round part, but the tinder sits in the long end, barely touching the drill. You know, it took me two weeks to learn that?

CARTER
It's always easy—if you know how.

NELSON
They know how.

STEVENS
It really works, eh?

NELSON
Sure. It's just applied friction. That's the key to any number of fire makers: the drill; the fire thong; the plow.

CARTER
I still prefer a good match.

NELSON
And you light it with friction, Doctor. The natives like matches, too. But if you don't have them, you make fire with your hands— and with your head. First principles. The character who made the first match knew about fire before he started. And somebody told *him* what those first principles were.

CARTER
I never looked at it that way.

ARVIK
Give me the larger sticks, quickly. The flame is starting to catch.

NELSON
They're right there, Arvik, right beside you.

ARVIK

We must take care of this fire. We must not let it go out till our clothes are dry.

CARTER

You know, Nelson, somehow I feel I'm discovering fire for the first time.

NELSON

February the 6th. I began my journal that first night, writing clumsily with my mitts on—by the light of that precarious, spitting little fire Arvik had made for us. And long after I fell asleep I could hear Arvik, busy at something, pounding and tapping and pounding at some inscrutable piece of metal, humming an Eskimo song.

NELSON

How is it coming, Arvik? Almost through?

ARVIK

It is slow. The canvas bags of the parachutes do not care if we have cold feet. They do not want to become shoes—and they fight the knife I have made.

CARTER

Cigarette, Nelson?

NELSON

Thanks.

CARTER

Stevens?

STEVENS

Nope. (*Coughing*.) I get enough smoke from that fire!

NELSON

Anything wrong, Stevens?

STEVENS

Nope.

ARVIK

Many times I have seen my mother sewing the kamicks. She would frown at this canvas. But we have no skins to use.

CARTER

Do you need any more of my sutures?

ARVIK

No, Doctor. I have enough for the last one.

(*Pause.*) Have you sewn many people with this needle, Dr. Carter?

CARTER

Quite a few.

ARVIK

You must have great skill to do that—inside a man's body.

CARTER

Takes a long time to learn.

ARVIK

Where does a man learn these things?

CARTER

We have special schools, Arvik. The same as you had in the Army—only they teach doctors. You watch others and read books and study.

ARVIK

I would like that.

CARTER

I can't make a shoe cover, Arvik.

ARVIK

Ha! My mother would laugh at these! "Did you not chew them, my son? Can a man keep his feet from turning to ice without furs? You are a senseless man to go away without skins or a woman to keep your clothes and light the fires."

NELSON

Woman—the indispensable tool. Anywhere.

ARVIK

Better than a knife! Better than blubber to fill a lamp! One can find a knife by splitting a rock. One can kill a seal.

CARTER

And you can't sleep with a knife.

ARVIK
No. That is true.

CARTER
(*Sighs.*) Ah, me. (*Choking from the smoke.*)

NELSON
A penny, Doctor?

CARTER
Nothing at all, Nelson. Just that I'd always imagined myself as an old man, having something witty or wise to bring to a crisis. And I haven't.

NELSON
What is it the manual says? Survivors should sing, laugh, tell jokes. Keeps up the morale and time goes quicker.

CARTER
I can't think of a joke about starving.

STEVENS
Old Mother Hubbard went to the cupboard
To find her poor dog a bone.
But when she got there—
(*Stevens begins to get shrill.*) Have some ice water, anybody! Nice fresh ice water! Melted continuously in a tin can!

CARTER
Shut up, Stevens.

STEVENS
(*Mimicking him.*) Shut up, Stevens. Shut up, Stevens.

CARTER
Shut up!

STEVENS
You shut up! I'm hungry, see. My guts are in knots drinking that stuff. So I want to make a joke. I'll make a joke.

CARTER
I'm twenty years older than you are, young man, and I—

STEVENS
You can starve at any age, old man.

CARTER
Why, you—

NELSON
Stop it! Cut it out, both of you!

STEVENS
Who put you in charge of the party?

NELSON
Nobody's in charge — you, me, or anybody else. We're in this together.

CARTER
What is this, Nelson—Eskimo logic?

NELSON
I don't care what you call it. All I know is we're sunk if we don't think, plan, work together—till we're out or till we're dead. I know that much from my time in the jungle.

CARTER
I apologize, Stevens.

STEVENS
Forget it. I'm sorry.

NELSON
We're sorry, Arvik.

ARVIK
It is because we cannot do anything. A storm which keeps men in the house for a long time, waiting, breeds a storm in the house, too. If the wind falls we must hunt tomorrow.

CARTER
Hunt? With our bare hands?

ARVIK
No. Perhaps I can make a harpoon.

NELSON
What are we going to hunt for, Arvik?

ARVIK
The sea contains fish, and the bearded seal waits under the ice for a harpoon. The fox and the wolf can be killed without guns. In my country a man can kill anything if he knows the way.

NELSON
February the 7th. About dusk the snow stopped. Arvik, Stevens, and I drove holes into the four-foot ice with a steel bar from the wreckage. Then we let down our lines, and (as Arvik would say it) the black salmon welcomed a hook that was nothing more than the key from an empty ration can, bent like a pin. Tomorrow we hike up the coast.

ARVIK
Nothing is alive. Nothing is stirring yet after the storm. Our feet are silent in the new snow.

CARTER
Did you ever see such a sight, Nelson? Look at that bay—not a mark, not even a ripple in the snow.

NELSON
Be happier if we saw some animal tracks somewhere. That's one thing you've got over the jungle boys, Arvik.

ARVIK
What is that, Jim?

NELSON
In snow you can track your game inch by inch.

ARVIK
Yes.

NELSON
I've watched natives in the South Pacific follow a trail by the way the leaves were disturbed. You can't see a thing, but they get all excited over a broken twig or a flat piece of grass. "Monkey here! Monkey here!" Sure enough, there's a monkey around.

ARVIK
They must be men of great knowledge.

NELSON
They are.

ARVIK
I think there will be a river beyond that ridge. Look at the clouds over there.

STEVENS
Nothing special about them, Arvik. Strato-cumulus, two thousand feet.

ARVIK
Do you not see the pattern?

CARTER
What pattern?

NELSON
You mean that break where the sun's coming through?

ARVIK
Yes. The sky is sometimes a map of the land underneath. When a valley is seen above there is one below. Let us go there—we may find fresh-water ice. Maybe some live willow branches, too.

STEVENS
I'll bet you five to one there's no river.

ARVIK
(*After a pause.*) I am wrong, Stevens. There is no river— only a deep cut into the land for a tongue of the sea.

STEVENS
You won your money, Arvik.

NELSON
There are a few pieces of driftwood.

ARVIK
Driftwood and something else. See where the wind has blown the beach clear of snow— that is old ice. It will give us fresh water.

CARTER
How can you tell it's old?

ARVIK
Look at it. It is blue and it shines. When you strike it, it will break like glass.

NELSON
It all looks the same to me.

ARVIK
(*Laughing.*) Is it possible? New ice is gray, milky. But that is old ice over there. It has hid from the sun under that cliff for many seasons. Now that the salt is gone, the water will be sweet.

STEVENS
Tell me, how did it get there?

ARVIK
Does someone ask why the sun is warm or the seas wet?

CARTER
Probably driven up by the wind, Stevens. I've seen pack ice jammed up at Pelly Bay in July.

ARVIK
I do not know. Maybe an angiut left it for us. The helping spirits know all about everyone.

NELSON
On February 9th and 10th, it stormed, and

I wrote in my journal: "Arvik is a mixture of technician and mystic, like most men. What observation can teach, he knows. What doing can prove, he accepts. Without knowing physics, he observes the effect of adiabatic changes in the atmosphere, and correlates a break in the clouds with an unseen valley. What meteorologist could do better? And no meteorologist would spot the old sea ice—in spite of knowing that sublimation removes the salt with time. Without books, he preserves the past. And yet, he believes in spirits.

"We have no food now. If it stops blowing tomorrow, Arvik and I will go after seals. He has made us two harpoons—shafts from driftwood, heads from the brass case of the plane's compass, lines from the nylon cords of the parachute. We will see."

ARVIK

(*Walking with Nelson in the snow*). There will be no caribou along the coast, Jim. When the sun goes away they follow it.

NELSON

You never keep caribou. Why?

ARVIK

What could we feed them—ice?

NELSON

Don't you ever think—

ARVIK

Wait! Let us be still. (*Pause.*) See the small rise in the snow. Something is coming up to breathe at a hole there. (*He runs through the snow.*) Quickly! Softly! (*Pause.*) Now! (*He plunges his harpoon into a pocket of water and ice.*)

NELSON

Did you get him?

ARVIK

It is too late. You have only one chance.

NELSON

It's the first hole we've found.

ARVIK

We are lucky. Now we know there are seals under this ice.

NELSON

It won't help if we don't get one.

ARVIK

You will stay here, Jim. I have scraped new snow over the hole which the seal has gnawed. The small stick is in place. If you see the stick move, drive the harpoon down with all your strength.

NELSON

I stood on the ice with my back to the wind, crouching over the hole. Arvik walked slowly in widening circles around me, probing the snow with a bent piece of wire—pausing, then going on. Then he stopped. He had found one. Time seemed to crawl as we watched the unmoving slivers of wood in the snow. It came to me that I was hunting for my life—directly—with nothing between me and this one objective. Knowing the shape of a mine shaft had no meaning in this environment. Nor the sound of a Geiger counter. The hand and the spear and the eye held all the answers to survival.

ARVIK

Nelson! Nelson! We have one! Come and drink the hot blood of the seal!

(*Pause.*)

CAST

For he's a jolly good seal,
For he's a jolly good seal,
Which nobody can deny. (*Laughter.*)

STEVENS

You know, Nelson, I thought you'd been stabbed. Your whole face was bloody.

ARVIK

He did not want to take it. I had to open his mouth, and then he choked!

NELSON

I never drank blood before. Almost scalded my face off.

ARVIK

You were cold from standing so long. That is why it was hot to your lips.

STEVENS
Do you think it has stewed long enough?

CARTER
Eat slowly, Stevens. It's going to be strong.

ARVIK
What will you eat first? A flipper? A piece of the lip?

STEVENS
Anything—anything but the guts.

ARVIK
Ah.

CARTER
For what we're about to receive, Lord, make us truly thankful. Amen.

STEVENS
Amen.

NELSON
Amen.

ARVIK
What is wrong? Does no one wish to eat?

NELSON
Grace before food, Arvik. It's a custom sometimes among us.

ARVIK
Like blowing sweet water into the seal's mouth. We do that so the dead seal will tell his brothers we gave him a drink. They live in the sea; they are always thirsty.

CARTER
Did you do it this time, Arvik?

ARVIK
Yes. On the ice, I melted snow in my mouth for the dead seal. His brothers will not avoid us.

CARTER
Amen.

STEVENS
Is it all right if we eat now?

ARVIK
Everything. Eat everything but the eyes. We must have them to keep evil spirits away if we travel to Pelly Bay.

NELSON
February the 12th. We have killed three seals now. Tomorrow we start for Pelly Bay dragging our gear on a sealskin sled. Arvik makes even the cold work for him. The runners are strips of sealskin well soaked with water and frozen rigid. We're going overland. Four men on the tundra. A hundred miles....

ARVIK
(*Shouting over a howling wind.*) We cannot stop here. To reach Pelly Bay with food we must not stop here.

NELSON
Carry on, Arvik.

ARVIK
Keep the slatted wood over your eyes, Stevens. Without sun, you can still go blind in the snow.

STEVENS
Okay, okay, okay!

CARTER
Can't something be done about the sled? It's getting heavier all the time.

NELSON
We're just tired, Carter.

STEVENS
You're crazy, Nelson. Feel it; it drags like a stone.

ARVIK
That will be the runners. We must renew the mud and the ice to make them run smoothly.

NELSON
It's a long way to water.

CARTER
Can't we stay here? Can't we build a shelter and melt snow?

ARVIK
Is that what is wanted?

CARTER
I'm tired. I'd like a rest. I'm an old man, Arvik.

NELSON
How far should we go, Arvik?

ARVIK
Five, maybe six, miles. We should do six miles before dark.

NELSON

We won't start again if we make shelter. Not before dark.

ARVIK

What is the wish of the others?

STEVENS

Fix the sled and I'll go.

NELSON

Carter—what about you?

CARTER

I'll go, if I have to. I'll go.

ARVIK

Take the mud bag from the sled. Water? We will make urine. That will save time. That will save lighting a fire.

NELSON

February the 19th. We have come sixty miles on the way. But the meat is running out. Carter is very tired. Arvik and I went searching for iron pyrites among the rocks. No luck. The fool's gold eludes us. But this fool stumbled into a crevice and twisted a knee. A painful reward for my ignorance of snow. Three matches left. Unless we find bits of pyrites, the blubber won't be much use. Forty miles to go.

STEVENS

Come on, Doc. On your feet. Sled's waiting for us.

CARTER

What day is it?

STEVENS

The same as yesterday; the same as tomorrow; forever and ever.

NELSON

It's the twentieth, Carter. We've been on the march eight days.

CARTER

Eight days—is that all?

NELSON

That's all.

CARTER

I'm not going, Nelson. I'm going to stay behind.

NELSON

Don't be crazy. You're coming if we have to carry you.

CARTER

Listen to me, Nelson, Stevens.

STEVENS

He's pretty bad. Ankles all swollen.

NELSON

We'll put you on the sled, Carter. We'll pull you. The three of us can manage.

CARTER

Ask Arvik to come here.

NELSON

He's fixing the sled.

CARTER

I want to see him.

STEVENS

I'll get him.

NELSON

Now let's take it easy, Doctor. Forty miles and we'll be in Pelly Bay.

CARTER

Don't try to confuse me, Nelson. And watch your knee. Or you'll be next.

ARVIK

What is it?

NELSON

He wants to see you.

ARVIK

Yes.

CARTER

You'll give me an honest answer, Arvik?

ARVIK

Yes.

CARTER

What chance is there of your getting through to Pelly Bay—with me on the sled?

ARVIK

It is not easy to say. We may find a cache— or kill a fox. Then we would all have new strength.

CARTER

Answer me.

ARVIK

(*Slowly.*) No. It is not likely.

CARTER

That's all I wanted to know.

NELSON

But, Carter.

CARTER

You heard him, didn't you? Now the three of you go like blazes for that Bay. If you make it—then you can learn how to live with your conscience. If you don't—what does it matter?

ARVIK

(*Pause.*) You are a good man, old man.

NELSON

What are you talking about? I'm not going to leave him here.

ARVIK

No, Jim, no. He speaks the wisdom of old men among my people. My own grandfather— not as old as the doctor but going blind—he left us one night for his long sleep on the ice. Without speaking. If the young and the strong ones are to live, the old and the weak ones must die. It is the way....

NELSON

February 22nd. This may be the last entry in the journal of James Nelson, mining engineer. Arvik and Stevens have disappeared over the last ridge of ice. And my hope goes with them toward Pelly Bay. I am alone now, without food, with my knee in the splints. I am afraid, and I keep a seal eye in my hand— for safety. What life I have left or hope to have again, I owe to Arvik—technician, mystic, man.

4. EDUCATION

We enter our society as infants, and as we grow up we also grow into our culture. This is true of all people in all societies. The process of growing into a culture is the process of learning its technical knowledge, its patterns of behavior, its attitudes and viewpoints. Anthropologists have come to call this process "enculturation," but we can refer to it more simply as "education." Since all culture is based upon learned behavior, it follows that all cultures must provide for the education of the young. The patterns of teaching vary, as do the things taught, but the process always involves two areas of learning.

The first of these is the learning of skills. It is this part of education that we emphasize in our schools—so that it is virtually synonymous with the word *education*. The complexity of our accumulated knowledge has made schools into one of America's major activities, and we not only carry on this education longer than almost any other people, but we have a great variety of technical schools. Few primitive societies have anything like schools for the education of their young. There the processes of manufacture and food-getting are so much a part of everyday life that they are constantly before the child. As in "progressive" schools, the child learns by doing. The girl helps her mother gather clay for pottery, or helps her aunt gather the necessary roots or grasses for basketry. The boy joins his father on the hunt or watches while he straightens and shaves the arrow shaft. The child is not merely allowed to watch, but given instruction and practice. He is constantly induced to learn that which must be known to maintain the economy. Where very special skills art required, this teaching is often highly organized—as in teaching the native doctoring craf to the shamans.

But the area of education that interests us most is the teaching of attitudes and values. The outlook of a people is constantly shown in actions as well as in words, and so it is communicated in thousands of little ways. Education for values begins therefore from the very earliest experiences, and continues throughout the growth of the child. Much that is learned is never given conscious formulation but rather laid down as the underlying assumptions upon which the more conscious attitudes are based. The deep influence of such undirected learning can best be seen in the way we learn our language. Man is capable of making an infinite variety of sounds, but he loses this ability when his culture focuses attention on just a few. Try to teach an English-speaking person the French *u* sound, or the difference between the *ch* sound in the German words *ich* and *ach*—perfectly ordinary and easy sounds to a child who grew up hearing them as important. So too with grammar. As shown in the Navaho illustration in "A Word in Your Ear" (Chapter 2), our notions of causation are subtly introduced to us as we learn our grammar.

The same applies to other things we learn. Consider, for instance, the attitude in our culture that a person should try to outdo others wherever he can. It is related to our ideas of competition in business, where, perhaps, it gets its philosophical justification. Many influences make a child aware of this idea. He is encouraged in sports, and he tries to win. He is given marks in school which compare him with his fellows. It is important that he pass in school, that he graduate. He must earn money if he is to satisfy his wants, and he earns it by work and skill. Much earlier he has probably heard: "Johnny started talking before he was a year old," or, "Eat oatsies if you want to be a champion." He thinks of himself in the comparative terms he has heard fond grandparents—and television commercials—use. These attitudes are so familiar that they seem—like any element of one's own culture—the very nature of behavior.

But a Hopi boy, as we will see in "Desert Soliloquy," does not hear these things. He works, because he must eat. But he does not work in competition with others. Games are not played to win, native education does not give marks, children are not compared with other children by fond grandparents. The Hopi way of life mutes competitiveness in favor of a personal subordination to the general group.

But this attitude is not characteristic of all primitive peoples. The Tlingit Indians, as we saw in "Stand-in for a Murderer" (Chapter 1), place great emphasis on individual accomplishment, and they are faced with constant comparisons of rank.

The important point is that each culture provides its young with models for behavior in terms of its own culture pattern, and the young fit themselves to the model. It is in precisely this way that the patterns of culture are continued through the generations.

Many anthropologists and psychologists see still more subtle and indirect forces at work. They feel that prolonged breast-feeding and relaxed attitudes toward toilet-training help the child feel secure in his relationships and therefore less competitive in his attitudes. Another influence is in the method of chastising the child when he misbehaves. In our culture this is the job of the parents, who have full responsibility. Among the Hopi it is rarely the parents, but usually an uncle, and more often an impersonal spirit. It may be a warning like the "bogey man" we once used, or it may be a relative dressed as a Katchina spirit, threatening to eat the child. When this happens, the parents take the side of the boy and help to "prevent" the Katchina from doing harm. Thus the child gets support from those closest to him, feels warmth and protection rather than resentment and hostility. Even when one parent scolds the child, the other parent will usually take his side. He is never isolated by punishment, never made to feel outside the group.

No culture lets its values and attitudes merely grow up in the child. It often makes some of them explicit. Values are usually presented in ceremonial occasions, which have heightened emotional content. Among the Hopi the boys have special initiations in which they are told the tribal values. Myths and tales provide other means of telling the young the values of the society. We, too, use these methods.

Education must provide the youth with the tools he needs to be a member of his own society. This means both the skills necessary for his livelihood and the attitudes required for participation in his own culture. We may admire the educational ways of the Hopi or some other society, but we cannot emulate them without altering the fabric of our own culture. A child reared by Hopi methods is not well trained for modern American life, though he may be ideally suited for the co-operative efforts necessary to getting a living on the southwest desert.

Education, the transmission of culture from generation to generation, is therefore a necessary process for the continuation of culture. All societies provide for education by processes that are direct and explicit, as well as those that are subtle and unintentional.

Desert Soliloquy

LEN PETERSON

❮❮

The scene is the southwest desert, at night. Naquima, a Hopi youth of eighteen, sits on the flat roof of his Pueblo house. He is faced with a decision which will determine the course of his life, and he conjures up the scenes that have made him feel and act as a young Hopi man.

The Hopi are one of several Pueblo tribes of the southwest, living in compact villages atop mesas. Below the mesas are their small farm plots, scattered in the arroyos where spring floods offer damp soil. Here they carefully plant corn, beans, and squash. The Pueblo Indians now have adopted sheepherding and other elements of Western culture, but their life remains rooted in the old traditions, the old rituals, the old social organization.

NAQUIMA

(*To himself.*) It has cooled off. The stars are very bright tonight. No clouds. We need rain badly. Mr. McCrea will be around first thing in the morning and I haven't decided yet. What holds me here? Tourists who drive through think it's the end of the earth and can't understand why we Hopi Indians go on living here in northern Arizona in the middle of the desert. And yet Oraibi, one of our villages, pueblos, is the oldest inhabited place in the whole United States. Life is hard, a good heart is needed—that is the Hopi way. I do not want to leave the Hopi way, that is why it is so hard to decide. My high-school teacher has got me a scholarship to the white man's university at Tucson. But—I will have to think with the head if I go away, and not with the heart. I feel more sure with the heart. That is the Hopi way. Even the story of my birth the whites (I have told it to them) will not believe. (*Remembered scenes and snatches of conversation are conjured up by Naquima.*)

GRANDMOTHER

(*Who delights in telling stories to wide-eyed children.*) The first time you were born a girl.

NAQUIMA

My grandmother liked to tell that story to me.

GRANDMOTHER

You were a fine girl. But when you were still wrapped up on the cradleboard you died. Your mother and father were very sad. They

buried you and thrust a digging stick into the grave. On the fourth day you climbed up the stick and came back to this house and waited in the ceiling to be born again, and this time you were born a boy, and we named you Naquima.

NAQUIMA

The whites say that is nonsense. But do they have a better story to tell their women who have lost a child? I do not look down upon the whites, but it is not easy to leave the Hopi way for the American way. The American way seems so complicated and difficult and—nervous. I watch a white mother in a cafe:

WHITE MOTHER

Douglas, sit there and behave yourself. We've only got ten minutes before we gotta catch the bus.

WHITE BOY

My ball's on the floor.

WHITE MOTHER

Leave it there; nobody's going to steal it. Sit up and eat.

WHITE BOY

Pickle—wanna pickle.

WHITE MOTHER

No, you can't have any more pickles. And don't play with your food. Eat those vegetables and grow up to be a big boy. See if you can beat Mama.

WHITE BOY

Sure I can! Watch me. I can beat anybody.

WHITE MOTHER

Look out, you're going to spill that glass of water! (*The glass goes over and water spills.*)

WHITE MOTHER

Oh, dear, all over everything, soaking wet. Never seen it yet to fail, I'm never going to take you out again. (*She slaps him.*) Get up! Don't just sit there and let it run all over you! (*The boy begins to cry.*) Bad boy!

NAQUIMA

White children cry a lot more than Hopi children. They're always being bawled out and

punished. They must do this, they mustn't do that. I am glad I was not a white child. But I have heard—criticism of the way our kids are brought up too.

TOURIST

Those poor Indian babies! I think it's terrible binding those babies on those cradleboards so they can't move.

NAQUIMA

I don't know who she was, that woman—some tourist passing through. But she had a lot to say.

TOURIST

With both their arms and legs tied down, I'm sure it retards them in learning things. And they must be very slow getting around to walking.

NAQUIMA

I should've spoken to her, but I didn't. Hopi babies who are bound and those who are not learn to walk at the same time.

TOURIST

And I think it's dreadful letting these children do anything they want. Really! No discipline at all!

NAQUIMA

Free as the breeze, huh, lady?

TOURIST

No schedule right from the beginning. Whenever a baby whimpers its mother feeds it. No toilet-training that I can see. And very small children—if they want a drink of black coffee or a piece of spiced meat, they get it. Anything they want. Completely spoiled.

NAQUIMA

And what's the harm in that, lady?

TOURIST

No wonder so many of their children die, with the kind of diet they get, and the unsanitary conditions.

NAQUIMA

She is right, we do have a lot of deaths. Maybe we should be more careful about what we feed babies and small children, and maybe the sanitary conditions could be improved. I have heard the government doctor say that too.

[MUSIC]

My own childhood. Do I remember so much, or is it the older people telling me about it that I remember? I don't remember being bound on the cradleboard, but I remember being carried around by my older sister, I remember climbing up on my mother to be fed, I remember her stopping me by putting red chili on herself. I was a toddler then and could say a few words.

NAQUIMA

(*Now aged two.*) Mama—want—Mama.

MOTHER

No, Naquima, you are getting too big.

NAQUIMA

Mama—want—

(*Again narrating.*) My brother, Lee, was coming along; that was why she weaned me. I remember the night journeys in the dark when I was very small.

MOTHER

Now that you understand, you'll go outside when you have to go, Naquima. You do that again in here and your uncle will come for you. Do you want that? Do you?

NAQUIMA

No.

[MUSIC]

NAQUIMA

Life seemed very hard having to get up in the night and go out, even just outside the door. When I got older I had to go to the end of the plaza. It was cold, it was dark. I'd hold back—until there wasn't time sometimes. The first thing I was ever punished for. My mother's brother, my Uncle Tuvaletztewa, came and carried me about the village and invited people to throw cold water on me.

UNCLE

Naquima will not obey his mother. Won't you help me purify him?

VOICE

Yes, Tuvaletztewa. Here. (*He throws water on Naquima.*)

NAQUIMA

(*Age 3.*) (*Choking and shivering.*) Oh! Oh! I will be good, Uncle. I will be good.

[MUSIC]

NAQUIMA

One other time I was taken out by Uncle Tuvaletztewa and rolled naked in the snow. I don't remember what badness it was for. Among the whites it is the father who is stern and punishes. That must be very strange. My father never punished me, or my brothers and sisters. We were always very happy with him. My mother sometimes slapped us or threatened us.

MOTHER

(*The propeller-like noise of a toy "bull-roarer" is heard.*) Naquima!

NAQUIMA

(*Now 4 years old.*) What?

MOTHER

Stop twirling that flat stick with the string and making that noise, or a bad wind will come.

NAQUIMA

What bad wind?

MOTHER

The neighbors will talk about you, you'll disgrace the whole family, if you make a strong wind come. That is not Hopi.

NAQUIMA

Oh, listen what a loud noise it makes, Mama!

MOTHER

I'll let the Spider Woman catch you in her web, or a coyote get you, or a Navaho, if you don't stop. (*The bull-roarer is abruptly stopped.*)

NAQUIMA

I've stopped, Mama. You won't let the Spider Woman get me?

FATHER

No, come here, Naquima. I won't let anything get you.

NAQUIMA

If anyone threatened or punished us, there was always somebody else around to comfort us so that we were never frightened or hurt for long.

MOTHER

Don't touch the fire, Naquima. It's hot. It'll burn you.

FATHER

Don't go near the edge of the cliff, Naquima. You might fall over.

NAQUIMA

Those were the only two really big don'ts in my life when I was very small. And I didn't hear them very often. Someone was always with me—my big sister or my mother—to see that nothing did happen to me. My childhood was very happy. And full of wonder. My grandmother telling stories filled the days with wonder.

[MUSIC]

GRANDMOTHER

The Sun is the greatest god of all. He is very strong. Every day—you see him, don't you?—he travels across the sky and heats and lights the world and makes life, makes you, makes me, makes the plants and the animals and the birds. And the Moon and Stars help him. And then there are the other sky gods, the Wind, the Lightning, the Thunder, the Rain, and the Rainbow. And Eagle and Hawk spirits who do many things to help us. And under the ground is Masau'u, the god of fire and death, who walks at night and protects us in our sleep. And Muyingwa who makes the seeds come. And the Corn-Mother and her Corn-Maidens who watch over the corn. And the Katchinas. And a spirit guide for each one of us.

NAQUIMA

(*Five years old.*) Grandmother, make a story about the Katchinas.

GRANDMOTHER

Long ago our people had a terrible drought; there was no water and no food and the Hopi tribe was starving. They heard strange noises from the forest at the foot of the San Francisco peaks. They went over and saw strange figures in gay costumes dancing and singing songs. They were Katchinas, spirits from the other world who had come with water and food to end the suffering of the Hopi tribe. Ever since then, from January to August, the Katchinas, the Eagle Dancer, Long Hair, Corn Maiden, Mud Head the clown, and all the others have come over from the San Francisco peaks and the Black Mountain every year to visit our pueblos. Some travel on the clouds and some underground and come up through the floor of the ceremonial chamber, the kiva. They come to dance and sing and help us with our crops and bless our homes and bring presents for the children if they're good.

NAQUIMA

What will they bring me this time when they come?

[MUSIC]

NAQUIMA

Oh, I remember the time I was not good and the Katchinas found out.

FATHER

(*Speaking as a Katchina with a heavy, menacing voice through a mask.*) Where is Naquima?

MOTHER

Naquima, the Katchina wants you!

FATHER

Where is he? Are you his mother?

MOTHER

Yes, what do you have for him? He has been hoping for a fine bow and arrows.

FATHER

No, he has been bad. I am going to take him away and eat him.

[MUSIC]

NAQUIMA

That was enough for me. I scurried into the house and hid under one of the couches. The

Katchina had a terrible face. I could still hear them.

MOTHER

No, don't take him away.

FATHER

Yes, he has been bad. Fighting with the other children and killing chickens. Where is he? (*Shouting*.) Naquima!

GRANDMOTHER

I am his grandmother. Please, don't take him away.

FATHER

We always eat the bad Hopi children.

MOTHER

If we give you some food, won't that do?

FATHER

No, I want Naquima.

GRANDMOTHER

Katchina, why don't you take my old man instead? He's not much use to me any more. Take him and leave Naquima.

FATHER

Which is your old man? This dried-up old fellow?

GRANDMOTHER

Yes.

FATHER

No, too tough. I want Naquima. (*Bellowing*.) Where is he?

MOTHER

Please, Katchina, he will be good, I promise you. His uncle will see that he is. He didn't mean to be a bad boy, and he won't be any more. Take this food, and leave Naquima with us. Please!

FATHER

(*Dubiously*.) He will be good from now on?

GRANDMOTHER

We will all promise that he will be a good boy, his mother, his uncle, his grandmother and grandfather. Take this food.

FATHER

All right, I'll let you keep the boy. Give me that basket of food. And since Naquima is

going to be a good boy from now on, give him this bow and arrow.

MOTHER

Thank you, Katchina. I'll go and find him and give them to him.

[MUSIC]

NAQUIMA

I was very grateful to my mother and grandmother for saving me from the Katchina. I was glad I got the bow and arrows too. I was glad about a lot of things those days. I was even glad when my father made me get up before sunrise.

[MUSIC]

FATHER

You are getting too big to be lying in bed in the morning, Naquima. Off you go to the far spring and wash.

NAQUIMA

(*Aged 6.*) My clothes—

FATHER

No, naked. Run so that you will get back here before the women get up and see you. From now on you will do this every morning so you'll get big and strong. And after eating would you like to come along and help me in the fields?

NAQUIMA

Oh, yes.

FATHER

Keep the birds away—and the prairie dogs.

NAQUIMA

And herd the sheep?

FATHER

Maybe. Hurry now, dash off and wash. The sun will soon be up.

[MUSIC]

NAQUIMA

Learning to work began like play. I tagged along behind my father and tried to do what I saw him doing. I helped my mother gather rabbitweed for baskets and dig clay for pottery. I planted melon seeds and kernels of corn. I carried dirt for my father when he put a new roof on our stone house. I felt important. The work I did—even when I was only six and seven—was important to my family. Just to survive here on the desert every Hopi must work hard and long. I was a child with responsibilities. But still I rolled my car tire, and played games, and teased the girls. I came and went pretty much as I pleased, I ate when I pleased, I explored where I pleased. And every now and then my father told me things about the Hopi way.

FATHER

Naquima, it is wrong to destroy plants and animals.

NAQUIMA

Will something happen to us for hunting these rabbits?

FATHER

We must not kill any more than we need. And we must ask the animal people to forgive us and not be too angry, because we kill only to live. Just the same as you and your mother asked the plant people to forgive you when you picked weeds for weaving.

NAQUIMA

We put food down beside the first weed we found.

FATHER

And you asked it to tell the other plant people how much you needed rabbitweed for baskets.

NAQUIMA

Yes, we didn't pick it.

FATHER

The whole world must work in harmony, Naquima. Nature, the gods, the plants, the animals, and men need each other and must work together for the good of all. There is no place for selfish men, or even for a selfish man among men; it would throw everything out of balance and endanger the whole universe. To be a good Hopi, Naquima, you will work for the good of your family, your clan, the village—

NAQUIMA

And the whole world.

FATHER

Yes. Praise what others do, but belittle what you do yourself, Naquima. Keep a good heart.

[MUSIC]

NAQUIMA

The only trouble was I had to go to the white man's school. I couldn't spend all day in the fields with my father. I had to sit at a desk. How we all squirmed on the nice days! We learned the white man's language, and we learned to read and write. Our teacher was Miss Talayesva, who had gone away and learned the white man's ways. She was all right. But our next teacher was Miss Wilson. She had queer ways.

MISS WILSON

(*At head of class, in a raised voice.*) Children, put up your hand as soon as you've finished the exercise. Now let's see who can get through these subtractions first. All right, start! (*Pause.*)

MISS WILSON: Naquima.

NAQUIMA (*Aged 8.*) Yes, Miss Wilson?

MISS WILSON

Why aren't you working on those subtractions? Don't sit looking out the window. Get to work!

NAQUIMA

I'm working.

MISS WILSON

You were daydreaming.

NAQUIMA

No.

MISS WILSON

(*Coming closer.*) Have you got any of them done? Let me see.

NAQUIMA

Working on them.

MISS WILSON

Let me see. Why, you've got them all done! So soon! Why didn't you put up your hand? Why didn't you tell me you were finished?

NAQUIMA
I don't know.

MISS WILSON
Why don't you know?

NAQUIMA
I don't know.

MISS WILSON
Don't you want to do well in school?

NAQUIMA
I was ashamed to do better than the other kids. I didn't want to be teased by them for showing off. I didn't understand Miss Wilson. I wished she'd leave me alone. But she caught me a number of times holding back.

MISS WILSON
What are you trying to be, saucy with me, Naquima?

NAQUIMA
No.

MISS WILSON
Don't you want to do well in school? Don't you want to get ahead? You could be a very good pupil if you wanted to be. Why don't you try?

NAQUIMA
I don't know.

MISS WILSON
What kind of an attitude is that? I notice it in a lot of the pupils here. Now where did you get this from? Tell me!

NAQUIMA
I couldn't explain to her. I didn't know how to tell her. But she must've found out from someone how a Hopi feels, because after a while she stopped all that stuff about getting through first or getting the highest marks. Even when we played basketball, we didn't like to keep score; it was better just to play. Miss Wilson was a good teacher, and I liked her, after she stopped picking on me. She got me interested in history and geography and lent me books. I guess she was the first one I ever knew who thought and lived the American way, where you worry a lot about getting ahead of everybody else.

FATHER
Here in the middle of the desert no one gets ahead unless we all get ahead. The threat of death from thirst and starvation hangs over all of us. We live and die together.

[MUSIC]

NAQUIMA
The time came when I was to go through the Katchina initiation and learn the real nature of the Katchinas and gain the right to take part in the Katchina dances. It was in my eighth year. The sixth day of the Bean Dance was the day of the initiation. I was prepared by a friend of my father's, Talasemptewa of the Gray Hawk Clan.

TALASEMPTEWA
Naquima, down in the kiva you will be whipped by one of the Katchinas.

NAQUIMA
Yes, I know. Will it hurt, Talasemptewa?

TALASEMPTEWA
They hit hard to purify you, my boy.

NAQUIMA
Do many of the boys who are whipped cry?

TALASEMPTEWA:
Some of them. But you will be brave, Naquima, won't you?

NAQUIMA
(*Not too sure.*) Yes, Talasemptewa.

[MUSIC]
(*Hopi ceremonial.*)

NAQUIMA
It was a long ceremony down in the kiva: prayers, singing, sprinkling us boys and girls with water and tying feathers into our hair, sand-painting, ritual, the Katchinas dancing. (*The dancers grunt in time with their turtle-shell rattles and bells.*)

NAQUIMA
What is that, Talasemptewa?

TALASEMPTEWA
The time has come, Naquima. (*Men beat on the earth roof of the kiva with whips.*)

KATCHINAS

(*Three Katchina dancers chant, in and out several times before coming close.*) U'huhuhu, u'huhuhu, u'huhuhu, u'huhuhu, u'huhuhu, u'huhuhu.

NAQUIMA

The Katchinas who were to flog us came down into the kiva, took their places around the sand mosaic on the floor—and one of the naked boys who was to be initiated was seized, placed on the mosaic with his hands held over his head. (*The sound of a whip lash, and a boy reacts with pain and fright; then a second lash and the initiate begins to whine.*)

NAQUIMA

They weren't light with the whip. I wanted to scramble up out of the kiva. I hoped something would happen and my turn would never come. And I hoped my turn would come soon and be over. Some of the children cried even before their turn, some held out right through the punishment—the cleansing. I held out against the first three lashes, but with the fourth blow (*there is the sound of a whip lash and Naquima blurts out in pain*) the pain was too great and I gave way.

TALASEMPTEWA (*Protesting*)

Did you have to hit him so hard?

NAQUIMA

But with that fourth blow the ordeal was over. I was ashamed and relieved. And at the end— at the end of the ceremony we were overjoyed to see the Katchinas whipping each other. (*Whip lashes are heard, increasing in intensity; there is angry grunting and yelping with pain.*)

CHILDREN

(*Yelping with delight and cheering and urging them on.*) Yes, hit him, hit him, hit him! More! More!

[MUSIC]

NAQUIMA

On the ninth day of the Bean Dance—the last day—we saw the Katchina dancers without their masks. They were men whom we knew. They included my father and my uncles.

TALASEMPTEWA

Naquima, you must tell no one what you have seen and heard during these ceremonies. Above all, you must not tell the children who the men are that wear the Katchina masks. In gratitude for their saving us long ago and watching over us ever since, we impersonate

the Katchinas. You will be able to take part in the dances now. You are growing up, Naquima.

[MUSIC]

NAQUIMA

We went through a very bad drought when I was ten, eleven, and twelve years old. Our three-year storage of beans and corn in the kiva almost gave out. I learned to wash myself with a mouthful of water to avoid wasting a drop. I learned how precious water is.

FATHER
Naquima, we will have to take the burros and move on west to get water and bring it back.

NAQUIMA
(*Aged 12.*) How far will we have to go, Father?

FATHER
I do not know. I do not think we'll have to go as far as the Colorado. I hope the Snake Dance will bring rain.

MOTHER
It will.

GRANDMOTHER
Oh, yes, this time it will.

FATHER
This time it must.

[MUSIC]

NAQUIMA
The ceremonies in themselves were never enough. They had to be made intense and alive before they could affect the rest of nature. Man can, my people believe, exercise some control over the orderly rhythm of the world with his actions, thoughts, emotions, and will. Man must, to avoid failure, see the world whole, and understand the relationship of all that goes to make up the harmonious ebb and flow, the decay and creation.

[MUSIC]

TALASEMPTEWA
Naquima, you are a man.

NAQUIMA
This year I went through my second initiation to become a member of the Horn Society.

TALASEMPTEWA
Naquima, you take on the duties and rights of a man. You will avoid quarreling and fights over petty things. You will be a good Hopi. You will be peaceful.

[MUSIC]

NAQUIMA
At school I have learned many things of the American way. All my teachers have told me I am a good student, and when I came under Mr. McCrea in high school he told me I

should go on to the university. He gave me extra work and instruction. And now he's gotten me this scholarship. But I still feel strange to the white man's ways. We have had many talks together after school, Mr. McCrea and I.

MCCREA
You could become an interpreter, Naquima, explaining Hopi customs to the whites, especially officials, and explaining American customs to the Hopi.

NAQUIMA
Mr. McCrea, there are some old Hopi men who say we will lose the Hopi way if we mix any more with the whites. We must keep to our own path.

MCCREA
Certainly, the Hopi way deserves preserving. But you can become rigid and stand still.

NAQUIMA
But our people say that when you have been away to a white university it is impossible to come back here, because they turn you into a white, in your thoughts and feelings.

MCCREA
You are threatened, Naquima, whether you stay here or go away. American ways are creeping into the pueblos. Why not face it with wisdom and a good heart? Be proud of your Hopi heritage, but don't be afraid to take from other worlds what might be useful in yours. Learn from the whites; at the same time you could teach them something.

NAQUIMA
What?

MCCREA
Aliveness within and serenity without. No desire for wealth, power, and prestige gnawing at the heart.

NAQUIMA
Hunger sometimes.

MCCREA
Yes, you have your battle with nature. But among yourselves you feel secure. People in

the other world, though they are richer, much richer—and more powerful, I suppose—can never be sure what kind of treatment they are going to get from their fellows. And it isn't just one man against another, but also each man battling within himself over conflicting values. He wrestles with them for a while, and then divides his life into compartments. It's called adjustment. Life is lived then in fragments.

NAQUIMA
Instead of whole.

MCCREA
If you could teach them to see things whole, Naquima—

NAQUIMA
Like the creatures in the Hopi world.

MCCREA
Yes, but it's a devil of a job to get them to.

NAQUIMA
If I go, maybe I'll end up leading a fragmented life.

MCCREA
Maybe. You'll probably be less happy than some of your friends who stay on here in the pueblo.

NAQUIMA
Then why go? For some kind of "success"?

MCCREA
No, Naquima. I wouldn't want you to go to pursue success, nor stay to pursue happiness. I've been hoping you'd just want to go because you're alive, curious. Well? Why don't you?

[MUSIC]

NAQUIMA
I still can't make up my mind, sitting out here on the roof all this time. The stars have moved. It's getting chilly. I'll probably not decide until the very last minute when Mr. McCrea comes for his final answer in the morning. Then I'll have to say.

[FINALE]

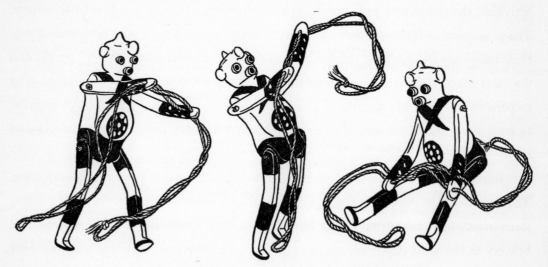

Katchina dolls

5. VALUES

A society is a group of people organized as a unit and sharing a common cultural heritage. The central organizing principle in any society is the values that its people have acquired as a part of their cultural heritage. For values give direction to the lives of the people, make meaningful their acts, and serve as a bond among them.

Values are sometimes defined as those broad principles which each culture assumes, and which underlie the specific acts of the people. In such a view, democracy and individualism are values in our society—just as "having a good heart" and self-effacement are values in Hopi society. Each culture has broad values of this type that govern conduct.

But we use the word differently here, as being those qualities, situations, and things that a people holds dear: the qualities of personality and character, the social positions and activities, the things that have special symbolic meaning for any one particular culture. The possession of these qualities, the enjoyment of these positions, and the ownership of these things are the marks of prestige. They differentiate between the "better" people and the "less good"—as that culture views the good. The Greeks used the word *arete* to refer to persons so endowed—and had a clear definition of what a man must be like in order to have *arete*. But all cultures, whether they have such a word or not, have a definition of *arete*.

But each culture has its own specific notion of the things that enter into having *arete*. The Indians of the American plains were a warlike hunting people. Warfare and hunting were most important to the plains Indians, and they recognized military prowess and bravery as the most important qualities of character. The most desirable activities were to belong to a military society, to have the visions that give magical power and strength, and to lead a war party. Owning horses and the privilege of honest boasts of valor were the prize evidences of attainment. Among the Hopi Indians of the Southwest, as we saw in "Desert Soliloquy" (Chapter 4), very different virtues were sought. A deep religious sense, the detailed knowledge of rituals, and a self-effacing character were all-important. To have the ceremonial knowledge necessary for being dance leader was to be "wealthy." As we turn from one people to another, we see that each has its own particular values, its own definitions of *arete*.

Values are a part of the cultural heritage. They do, of course, change with time; but they often have a long life. That the young should ordinarily seek the values that their elders hold important is quite natural, when we consider the situation. For one thing, they are told to. But this is not so important as the fact that the young people see that the old people who possess the valued qualities are viewed with prestige; they see such people influencing others, and see that they also have the maximum satisfactions the society can provide.

In all cultures there are symbolic representations of values: things to possess, privileges to be enjoyed, crests, emblems, memberships. The variety of such symbolic representations are very great. Man's imagination has run riot in devising symbols for values—rare skins, sacred stones, modes of birth, copper shields are among the items found in various parts of the globe—and our own symbols are of many similar kinds. The symbol serves as the public proclamation of the *arete*, and at the same time offers a concrete goal to behavior. Consider the logic from the standpoint of a young person growing up in his culture: "I want to be thought well of, like such and such an elder. He has certain goods and privileges and therefore I must have them, too. To get them, I must act according to prescribed canons of behavior—then I, too, will be what I (and my culture) want me to be."

The logic is circular, to be sure. But it is precisely this circularity in reasoning that acts as the basis for cultural continuity—to want what is valued and to value what is wanted. In final analysis, it makes little difference what the symbols of *arete* are, so long as all people recognize them, and will shape their behavior in the prescribed manner to get them.

Not all cultures allow for the attainment of values by all. In some societies, valued positions are determined by heredity; this is true of the feudal estates of Europe or the castes of India. The same was true in ancient Greece, where the *arete* of the Greek citizens was not available to a large slave class. These slaves probably also had a set of values to which they directed their attention, but we do not know what these were. Sociologists distinguish these caste positions by calling them *ascribed status*, as distinct from the *achieved status* of our own society, and of the plains Indians and others. We will return to this point in "All the World's a Stage" (Chapter 10). The bravery of the plains Indians was important to the nature of their hunting activities, while the self-effacement of the Hopi was an adjustment to an environment that required close co-operation for its proper exploitation. But where the economy makes less rigorous demands upon the social organization, there is more freedom of choice. The nature of values can, however, exert a strong influence upon the history of the society itself. Where values place sharp emphasis on certain forms of activity, they express the spirit of the culture and leave a strong imprint. The high value of musical accomplishment in nineteenth-century Germany, and the similar emphasis upon painting in Renaissance Italy and nineteenth-century France, are examples of such specialized emphasis on value. Modern America places similar emphasis upon mechanical proficiency and utilitarian inventions, so that while a German youth might be studying the violin after school, an American boy will be tinkering with a car. Cultures may be quite alike in their general features, but differ in spirit just because of the difference in values.

This was the case in ancient Greece, where each city had its own values, though in basic features all were similar. "When Greek Meets Greek" offers an example to show how the values differ, and how, in each community, the youth takes over the values of the culture and makes them its own. Sparta had those values of self-denial and endurance that made for toughness and "strength of character." We acquired similar values from our Puritan tradition of hard work and self-denial, though they were not expressed in just the same way. Athens, the center of the liberal Greek inheritance, emphasized the values of esthetic satisfaction, philosophical speculation, intellectual independence, and the good life. This tradition also is familiar to us, and much of it is embodied in our political life as well as our general attitudes.

We must remember that in each culture the people believe in their own values, which have great meaning to those who participate in the culture. To be sure, we (as outsiders) cannot entirely escape judging the values of others; but we must do so on the basis of general principles rather than prejudice. Do the values lead to a successful preservation of the society in terms of its own conditions of life? Do the values provide for the people themselves both the motivations and satisfactions that allow them to have a full life? Are the values attainable, or are the individuals frustrated in their attainments? Do the values lead to peaceful world relationships? Such questions can well be raised in judging the values of any people, without applying our own specific value judgments.

When Greek Meets Greek

LISTER SINCLAIR

❮❮❮—❮❮❮

The scene opens in Athens of the Fifth century B.C., with Pericles giving his oration over the recently killed in battle, setting forth the values his people held dear. The scene shifts between Athens and Sparta.

PERICLES

Heroes have the whole earth for their tomb; and in lands far from their own where the column with its epitaph declares their merit, there is enshrined in every breast that more notable inscription that is written in the hearts of men.

[MUSIC]

NARRATOR

This city, between the barren hills and the sea, is Athens, 2500 years ago; and this is its most beautiful suburb, where those who died for the city are buried with public honors. On the platform beside the sepulchre, stands Pericles; he is the leader of the city of Athens in the war that has just begun between Athens and her great rival city, Sparta. Pericles is speaking the funeral oration over the Athenian dead of the first year of the war.

PERICLES

(*Continuing.*) These take as your model, and judging happiness to be the fruit of freedom, and freedom of valor, never decline the dangers of war. For it is not the miserable that would most justly be unsparing of their lives; these have nothing to hope for; it is rather they to whom continued life may bring reverses as yet unknown and to whom a fall, if it came, would be most tremendous in its consequences.

NARRATOR

The speaker is pointing out the virtues of the patriots, and telling the Athenians to follow in their footsteps. He has reminded the people of the traditional values of Athens: liberal thoughts, and sumptuous and delicate taste in art, philosophy, and living; and the things that symbolize these values—dying for their country, spending their money wisely on beautiful things, and taking a vigorous part in public affairs. Values are symbolized by specific honors and achievements.

[MUSIC]

NARRATOR

Now here is Sparta. Sparta has her values too, and to this day we call them Spartan. There is no speech for her dead. Instead there are funeral games at the tombs of Spartan heroes. The Spartan values are the four pagan virtues —prudence, justice, temperance, and fortitude —but they are all surrounded and encompassed by obedience. Sparta is a city of soldiers, and the highest mark of Spartan approval is election to a military lodge or fraternity.

[MUSIC]

NARRATOR

This is the house of an Athenian gentleman. The torches are lit, and the brilliant painted statues gleam in their light. Slaves are running about with wine and food; the master of the house smiles and receives his friends, for tonight his wife has borne him a son.

ATHENIAN FATHER

A son! I shall sponsor the performance of a tragedy at the very next festival so that the public may see how much I appreciate this honor from the gods.

OLD FRIEND

The city he will help to govern will be a far greater place than this.

ATHENIAN FATHER

(*Pleased*) You think he will grow up to govern the city?

OLD FRIEND

Obviously, since he's chosen his father so wisely. (*The Athenian father chuckles.*)

ATHENIAN FATHER

Do you know I've a good mind to let him start in public life tonight! Call one of the girl slaves! He shall be brought out and shown to my friends.

OLD FRIEND

He won't make an eloquent speech in front of this audience.

ATHENIAN FATHER

(*Who is by now a little merry*) Make a speech! I'll wager he'll deafen us with his eloquence!

OLD FRIEND

No takers! But seriously, leave the child alone. Let him sleep.

ATHENIAN FATHER

He is my son. I wish to show him to my friends.

OLD FRIEND

Of course, but—

ATHENIAN FATHER

Athens will not prevent a father ordering his son as he sees fit.

OLD FRIEND

Naturally, but—

ATHENIAN FATHER

It's a free city. I'm a free man; so's my son. We'll do as we please, my son and I.

GIRL SLAVE

My master had some command?

ATHENIAN FATHER

Yes. Go into the inner room and bring out my son.

GIRL SLAVE

Yes, master.

OLD FRIEND

Consider; the child's not twelve hours old yet.

ATHENIAN FATHER

Not six hours; barely three.

OLD FRIEND

Then let him sleep.

ATHENIAN FATHER

Sleep—rather than come forth and hear the applause and approval of his fellow citizens?

GIRL SLAVE

Master.

ATHENIAN FATHER

Well, where is he?

GIRL SLAVE

Master, your wife begs you to let him lie in his cradle. She begs you to remember he is very tiny, and—

ATHENIAN FATHER

My wife begs *me*, his father, to remember things about my own son! Impertinent woman! This is female emancipation for you!

OLD FRIEND

Scandalous.

ATHENIAN FATHER

Bring him out at once.

GIRL SLAVE

Yes, master.

ATHENIAN FATHER

I must apologize for my wife. She behaves as if the child were as much hers as mine. She must have forgotten that the finest woman is the one who is least talked about among the men, whether for good or bad. Look, here comes the slave, with my son in her arms! Gentlemen, may I present to you Demarchus, son of Rhamphias. Gentlemen, my son! (*The guests murmur elaborate approval.*)

ATHENIAN FATHER

Well, my boy, what do you say to that? (*The child roars and the guests break into laughter.*)

ONE

He sings like a nightingale! He'll have a fine voice and enchant his friends with melody.

TWO

See him double his fists! He'll be a boxer, and take the wreath at the Olympic games.

THREE

Look at him kick his legs. I say he'll win the

foot race, and take the Olympic crown for Athens.

ATHENIAN FATHER

(*With a depreciatory laugh.*) Of course, with a child so young—

THREE

No, no, you can see it already.

ATHENIAN FATHER

He's not a day old. I expect he can hardly walk yet, let alone run. But my brother was one of the greatest runners of his day.

OLD FRIEND

I'll give him the best fortune of all. He'll be a great man and a great Athenian. He'll travel to all civilized cities.

ATHENIAN FATHER

How do you know?

OLD FRIEND (*Half joking.*)

Because his clever father will send him. But he won't be spoiled.

ATHENIAN FATHER

Certainly not!

OLD FRIEND

He will grow up to combine daring and deliberation. When he ascends the speaker's platform, the whole assembly will be silent, and when he steps down again, he will be saluted by a roar of approval like the thunders of the wine-dark sea, as everybody hurries to vote to approve his suggestions.

ATHENIAN FATHER

When he grows up, the boy shall be told how notable citizens, patrons of the arts, lovers of beauty, lovers of philosophy, athletes, and men of affairs gathered around his cradle. And, gentlemen, he shall be taught to honor your names, and to follow in your footsteps!

[MUSIC]

NARRATOR

The Athenian boy was born to be liberal and patriotic, and a man of affairs, expert at persuading other people to his views. At his birth, he was surrounded by notable citizens, whose notability came from these very same values, and who naturally trained him to imitate themselves.

[MUSIC]

NARRATOR

That same night, a Spartan boy was born, and this bare building is a Spartan house. In his plain tunic, the Spartan father sits, and beside him sits the mother, pale but composed. They too have slaves; but there is no banquet. They are waiting for the elder of the tribe into which the boy has been born.

SPARTAN FATHER

I think I hear his footstep now.

SPARTAN MOTHER

Shall I light a torch?

SPARTAN FATHER

He can walk in the dark. Avoid vanity. (*Pause.*) Did you bathe the child?

SPARTAN MOTHER

Yes.

SPARTAN FATHER

In wine?

SPARTAN MOTHER

Yes.

SPARTAN FATHER

A strong child bathed in wine grows stronger; a weak child dies. The better for everybody.

SLAVE

Master, a word with you.

SPARTAN FATHER

Speak.

SLAVE

The elder is at the gate.

SPARTAN FATHER

Admit him. Then bring our son.

SLAVE

Yes, master.

SPARTAN MOTHER

I find waiting hard.

SPARTAN FATHER

Do not show it. Remember, the child does

not belong to the parents but to the city. Here comes the elder. Greetings and welcome.

ELDER

Greetings.

SPARTAN MOTHER

Greetings.

ELDER

A child has been born in this house.

SPARTAN MOTHER

A boy.

ELDER

We are here to inspect it for the city.

SPARTAN FATHER

The slave is fetching it.

ELDER

If the child seems strong, you will bring it up, and it will be allotted for its upkeep one of the nine thousand shares into which the city is divided. If it is not strong, it will be removed from you now, taken to the hill of Taygetus, and cast down into the ravine of the Apoth-etae.

SPARTAN FATHER

Why bring up a weakling?

SLAVE

Master, the child is here. (*The child cries very gently.*)

SPARTAN MOTHER

Sir, here is my baby. Examine him, and tell us if he is to live or die.

ELDER

Lay him on the stone bench. (*The child whimpers a little at this.*) His limbs seem strong and well shaped. He is large and vigorous. But his lungs seem weak.

SPARTAN MOTHER

He does not cry because he is brave.

ELDER

(*Sceptically.*) Hm! (*Pause.*) Perhaps. (*Pause.*) This is your fourth son?

SPARTAN FATHER

Yes.

ELDER

Are you its father, or did you invite some admirable citizen to raise you a child from this plot of good ground, your wife?

SPARTAN WIFE

Not for this child. I did so for my second son; but he was killed at the age of seven in a sword fight.

ELDER

The child seems strong. Bring him up to be a boy whom the city will be proud to take.

SPARTAN FATHER

The fourth son exempts me from further public service.

ELDER

One of your sons is dead. But three sons exempts you from further military service.

SPARTAN FATHER

That I do not wish. I am a nobleman of Sparta, and therefore a soldier. Therefore, also, though I do my duty in public life, I long for the city to order me to retire from the tediousness of government, and live once more like a man.

ELDER

Public life is a bitter duty. (*Turning to the wife.*) I hope you are proud of your sons, madam?

SPARTAN MOTHER

If they do something to make me proud. They are learning obedience, but none has been elected to a military lodge, nor have they been given a chance to defend the city, whose walls they are.

ELDER

You are right, madam, the city is well fortified whose walls are of men, not bricks. It is a great honor to raise soldiers for Sparta.

ELDER

Shall you enter the boy in your own lodge?

SPARTAN FATHER

I shall bring him up to be a good citizen, and I hope he may be found worthy of election. First let him learn to obey.

ELDER

What do you wish, madam?

SPARTAN MOTHER

To win the Olympic crown.

ELDER

Have you been to Athens, to set your heart on vanity?

SPARTAN MOTHER

I wish it because the Olympic victor may fight next to the king and may perhaps be fortunate enough to die there.

ELDER

Good. I must go. No doubt, you will stay this evening with your wife.

SPARTAN MOTHER

He will not. A man may eat at home if he has sacrificed to the gods, or had success in hunting. My husband has done neither, so he will eat in the mess hall of his lodge with his fellows.

ELDER

A good answer. Fortunate child, to be born in a house so full of duty and obedience.

[MUSIC]

NARRATOR

The Spartan was taught only enough reading and writing to obey orders; the rest of his education was aimed toward making him endure pain and conquer in battle. When he was seven years old, he was enrolled in a military company, with other little boys; his hair was kept close-clipped, and he ran about naked, if possible even in winter. He was given very little food, so that he was forced to try and steal his dinner. This was to make him energetic and self-reliant. But to make sure the stealing was not just a formality, he was severely whipped, if anyone should happen to catch him at it. (*Callias, aged about seven, runs in howling and crying.*)

SPARTAN MOTHER

Callias! Silence!

CALLIAS

(*Whimpering.*) Mother.

SPARTAN MOTHER

I only understand human talk, not kitten talk and puppy whimpers.

CALLIAS (*Collecting himself.*)

Mother, I was badly whipped.

SPARTAN MOTHER

What had you done to be whipped?

CALLIAS

A man caught me stealing bread.

SPARTAN MOTHER

Disgraceful child!

CALLIAS

I'm so hungry, I *have* to steal.

SPARTAN MOTHER

Of course you have to steal; but how dare you let yourself get caught? Who will ever want you in a military lodge? Do you think you'll grow up to be a brave and cunning soldier, if you even get caught stealing bread, and then come whining to your mother about it?

CALLIAS

But he hurt me. Look at the blood.

SPARTAN MOTHER

Nobody can hurt a soldier. Did you tell him you had stolen?

CALLIAS

Yes.

SPARTAN MOTHER

You should have died rather than admit it. Do you think the heroes who founded Sparta would have *admitted* stealing? You should have lied to the man. Many years ago a boy like you stole something. He stole a fox; and just as he was getting away with the animal hidden under his coat, the owner came out and began to speak to him, not suspecting anything. Do you know what the boy did?

CALLIAS

No, mother.

SPARTAN MOTHER

Rather than let it be known, he stood and talked without showing a sign, and allowed the fox to tear out his bowels with its teeth and claws, so that suddenly he fell dead on the spot. Was this right?

CALLIAS

That was right.

SPARTAN MOTHER
Then remember it. Be like the boy with the fox, and you may grow up to join a military lodge, and fight beside the king!

[MUSIC]

NARRATOR
While the Spartan boy was being taught the values of his city, and how, if he respected them, people would respect him and give him the proper honors, the Athenian boy was being taught exactly the same. But *his* circle of respect moved round a different set of values—Athenian values.

ATHENIAN FATHER
Now *you* take the stick and draw in the sand any triangle.

DEMARCHUS
(*Also about seven.*) Like this?

ATHENIAN FATHER
Good. Now mark for me the middle points of each side. Good. Now draw lines from each angle of the triangle to the middle point of the side opposite. Three such lines.

DEMARCHUS
Like this, Father?

ATHENIAN FATHER
Good. Now the proposition says that these three lines run through a point. How shall we set about the proof?

DEMARCHUS
I don't know.

ATHENIAN FATHER
Well, let us consider.

DEMARCHUS
And I don't care.

ATHENIAN FATHER
Why not?

DEMARCHUS
Because I want to go and play.

ATHENIAN FATHER
(*Pretending to make a new start.*) Yesterday, my boy, we went near the assembly, and saw the beautiful new buildings they are putting up on the rock of the Acropolis.

DEMARCHUS
They had a big hoist, and lifted up big stones like—like wagons. Do you have to learn geometry before you can hoist up stones like wagons?

ATHENIAN FATHER
Yes, you do; but that isn't the reason why *you* learn geometry.

DEMARCHUS
Isn't it?

ATHENIAN FATHER
No. Do you remember the quiet man we saw watching—with the big helmet? That was Pericles; and he is the statesman who is making the city famous and beautiful by ordering all those fine buildings. Now you'll grow up to be a fine man like Pericles, and people will listen to what you'll have to say; and fathers will take their little boys and point to you.

DEMARCHUS
Why?

ATHENIAN FATHER
If you want to be a great man, you must learn geometry and philosophy so that you'll be full of wisdom, and able to think brave new thoughts to make Athens even greater than she is already.

DEMARCHUS
But I thought Pericles was a great soldier.

ATHENIAN FATHER
He's a great soldier as well. He must be both. And so must you. Now let's get on with it, and learn some more geometry.

[MUSIC]

NARRATOR
The Athenian boy is being gently looped within his circle of values, just as the Spartan boy is being looped within his. Everybody's circle of values goes the same way. Certain things are good. The men who have these things are great men. If *you* want to be a great man, you must learn to have the valuable things great men have—not only virtues, but honors, and public awards, and position. So

the circle goes. In Sparta, the good things were the private life, frugality, and obedience; in Athens, public life, love of beauty, and the questioning open mind. And of course as the boy grew older, these values became more and more familiar.

DEMARCHUS

(*Now about fourteen.*) Father, there's a craftsman at the door selling fine bronze brooches with enamel on them. I should very much like to buy one.

ATHENIAN FATHER

Why, Demarchus?

DEMARCHUS

They're very beautiful; and I want lots of beautiful things. When I have enough money, I shall buy gold and ivory, and put on plays. At present, though, perhaps I'd better just buy a bronze brooch.

ATHENIAN FATHER

Well, you have your own money, and you couldn't spend it better than on something beautiful so that everyone will see your good taste. Show us the brooches.

CRAFTSMAN

Here, sir.

ATHENIAN FATHER

Yes, I see. I see. Which do you like, Demarchus?

DEMARCHUS

I like this one.

ATHENIAN FATHER

Why?

DEMARCHUS

Because it's beautiful.

ATHENIAN FATHER

Why?

DEMARCHUS

Because the design has unity, while the details have variety. Because all the parts have a just balance with one another, and so don't exist just for their own benefit but for the good of the whole brooch. That is what's meant by beautiful.

ATHENIAN FATHER

Very good. And I think you've made a good choice.

CRAFTSMAN

The young gentleman has learned excellent taste.

DEMARCHUS

How much is this brooch?

CRAFTSMAN

Three drachmae. The materials alone are very

costly; this filigree here is made of the finest soft silver.

DEMARCHUS

(*Uneasy.*) Oh. Somehow, now that I look again, the proportions don't seem quite right. But this one here seems very fine.

CRAFTSMAN

(*Flatly.*) It is not as good as the first one.

DEMARCHUS

What do you think, Father?

ATHENIAN FATHER

I think you don't have enough money, and you're ashamed to admit it! (*Father and the craftsman chuckle.*) How much do you need?

DEMARCHUS

Well, I have it, all but a few obols.

ATHENIAN FATHER

Never be afraid of admitting poverty. It's not shameful. What is shameful is to be poor, and then not struggle against it. Well, how are you going to struggle against your poverty?

DEMARCHUS

This afternoon, I must go to the stadium and throw the discus and the javelin. If I can beat all the others, will you give me the extra money?

ATHENIAN FATHER

Will the craftsman keep the first brooch until evening?

CRAFTSMAN

Certainly.

ATHENIAN FATHER

Then, if you beat all the others at discus and javelin, we'll see what can be done. Do you think you have a chance?

DEMARCHUS

Yesterday I beat them at those games and at the foot race as well.

ATHENIAN FATHER

So I've been tricked, eh? Never mind; perhaps we're raising a victor at the Olympic games as well as a judge of brooches.

[MUSIC]

NARRATOR

While the Athenian lad was being taught the value of beauty, and wise spending, the Spartan lad was being taught the value of honor and military virtue, by means of the special Spartan teaching method of putting cases and then asking questions.

ELDER

Boy.

BOY

Sir.

ELDER

In another city, there is a man who has learned to imitate the nightingale to absolute perfection. I ask you if you would like to hear him.

BOY

Sir, very much indeed.

ELDER

A bad answer. Do not fly after vanity. You do this too much. This time I shall punish you severely. Come here, and let me bite your thumb. (*Pause.*) Make no sound. (*Pause.*) There. Wipe off the blood and return to your seat. What is the right answer if you are asked

to hear a man who imitates the nightingale?

CALLIAS

Sir, I have heard the nightingale itself.

ELDER

Good. Now, Callias.

CALLIAS

Sir.

ELDER

Our ancient king and lawgiver, King Soas, was once besieged by the Clitorians in a very dry place. He had no water and had to come to terms. The conditions were that he would restore all his conquests, providing he and all his men might drink of the nearest spring. After all the usual oaths and ratifications had been exchanged, so that both sides were bound to the outcome, King Soas called his soldiers together and offered his kingdom as a reward to the man who could refrain from from drinking. But they had all gone without water for so long that not a man could bear to refrain, especially with all his comrades drinking. So they all marched down to the spring, and each in turn drank his fill, until at last along came the king, and sprinkled his face, without swallowing one drop. Then he marched off in the face of the enemy, because according to the oaths and articles he and all his men had not drunk of the water. Callias, was this well done?

CALLIAS

Yes.

ELDER

Why? (*Pause.*) Consider well. He who knows what to speak knows when to speak.

CALLIAS

Because he conquered his enemies by conquering himself.

ELDER

Good.

CALLIAS

But I do not believe he was leading an army of Spartans.

ELDER

Why?

CALLIAS

If that had been a Spartan army, not one single man would have been coward enough to drink!

NARRATOR

So by example and teaching, by questioning and answering, and by the steady pressure of society, the Spartan grew to be a young man burning with Spartan ambition to earn Spartan prestige by winning Spartan values. And, as usually happens, these values that he struggled after were no longer the original values, but rather the special honors given in exchange for them. Therefore, the day of his achievement really came when his father introduced him at the military lodge where already he had sat for years at the feet of the experienced men. Standing up, his father presented him.

SPARTAN FATHER

Sirs, I here present my son, Callias. I have trained him myself to give to the city. He is obedient. And he is healthy; you have all seen him naked at the games, with the other young men and women. I submit him for membership in this military lodge.

ELDER

Callias, your father thinks you deserve membership in this lodge. If elected, will you uphold the rules?

CALLIAS

Yes.

ELDER

Through that door no word passes.

NARRATOR

A secret ballot is held. A single vote against Callias will disqualify him. (*Pause.*) Callias is elected!

ELDER

Callias, these fifteen men are now your comrades. In war we fight together; in peace we eat together. Remember that when King Agis returned home victorious he wished to eat privately with his queen, but this was refused and the king was heavily fined. Every man should always be proud to eat at his lodge. Sit down with us now, and eat the black soup.

SPARTAN FATHER

Callias, you are no longer my son; you are my comrade. You are a Spartan.

[MUSIC]

NARRATOR

The young man has become as much a Spartan as he can be, short of dying in battle for his city—and this he will do later.

In Athens, it was the same. The Athenian youth grew up to be a young man burning with Athenian ambition to win Athenian prestige by achieving Athenian values. As usual, the target soon became the public symbol that meant he had achieved the values. In this case, of course, he became a real Athenian citizen on the day the old men paid attention to his views on the behavior of Athenian leaders.

DEMARCHUS

No matter how great a leader he is, Pericles should be sent into exile at once; he should be ostracized.

OLD FRIEND

Is it wise to send our general into exile at the very moment when our guardianship of Greece is being challenged by the insolence of Sparta?

DEMARCHUS

He does not trust the people; therefore, he is unfit to be a leader of a democracy, and any good things he may have done have been done rather by accident than by design. What about the statue of Zeus he ordered for the city?

ATHENIAN FATHER

Now, my boy, you can say a lot against Pericles, but you cannot bring up that ivory-and-gold statue against him. He cleared himself absolutely.

DEMARCHUS

Of what?

ATHENIAN FATHER

Well, of stealing the gold the city had given him to make the statue. Pericles gave orders that all the gold parts should be made detachable, and detached they were, and weighed in public so that every grain of gold was accounted for.

DEMARCHUS

By clearing himself of the charge of stealing gold, Pericles convicted himself of the charge of contempt for the people.

OLD FRIEND

Why?

DEMARCHUS

Statues are not usually made with the gold parts detachable. He was simply preparing in advance for base insinuations.

OLD FRIEND

As it turns out, rightly. The insinuations were made. We Athenians are sometimes hard on our leaders.

DEMARCHUS

Not at all. A leader of a democracy must always account for his actions to the people.

ATHENIAN FATHER

Very true.

DEMARCHUS

But this doesn't mean he should always behave as if he expected the people to do their worst. We called his honesty into question, and we had a right to do it. But he, by protecting his honesty so craftily, showed that he was not trusting us. Therefore, he should be ostracized, and I shall go now and talk some more to the young men and arrange that it be done. Excuse me.

ATHENIAN FATHER

He's a very bold boy, to send the general into exile on the brink of war.

OLD FRIEND

He's a bold and audacious boy—clever. He will go far in Athens. With all that cunning, he will be looked up to. One couldn't help being impressed with what he said about Pericles.

ATHENIAN FATHER

Were you really?

OLD FRIEND

Much impressed. He thinks fearlessly and acts courageously. He isn't afraid of criticizing his leaders, and using his head as much as possible. You've brought up your son to be a true Athenian.

[MUSIC]

NARRATOR

For each boy, the circle of values is complete. For the Spartan, the main value is unthinking obedience, and its main symbol is election to the military lodge. For the Athenian, the main value is unobedient thinking, and its symbol is acceptance as a man of affairs. And the circle continues with these young men, now grown, each influencing the growing boys to follow in his own path and to try to gain the same recognition.

But both Athens and Sparta shared the value of patriotism, and symbolized it by dying honorably for the city. The Athenian and the Spartan died face to face on a Greek battlefield, 2500 years ago.

[FINALE]

6. GROUPS

₭₭₭

People everywhere belong to families, to clubs, to cliques. Everywhere they cluster together on the basis of some common interest. Perhaps they all went through initiations together; perhaps their mothers all belonged to the same clan; perhaps they all spend their time making boats. You belong to a number of such clusters: your family, your coterie of friends, your graduating class, your professional association or union. All these are groups.

A group is any number of people who share a common interest and feel themselves to be a unit for some particular purpose. Some groups are very large. In a sense, the whole society is a group. But for many purposes the small, intimate groups are the most important. Whether large or small, groups have certain features: they are bounded by a psychological barrier that distinguishes member from outsider, they share a common interest, and they have some form of internal organization.

Groups are the building blocks of society. All of us live our lives within groups, from the moment we are born and enter into our family or clan, to the time we die and are laid away by our burial society—or our clan. In some societies, the soul is considered to be a member of the group before it is born as a man, and to continue as a member even after his death. Groups are so obvious and ordinary a part of our daily lives that we tend to overlook them, and certainly we are largely unaware of the importance they have in the organization of society and the continuation of culture.

Groups are of two basic kinds—those to which we belong because of circumstances over which we have no control, and those we join by choice or for some reason. The best example of the first group in our society is our family, or our ethnic group, or our nation. The time, place, or circumstance of our birth usually determines our membership in such groups for life. Clubs, cliques, unions, and professional associations are groups that a person joins for some reason of his own. These groups are more common in American society, but in primitive societies most groups are set by circumstances of birth—though of course both types are found in every society.

Groups are necessary to society. It is through them that things get done. If we want to build a bridge, elect a candidate, or start a movement, we need to organize people for action. It is through the co-operative action of groups, organized to specific, more-or-less clearly recognized ends, that the business necessary for maintaining the society is performed.

Groups also are necessary for culture. It is within the circle of the groups to which you belong that you obtain most of the attitudes and patterns of behavior of your culture; the groups to which a person belongs bring him the attitudes and understandings of the culture of which he is a part. The family is the most important group for setting our cultural attitudes, because we are in it earliest (when we are infants and are most pliable), because we are a part of it longest, and because our most important needs are met by it. We take it for granted that the parents will tell the child the things he is expected to know— and this is true of all cultures. But the family is not the only group from which we take our culture. We saw how the Katchina dancers in "Desert Soliloquy" (Chapter 4) initiated the Hopi boy and brought him into the Katchina society group, where new ideas and values of Hopi culture were told him. We have all had similar experiences when we joined a club, or a fraternity, or a gang of fellows and learned the particular attitudes and values that this group considered the right ones.

Groups are necessary for the individual. It is from the group that the individual gets support in his actions. We get not only support for our daily tasks, but also the important psychological support to reinforce our attitudes and give us security in our course of action. The most dramatic example of such support comes from studies of soldiers in the military situation: a single straggler, away from his own outfit and his established friendships, is found to be a poor risk at the front, and should not be used as replacement; whereas a group of two or three buddies may continue to fight as well as ever. The drama of this example is based on the inherent drama of warfare, but the same is true of the ordinary actions of our daily behavior. Consider the development of fads—would a youth dare to adopt some exotic piece of clothes or a new haircut if he didn't have the support of some intimate group? There are many times that we have the courage to act only when we see that others are doing the same thing. In groups there is strength.

This support also supplies strength in adversity. In every society, at the crises of life, the person involved finds support in his group, and often in a ritual way. One of the greatest tragedies that can befall a person is to sense that he belongs to no group, can take support from no established intimate contacts. One of the most poignant of all sociological documents tells of a "dweller in a single room," a girl who was disowned by her family for going to the city, and who found no associates, no neighbors, no persons to whom she felt a bond. In her own words, "there was nobody who would care what I did."

Though there are many different kinds and sizes of groups, it is the small and intimate ones that are most important to us. Sociologists call these "primary groups," not only because they come first, but because they are first in our minds and hearts. They are the small, face-to-face associations within which we enact our daily lives. Among the members of such groups we find our closest emotional ties. Just because we care most about them, they have the greatest influence upon our behavior, our thoughts, and our feelings.

Group membership also requires group loyalty. The degree of loyalty depends upon the importance of the group to us. This again is seen most clearly on the battlefield, where many a soldier has sacrificed his life to save his buddies—the act that motivated Datgas in "Stand-in for a Murderer" (Chapter 1) changed to our cultural context.

There are ways in which modern society differs from primitive societies, and one of these is in the nature of group affiliations. In most primitive societies there are relatively few groups and a person rarely belongs to very many. Even when he does, some of the members of one group are apt to belong to others. But in our society each person generally belongs to many different groups at the same time. And these are organized so that he may be the only member of his family belonging to his club, the only member of his club belonging to his church, the only member of his church belonging to his work group. Since the group sets attitudes and behavior for the individual, he may find himself torn between different patterns of behavior and diverse values. Modern society, in allowing for more freedom of choice, more variation, often makes it more difficult for the individual to steer a clear course of action and to gain strength from group support.

You Are Not Alone

GEORGE SALVERSON

>>>->>>

The universality and variety of groups is demonstrated to a naive Solo by a man somewhat professorial in type—who knows that life is lived within the orbit of groups. Solo and Gregarious are not bound by time and space; they are invisible viewers of the world.

SOLO
You're not going on this bus ride, too!

GREGARIOUS
You didn't think you could go alone?

SOLO
I'm sick of people. I'll take this trip alone, solo, by myself.

GREGARIOUS
Not without me.

SOLO
What?

GREGARIOUS
You can't be alone.

SOLO
Why?

GREGARIOUS
If you were alone, you wouldn't exist.

SOLO
(*Incredulous.*) Huh?

GREGARIOUS
As long as you exist, there are crowds riding with you.

SOLO
What crowds?

GREGARIOUS
Crowds you created, and crowds that created you.

SOLO
Is that where this bus ride will take us?

GREGARIOUS
That's where it goes and how it goes.

SOLO
For Pete's sake, stay with me. I might get lost.

GREGARIOUS
Let's go. (*The bus pulls away with Solo and Gregarious.*)

[MUSIC]

GREGARIOUS
Now just look around at the people on this bus, with all their invisible crowds.

SOLO
I'm busy.

GREGARIOUS
Busy?

SOLO
Looking at the blonde in the next seat.

GREGARIOUS
Ah. Very nice.

SOLO
Yes, and alone, too.

GREGARIOUS
Come, she's only eighteen.

SOLO
Yes, and alone, too.

GREGARIOUS
What do you mean, alone? I'm here.

SOLO
(*Scornfully.*) Huh!

GREGARIOUS
We're all here, with her, in this bus. A bunch in a box, riding through the streets.

SOLO
But we haven't been introduced.

GREGARIOUS
Nevertheless, we have something in common here, a relationship enjoyed by no one else.

SOLO
But does she know that?

GREGARIOUS
We are the only people in the world riding on this particular bus.

SOLO
Practically a secret society.

GREGARIOUS
And we have crowds riding with us. You have crowds riding with you, and she has quite a crowd with her, too.

SOLO
Crowds? What crowds? I don't see any crowds.

GREGARIOUS
Invisible groups crowded in with you.

SOLO
Here I am only trying to look at a pretty girl. Why get me tangled up in invisible groups? Are you trying to be mysterious? Explain yourself!

GREGARIOUS
All right. Calm down. I'll put it to you simply.

SOLO
Okay—simply!

GREGARIOUS
Ahem. In every social system the people are divided into entities, or units, which we may call groups.

SOLO
(*Intently.*) Mhmmm.

GREGARIOUS
These groups are formed for the purpose of taking the necessary significant actions for the maintenance of the social system.

SOLO
Mhmmm.

GREGARIOUS
These entities or groups may be defined as any number of individuals who share certain common interests and who recognize themselves as forming a solitary social entity with respect to some kind of action, and which distinguishes them from non-members.

SOLO
(*Blankly.*) Uh?

GREGARIOUS
Each individual belongs to many groups, and to each group he has a specific responsibility, and his relation to the group will define his role or position. The individual acquires his attitudes, feelings, and values through the group, though different groups may communicate conflicting values. Thus the group tends to set the individual's behavior and support him in his actions. And very important to us all—the group has structure.

SOLO
Uh. But does the blonde know that?

GREGARIOUS
(*Smiling.*) Well, you see what I mean.

SOLO
Oh, sure. Only—

GREGARIOUS
Only what?

SOLO
Only what do you mean by all this about groups?

GREGARIOUS
(*Sighs.*) In every social system the people are divided into entities. (*Breaks off.*)

SOLO
(*Concentrating.*) Yeah?

GREGARIOUS
Never mind that. Let's get back to us on this bus.

SOLO
Yeah, that's a group. So?

GREGARIOUS
Well, not a group now, though of course we're all in this thing together. But let something happen, and we'll be a group. Suppose that driver made a U-turn and started back. We'd form a protest group in a hurry. Somebody would take the lead, others would help, and we'd all back each other up. We'd be a pretty effective group pretty fast.

SOLO
And I'd be on speaking terms with the little blonde.

GREGARIOUS
It's that feeling of common interests that is necessary for real unity of action.

SOLO
You said it. But it isn't a group after all, and the little babe is alone.

GREGARIOUS
No, she's not alone. Besides the people on this bus, there are other, important groups of people riding with her.

SOLO
Where?

GREGARIOUS
In her thoughts, feelings, attitudes, reactions.

SOLO
She's avoiding my eye. Wonder what she's thinking?

GREGARIOUS
If you see her thoughts, you'll see some of the people with her.

[MUSIC]

GIRL
Wish that man wouldn't stare. Makes me think of Bill last night. Some blind date! Why'd I let him kiss me? Scared he'd tell the gang I'm a dull date. Who cares—the dough-head doesn't fit in with the bunch anyway. Wonder how the girls at the club will like my new hat? Wish that man wouldn't stare. Mom says men who stare aren't nice. She said it! I could give him a dirty look. No, Dad would say it's too far beneath me to matter. Don't give him the satisfaction of knowing he even exists.

[MUSIC]

GREGARIOUS
No, that girl is certainly not alone. And she has much in common with unexpected kinds of people of whom she may never have heard. (*The bus stops and the door opens. Street voices are heard outside.*)

SOLO
Well, she hasn't enough in common with me. Aw, she's getting off the bus.

GREGARIOUS
Let's go along.

SOLO
What?

GREGARIOUS
I want to follow this up.

SOLO
A pleasure.

GREGARIOUS
What a mob of indeterminate people, flooding along the street.

SOLO
You said it. Don't lose her.

GREGARIOUS
But not so indeterminate, either. There's an invisible arrangement of all this humanity.

SOLO
(*Bumps into somebody who wasn't looking.*) Whoops! Pardon me, mister. Wish they'd arrange to keep to the right.

GREGARIOUS
Over there, newsboys talking. Members of a group. There are two lovers.

SOLO
Well, now! They're alone, anyway!

GREGARIOUS
Little group of two. Look, couple of clergymen talking together by the cafeteria. Members of—

DRUNK
(*Calling in distance.*) Taxi! Hey, taxi!

GREGARIOUS
Two drunks, looking for a taxi to get them home.

SOLO
They've taken on a lot in common.

GREGARIOUS
Endless little groups in the mass, and all interwoven with other kinds of groups. The girl there has something in common with all of them, and with all people throughout all time and space.

SOLO
You mean she's a biped?

GREGARIOUS

I mean that all people in all times and places are the members, the creators, and the products of groups. They all act as members of a group or combination of groups. They can act in no other way.

SOLO

A minute ago you were being mysterious. Now you're being obvious.

GREGARIOUS

Not as obvious as it seems. It's a fact pervading all human life, with vital consequences to both society and the individual. Neither of us can exist without it.

SOLO

Neither of whom?

GREGARIOUS

Neither society nor the individual.

SOLO

What can't they exist without?

GREGARIOUS

(*Exasperated.*) I'm telling you! Groups!

SOLO

Let's get out of this mob. I can't hear you think.

GREGARIOUS

All right. That's easily done.

SOLO

(*Relief.*) That's better. Don't tell me it isn't good to be alone.

GREGARIOUS

It wouldn't be if you could. But since all men are affiliated with groups—

SOLO

There you go again!

GREGARIOUS

Maybe we'd better follow that young lady home.

SOLO

Much better.

[MUSIC]

GREGARIOUS

All right, here she is, helping her mother to set the table. Now, examine her.

SOLO

You don't have to twist my arm.

GREGARIOUS

Don't you see that she's not a separate entity floating in space?

SOLO

(*Admiring.*) She walks as though she were!

GREGARIOUS

Please concentrate!

SOLO

I am!

GIRL

But, Mother, why are you getting so old-fashioned all of a sudden? It was only a goodnight kiss.

MOTHER

I'm not getting old-fashioned. But kissing a boy you don't even like, simply because you're afraid of what he'll tell the other boys—it seems to me that's a reason for not kissing him.

GIRL

Oh, Mother, you're oversimplifying.

MOTHER

It's not right to kiss people for political reasons. It should be a personal thing—an expression of genuine affection.

GIRL

(*Laughing.*) Dear Mother. Then here's an expression of affection for you. (*She kisses her mother quickly on the cheek.*) Now what about that new dress? I simply have to have it! You know what the girls will say if I turn up at the dance in some antediluvian rag!

MOTHER

Oh, all right. But don't tell your father. You're not supposed to have more new clothes right now.

GIRL

Oh, he won't notice. You know how he is about clothes!

GREGARIOUS

See?

SOLO

What am I supposed to make of that?

‒‒

GREGARIOUS

This girl is a member of a group.

SOLO

(*Contemptuous.*) Well, sure, if you mean a family.

GREGARIOUS

Yes, but there's another group within the family. Mother and daughter, who have things in common—like new clothes. And father is outside this little subgroup, and probably feels it.

SOLO

Poor Papa.

GREGARIOUS

Don't worry about him. He's down at the corner lot pitching ball to his young son—another subgroup. By the way, did you notice the family group, through mother, communicating rules and values to daughter?

SOLO

To kiss or not to kiss?

GREGARIOUS

Mhm. Just a minute.

MOTHER

Your Aunt Minnie's coming Saturday, so you'll have to give her your room, dear.

GIRL

Oh, Mother! You don't even like Aunt Minnie. Why does she have to stay here?

MOTHER

Now, dear, blood is thicker than water. You wouldn't want her to go to a hotel.

GIRL

Oh, I suppose.

GREGARIOUS

Well?

SOLO

Well, what?

GREGARIOUS

After all, it is a family, even if it is full of little subgroups. There is a feeling of family, and those who aren't family are outside—even if sometimes preferable. There's a kind of structure here, too. The little groups work together

individually, but they gather together and work in another way as the total family—with the head man at the top, a captain. The father.

MOTHER

Now, don't worry about the dress. I'll handle your father.

SOLO

Are you kidding?

GREGARIOUS

Pressure group. Merely a detail, depending on the particular society in which you live. If you're a Hopi Indian, the mother runs the household. If you're a modern American, the boss is—

SOLO

Yes?

GREGARIOUS

Merely a detail. Let's have a look at the young lady talking to her friends.

[MUSIC]

GIRL

Oh, Bill was the original blind date. Was I disgusted when he kissed me.

GIRL FRIEND

Why? What did he do?

GIRL

Nothing. I just don't like him, that's all. Why do I have to kiss every Tom, Dick, and Harry just because he takes me out?

GIRL FRIEND

What's the harm? He's clean, isn't he? He washes.

GIRL

Kissing should be a personal thing, because you like somebody—not for political reasons.

GIRL FRIEND

Oh, kissing, sure! But that kind of kissing, that's just polite. It's just something you do—like wearing your hat in church.

[MUSIC]

SOLO

Well, how do you like that!

GREGARIOUS

Interesting. The girl's a member of another group, with some attitudes that conflict with those of her own family group. Let's go to church.

SOLO

What?

GREGARIOUS

Church. Here we are. (*We hear the organ and the coughs of the congregation.*)

SOLO

Why church? It isn't Sunday.

GREGARIOUS

It is now. And here's the whole family, lined up in its favorite pew. Complete with all its little subgroups, acting in unison as a whole family.

GIRL

(*Urgent.*) Dad, I haven't anything for the plate.

FATHER

(*Reproving.*) I told you to budget your allowance. Oh, well, here's a quarter.

GREGARIOUS

The little subgroup conflicts go on.

SOLO

To budget or not to budget.

GREGARIOUS

Mhm. But that's now secondary to the role of family in church membership. In fact, the family has become something else, and each member is acting differently for the occasion. They are now members of another group— the congregation. And that's a group full of subgroups: families, and other kinds.

SOLO

Just a minute. Got a dime?

GREGARIOUS

Hmm? A dime?

SOLO

Oh, well, make it a quarter.

GREGARIOUS

Here you are.

(*The collection plate is passing.*)

GIRL

Mom, look at that stuck up Mary Miles, in the choir. Thinks she's good because she's loud.

MOTHER

Now, dear, don't be unkind. I do believe she has her claws into our poor bachelor minister.

FATHER

Will you females please stop that gossip?

GIRL

Oh, Dad, why do you men let that woman pull the wool over your eyes?

MOTHER

She entertained for him last Wednesday. I don't see why we shouldn't have a dinner for him some time.

FATHER

Maybe the poor guy would like a little peace.

GIRL AND MOTHER

Oh, really!

GREGARIOUS

Did you hear that?

SOLO

(*Chuckling.*) I did. Your subgroups are getting complicated. Male against female. Female against female. The members of the choir, the members of The Close Friends of the Minister, the members of The Society for Criticizing the Close Friends of the Minister. You have groups here, all right.

GREGARIOUS

Yes, and each group has its members and non-members, with psychological barriers existing between member and non-member. But look over the congregation. There are other kinds of groups at work here.

SOLO

I'll be doggoned. There's Inspector Clancey of the vice squad. Imagine him in church!

GREGARIOUS

And there's Bill McIntyre, the union business agent.

SOLO

Mike Billings, from the shoe store. He's in the board of trade, isn't he?

GREGARIOUS

Members of innumerable groups—groups that divide up the work of society, and provide the machinery to get the work done, as no individual could hope to do it.

SOLO

You said that before on the bus, I think.

GREGARIOUS

Groups formed for the purpose of taking the necessary significant actions for the maintenance of the social system.

SOLO

I think that's what you said.

GREGARIOUS

Just as these family members cease to be the family and become congregation, acting differently, thinking and feeling differently as congregation members. Just as these subgroups within the congregation, acting as bricks that construct the whole church membership, work together as one to accomplish the work of the church.

MINISTER

(*Making an announcement from the pulpit.*) Friends, we have a letter of thanks here from the Hospital for Children. I know that we all rejoice in the opportunity our church was given to help build the new wing, and to each of us must come some feeling of humble gratitude that we have been able to assist these little afflicted ones.

GREGARIOUS

Groups within families. Families sometimes divided among subgroups within a congregation. The individuals reacting, now according to one group, now according to another— as mother and daughter versus father; or as family together, to supply the collection; or as member of the choir; or again as members of the large group, the congregation. With the work of the church, like the work of society as a whole, divided, creating differences among individuals—but thereby achieving the work and accomplishments of the whole inclusive social unit.

The service is over. Shall we go?

SOLO

Say, I get what you're after. You mean, nobody is an isolated individual.

GREGARIOUS

Exactly!

SOLO

Everybody is attached to some kind of group.

GREGARIOUS

Right.

SOLO

And these groups are part of larger groups.

GREGARIOUS

Quite.

SOLO

And, furthermore, everyone is involved in several groups of different kinds.

GREGARIOUS

Definitely.

SOLO

Then why didn't you say so?

GREGARIOUS

Didn't I?

SOLO

And where does it get us?

GREGARIOUS

Why, it's through these groups that we are actually in contact with society, and from which we acquire our attitudes. And we not only acquire them but express them as we are expected to by the group in question.

SOLO

What do you mean? I don't change my ideas for this or that group.

GREGARIOUS

Let's look at this girl's father. See how many people he is, according to his group affiliations.

SOLO

How many people?

GREGARIOUS

Here he is at the taxpayer's association.

FATHER

This city is rapidly going to the dogs, due to scandalous inefficiency on the part of the civic authorities.

GREGARIOUS

Now he's at the chamber of commerce.

FATHER

We have the fastest-growing city in America, due to the enlightened and progressive outlook of our energetic civic authorities.

GREGARIOUS

But now see him as a member of the executive, at work in a big department store.

FATHER

I don't know what we're coming to. The demands of the employees are going to put us right out of business!

GREGARIOUS

Yet here he is again, presenting a watch at the store's 25 Year Club.

FATHER

I have always said, it is the employee who makes this business what it is, and we shall all go forward together.

GREGARIOUS

Well?

SOLO

That's all one man?

GREGARIOUS

The member and product of several groups—not to mention his church, the schools he went to, the gangs he played with as a kid, or groups to which he belongs through no choice of his own.

SOLO

In this free country?

GREGARIOUS

Such as the descendants of Scottish immigrants.

FATHER

(*Raptly.*) Ah, I've always said it, and I'll say it again: the greatest writer in the history of the world is bonnie Robbie Burns!

GREGARIOUS

All of these varied groups contribute to his thoughts, feelings, attitudes, actions, and re-actions, according to the group in question.

SOLO

That's no man. That's a crowd.

GREGARIOUS

And that's what I said on the bus: there are crowds riding with you. I also said that each individual belongs to many groups, and to each group he has a specific responsibility, and his relation to the group will define his role or position. But there's more to this. Like a cup of coffee?

SOLO

If aspirin goes with it.

GREGARIOUS

Let's go in here.

SOLO

This juke joint!

(*They open the door and get the full clatter and the juke box like a blast in the face.*)

[MUSIC]

GREGARIOUS

(*Calling over the noise.*) Come on. It's very interesting.

SOLO

(*Nervous.*) Not so fast. Who's that bunch in the corner booths?

GREGARIOUS

Doc's bunch.

SOLO

Who?

GREGARIOUS

Doc's bunch. A free street-corner association. This is one of their regular meeting places. Watch night after night, and you'll find they always sit in the same booths, and in the same positions. That's Doc in the corner. He's the leader. Where he's sitting—that's the seat of honor, so he always sits there.

SOLO
Why is it the seat of honor?

GREGARIOUS
Because he always sits there.

DOC
Jack, what's this about you and Alec?

GREGARIOUS
That's Doc.

JACK
I don't know, Doc. Must be off my game. When him and me play by ourself, I can't win. He ruins me.

GREGARIOUS
That's Jack. He's a lieutenant.

SOLO
Lieutenant? Is this an army?

GREGARIOUS
It's a group, and groups, my boy, have structure.

JACK
Yeah, he's steaming up to ruin us all in the match tomorrow.

SOLO
What are they talking about?

GREGARIOUS
Bowling. It's religion with them. Listen!

DOC
Listen, Jack, you're the best man in a team match. But you brood too much. You let Alec tell you he can beat you, and you get to believe it. But you're a better bowler. Next time you'll take him. Guys like him wouldn't know how to act if they won. Next time, you'll take him.

SOLO
Who's this Alec they're talking about?

GREGARIOUS
He's down at the bottom of the structure. And he's been beating the lieutenant in private matches.

SOLO
So what?

GREGARIOUS
So it's a team match tomorrow. He'll have the whole gang to contend with. They won't let him beat the lieutenant in a group situation.

SOLO
What'll they do, break his wrists?

GREGARIOUS
Hardly.

DOC
Steaming up to ruin us, is he? If he gets out in front, we'll steam him, all right. He'll get plenty of noise and argument.

GREGARIOUS
I have a feeling Alec won't be able to win, no matter how hard he tries. He'll be going against the group, tension will tighten his muscles and wreck his score.

SOLO
But how about this other fellow who has to beat him?

GREGARIOUS
He'll have group support. It'll be the right thing, the accepted thing, for him to win. He'll rise to the occasion. After all, the group has structure, and knows how to maintain it. Those boys all play a different game when they are together than they do as individuals, away from this particular group.

SOLO
(*Disturbed.*) Is this on the level?

GREGARIOUS
Certainly.

SOLO
I don't like it.

GREGARIOUS
Why?

SOLO
I don't know.

GREGARIOUS
It's in the group that the individual finds not only his attitudes but his strength and support. And this fact is important to our whole society.

SOLO
I don't like this joint. Let's get out.

GREGARIOUS

All right. Let's go visit some Tlingits.

SOLO

Yes, come on. (*He pauses and then does a double take.*) Some what?

GREGARIOUS

Tlingits.

SOLO

What are Tlingits?

GREGARIOUS

Indians. Alaskan Indians.

SOLO

All right, let's go. (*Another double take.*) Indians!

GREGARIOUS

Sure.

[MUSIC]

GREGARIOUS

This whole business of group responsibility is so important that a man will sacrifice his life for it. There's a Tlingit, now, ready to do just that.

SOLO

Looks to me as if he was going to battle. War dress, spear.

GREGARIOUS

He's going to get himself killed.

SOLO

Suicide?

GREGARIOUS

No. He has to pay for a murder.

SOLO

Oh, an execution. You mean, this Tlingit murderer gets all dressed up for his execution?

GREGARIOUS

He's not a murderer.

SOLO

Then why the execution?

GREGARIOUS

A member of his clan did it. Since the clan is his most important group, he gives his life to even the score with the other clan.

SOLO

Hey, hold on. Why don't they give it to the real killer?

GREGARIOUS

He's not important enough.

SOLO

An important guy takes the rap?

GREGARIOUS

It was an important man who was killed. By Tlingit Indian law, our Indian is just right to pay the score and avoid a major war. So he gives his life for the sake of his group, going into mock battle, fully armed, but letting himself be killed for the safety of the clan.

SOLO

That's a savage custom.

GREGARIOUS

Savage? Come on out on a modern battlefield.

SOLO

What?

(*We begin to hear the noise of battle, getting louder and more violent.*)

GREGARIOUS

Battlefield. Keep your head down.

SOLO

Real bullets?

GREGARIOUS

Things are bad, too.

SOLO

We're losing?

GREGARIOUS

Been falling back. Just formed a new line.

SOLO

How did I get into this? The enemy's coming!

GREGARIOUS

Keep behind those gunner boys, there.

SOLO

Gunner boys?

GREGARIOUS

The gun crew. They were separated in the battle—lost their parent outfit. But they're still together as a crew—a group.

SOLO

A group?

GREGARIOUS

Look how they are holding that line, like a rock!

SOLO

That's all very well, but who's next to them?

GREGARIOUS

Stragglers. In the mix-up, they lost their outfits. Now they've gone back into the line as individuals. Without their own groups.

SOLO

What's the difference? They're soldiers, aren't they?

GREGARIOUS

Good ones, too.

SOLO

Then what are you worried about?

GREGARIOUS

That straggler, over there, side by side with strangers. I'm worried about his thoughts.

STRAGGLER

What a lousy oufit, this is. Don't know any of them fellows. These gunners—they okay? Don't even know their names. Not like the old bunch when it was together. A real fighting bunch. Stood by each other. Men worth fighting for. Don't mind taking it so long as I knew it was either me or Joe or Pete. Now where are they? I'd be dead too, if I hadn't tossed that live grenade away. These guys— who are they? They wouldn't put themselves out for me. I'm getting out of here. Let somebody else fight this war. It's me for cover, and stay alive.

GREGARIOUS

Keep your head down. By the weakness of a group, the individual may lose his ideals of honor and courage. By the strength of a group, a nation may be saved. So those gunners are going to stay, and die if they have to. Let's go home.

SOLO

Yeah, come on.   [MUSIC]

SOLO

(*Sighs with relief.*) Whew! Glad to be out of that. (*Then with anger.*) And what did we prove by it?

GREGARIOUS

That all men affiliate with groups, and that this is a life-and-death matter of survival to both individual and society. The individual gains his strength and attitudes from his groups. Groups are the units, the building blocks, that create the structure of society. And from them, society, like the individual, gains its strength and its attitudes.

SOLO

And weaknesses?

GREGARIOUS

Something to think about, isn't it! Here's our bus. (*We hear the bus coming up to a stop.*)

SOLO

Bus? Are we back to this bus again?

GREGARIOUS

All aboard. (*The bus pulls away with Solo and Gregarious.*)

SOLO

Say, there's that girl again.

GREGARIOUS

The pretty one?

SOLO

Yes, and alone, too.

GREGARIOUS

Alone?

SOLO

(*Chuckles.*) Except for the crowd that goes with her.

GREGARIOUS

No, not alone. This bus, this little ephemeral collection of travelers, and this girl alone who is never alone, are involved with countless groups. Groups that keep the bus moving, the traffic flowing, the girl fed and clothed, and dreaming the dreams she dreams.

SOLO

Yes, and avoiding strange men, like me.

GREGARIOUS

That's not a conglomerate mob, out there on the sidewalks. (*The noise of the crowd comes in and rises with increasing numbers to a crescendo*.) It's a kaleidoscope of groups, groups of men, women, children, dividing the work of the nations and the world. Providing the faith and courage, and fears and doubts, of the individual. A massive invisible interplay. Even if you are isolated to outward appearance, hidden on some lonely northern island, you are not alone.

[FINALE]

7. FAMILY

Of all the groups we belong to, the family is the most important. This is true in every culture. But what the family is, how it is organized, who is important to it—these things are different in different cultures. And the way the family is organized is very important to the way people feel and act.

Nobody should be surprised to learn that the family is universal. It is necessary for the sexes to co-operate in having and in rearing children, and the family may be defined as the arrangement for just such co-operation. Because rearing children is so important, there must be some regular means of doing it, and everywhere there are rules about marriage and family arrangements. But people are surprised—even shocked—when they learn that family arrangements may be very different. To us the family means husband and wife and their unmarried children; or sometimes it means the whole group of kinfolk that we know and think of as being related. But this part of the family is not so important to us.

Most people think of family in these two ways. There will be a marriage and the children from that marriage, and also some larger group of kin. But marriages are not always the same as they are with us. Some people allow one man to marry many wives so that he will have several sets of children; some allow a woman to have several husbands. In a few societies, several men and women are married to one another and have one large household. This is one way in which families vary.

When we marry, we generally take a house or apartment separate from our parents and our in-laws. But some people never do this. In some societies the bride moves into the household of her husband, as in the Chinese village family. In some the groom moves into his wife's family. Usually, where there are such arrangements, the small family is thought of as merely a part of the larger group of kin. Then it is the large family that matters, and the parents on one side or the other are a part of the family—while those on the opposite side are not. Arrangements of this kind are spoken of as lineages (as with the Chinese) or as clans (as we saw among the Tlingit in "Stand-in for a Murderer"). This is another way in which families vary.

In our family the man usually earns the living, and the woman looks after the home and cares for the children. Such co-operative arrangements and division of the work and responsibility are found in most societies, though not in just this way. In some societies the women do most of the food-getting, and in nearly all of them they help. There is usually some arrangement also for division of authority. In our society the father is supposed to chastise the children and see that they live according to the rules. But this is not the way it is always done. Naquima in "Desert Soliloquy" (Chapter 4) thought it strange that a father would punish the children, for among the Hopi it is always an uncle who does that. In the Trobriand Islands there are clans, and the children always belong to their mother's clan. The father, who always belongs to a different clan, is not responsible even for feeding his children or seeing that they get a proper education. He is usually fond of his sons and acts like a kindly uncle. The man who chastises, who supports, and who sees that his children are properly reared is really an uncle—a brother of the mother. Meanwhile, the father will be taking care of his nephews—his sister's sons. Among the Trobriand Islanders the clan is reckoned through the mother, so that a boy will belong to the same clan as his mother's brother or his sister's children, but will belong to a different clan from his father or his wife or his own children. The family is the clan, and that is the important group.

Family arrangements are not merely matters of custom; they have deep significance for behavior. For within our family arrangements we find a pattern of relationships that tend to establish our attitudes toward people in general. Some anthropologists feel that the way behavior is set within the family is a representation-in-small of the way the society as a whole is operated. Or, perhaps, it should be stated the other way about—that the relationships within the family are projected into the whole society by the individual. After all, the child learns his family relationships first, and learns about the rest of society only later. It is not surprising that he should carry into his outside relationships the attitudes developed within his family circle.

For instance, consider a society where there are several women to whom the children look for motherly support—several women who may nurse them, feed them, scold them, give them affection. In such a society there is less apt to be a feeling that a person can have only one wife—that love can be received from only one person. In a society where the father is a stern disciplinarian, remote and hard, we may expect to find attitudes that the boss or the schoolmaster should be stern; or we may even find that the political system will reflect such strictness of rule and authority. Some anthropologists believe that these family attitudes in Germany contributed to the acceptance of Hitler and Nazism.

In recent years in the United States, the father's role has come to be more that of a "buddy" than of a disciplinarian. We generally view family life as a democratic one, where the father's influence is through persuasion rather than discipline. We can also see such attitudes in our schools where, for instance, the teacher is not supposed to punish the child. Modern industrial relations also stress the importance of the "good guy" boss. There are many exceptions, just as there are many cultural influences in America; this is only a general rule.

It is also important to appreciate that the family organization is influenced in many ways by the economic life of the people. Nearly everywhere that farming is carried on as a peasant activity, we find a lineage system held closely together by its landholdings. In these families, work is carried on by the larger family group as a single enterprise. In our society usually only one member earns the living. Where two or more family members are working, they will usually be working for separate wages or salaries. This tends to divide their interests and make them more independent of each other.

Each family system has its sources of strength and weakness. If we compare the Chinese peasant family with our own, we can see this. The Chinese family emphasizes unity and gives strength and support to its members, but the freedom of each person is lessened by the demands of family ties. The American family is discontinuous, it is small, and it offers less strength and support to each member. If a man dies, his widow may be put entirely on her own, and children do not regularly support their aging parents. But the system does give more freedom of action—particularly to the youth—and allows them more opportunity to find their own way and serve their own interests. We might well argue over which system is the better scheme for personal satisfaction; but it is hardly doubtful that our family pattern is better adjusted for life in America, with its rapid changes and need for free movement.

Home, Sweet Home

LEN PETERSON

‹‹‹-‹‹‹-‹‹‹-‹‹‹-‹‹‹-‹‹‹-‹‹‹-‹‹‹-‹‹‹-‹‹‹-‹‹‹-‹‹‹-‹‹‹-‹‹‹-‹‹‹-‹‹‹-‹‹‹-‹‹‹

*The scene opens on two men in a living room.
The radio is playing the opening bars of "Home,
Sweet Home."*

[MUSIC]

DON
Would you mind turning that off, George?
It's too gooey for me.

GEORGE
(*Laughs.*) Perfect timing, that, right in the
middle of your beefing. Doesn't it sweeten
you up a bit?

DON
No.

GEORGE
Doesn't cheer you at all?

DON
I'll turn it off. (*He does so.*)

GEORGE
Do you know that song was written by a man
who never had a home?

DON
No family man would write it!

GEORGE
Makes a fellow sound comfortable, doesn't it,
Don, calling him a family man?

DON
There isn't anything more uncomfortable. The
wife, my kids, the in-laws—

GEORGE
(*Amused.*) I know exactly how you feel. I had
it worse than you a few years back.

DON
Our whole idea of family needs changing.

GEORGE
How?

DON

I don't know. But this isn't working.

GEORGE

Don, I was in China just after the war on a special food commission: livestock and poultry diseases. And I came to Nantao, the village where my father was born. It was a mythical place to me—the home of my ancestors.

DON

Are you going to suggest I ought to switch over to the Chinese family system?

GEORGE

I was well received in Nantao.

[MUSIC]

FU

Then we are cousins, George. George—that is a strange name.

GEORGE

It's an American name, Cousin Fu.

FU

But you have kept the family name, Wang.

GEORGE

Yes.

FU

I have heard stories of your father who went away to America. He did not come back, but you come.

GEORGE

Never thought I would.

FU

You and I have the same grandfather. See, here is his name and his accomplishments on this plaque. Died at the age of sixty-eight.

GEORGE

You have quite an impressive family shrine here in your house, Cousin Fu. Are these offerings to ancestors, these bowls of fruit, incense, flowers?

FU

Yes, and to the gods. You will want to see the clan temple too. Over half the people in Nantao belong to our clan.

GEORGE

Well! Could we wander around and meet some?

FU

Yes. And I will show you our family graveyard.

GEORGE

Fine, fine.

[MUSIC]

FU

There is my father. I thought he might be down here at the graveyard. His tomb has just been finished. He is very proud of it.

GEORGE

His tomb?

FU

Yes. Come along and meet him.

GEORGE

Fine and healthy-looking old gentleman.

FU

My dear father.

HENG-SHEN

Fu, the inscription on my stone looks well.

FU

We have a visitor, a son of Ping who went to America.

HENG-SHEN

Son of Ping?

FU

George Wang.

HENG-SHEN

From America? Oh, you must tell us about our kin in America. Years ago Ping registered your name with the clan temple and sent money. But we never heard from him again. How many sons did Ping have?

GEORGE

Two sons and a daughter.

HENG-SHEN

And how many grandsons?

GEORGE

Three so far, and five granddaughters.

HENG-SHEN

What honors have been bestowed on our kinsmen in America?

GEORGE

I don't know. What do you consider an honor?

HENG-SHEN

Have you seen our family shrine?

FU

Yes, I showed it to him.

HENG-SHEN

Heaven has been good to our family lately.
When Ping left Nantao, the Wang clan knew
only ill fortune. But now we are prospering.
These things happen to families. Will you
come and look at my tomb?

[MUSIC]

GEORGE

The talk was light-hearted and lively beside
Heng-shen's tomb. He asked a stream of
questions about the Wangs in America, and
in turn related a good deal about our common
ancestors, whose tombs lay all about us under
the trees. It began as an idyl, that stay at the
home of my cousin in Nantao. My work
hadn't started, and the Communist sweep
had not yet reached that far. Life was casual;
I had time on my hands. I loafed about, ab-
sorbing the warm summer sun and the past
and a new sense of family. Oh, I was very
aware of family.

FU

Do you want me to hide you away, George?
Are you growing tired of all the Wangs hunting
you out and bombarding you with questions?

GEORGE

No, I am enjoying it. In America we ask about
relatives, too, but here they are much more
serious about it, even about relatives eight or
ten times removed. The American family
circle used to include more relatives, but now
generally speaking only the man and his wife
and their children are included; and sometimes even some of those feel on the outside
of the circle.

FU

The man's father and mother are not part of
the family? The man's ancestors?

GEORGE

(*Chuckles.*) Ancestors? Americans are a people
on the move. They can't be bothered lugging
their ancestors around with them. My father
stuck to Chinatown in San Francisco. I am
the halfway child. My children are real
Americans. It has taken three generations;
that is a long time to Americans. My children
speak only English. They don't want to know
anything about their ancestors.

FU

You are unhappy about it?

GEORGE

After all, they are Americans. Why shouldn't
they live as Americans? I'm American—more
American than Chinese.

FU

Yes, you seem to be.

GEORGE

Sometimes lately I have felt like a man without
any family, completely without ties. The only
thing that mattered has been my work.

FU

I cannot imagine that.

GEORGE

When work is a passion as mine is, it is not
so bad. But, on the other hand, my poor
wife—

HENG-SHEN

There is going to be a full moon tonight.

FU

Yes, Father.

HENG-SHEN

Warm. You were out in the fields with Fu all
day, George?

GEORGE

Yes, Uncle Heng-shen.

HENG-SHEN

You did not work too hard?

GEORGE

I enjoyed it.

HENG-SHEN

Fu, you will take those hens to market in the
morning?

-»»

FU

Yes, Father.

HENG-SHEN

And bring back some paper to mend the windows.

FU

Ch'in thinks we are rich enough to put glass in some of the windows.

HENG-SHEN

Fu, you are listening too much to that wife of yours. Her parents have no glass in their windows. Bring back wax paper for the windows.

FU

Yes, Father.

HENG-SHEN

Have you fed the ox yet?

FU

(*Leaving.*) I was about to do so, Father.

HENG-SHEN

My daughter-in-law has been influencing Fu too much since my wife died and she became the woman of the house. Up until now Fu has been a dutiful son.

GEORGE

How differently you would fare in my country, Uncle Heng-shen. There the young people boss the old, and the women—ah, it is a woman's country. Seventy per cent of the wealth in America is in women's hands.

HENG-SHEN

It sounds like the Communists—everything for the young, women behaving like men. There is no sense to it: upheaval, upheaval, unrest, no stability. If you were looking for wisdom would you look among women? Would you look among children?

GEORGE

(*Only half seriously.*) I suppose among old men of experience.

HENG-SHEN

Where else on this earth?

GEORGE

Some will argue that was fine when things

changed little from generation to generation, but we're astride a runaway jet today. A man of forty doesn't stand much chance giving advice to a youth of twenty; a man of seventy attempting it is considered ludicrous.

HENG-SHEN

In the youth's opinion.

GEORGE

But I believe in change!

HENG-SHEN

Are there more fools made by expecting changes, a brand-new world, or more fools made by looking back and taking guidance from the past?

GEORGE

I probably won't live long enough to answer that one, Uncle Heng-shen, but my heart is with the fools who peer on ahead.

HENG-SHEN

Like a dog that is led astray by every new odor his nostrils pick up. You trot to left, to right, around in circles. Where are you going now?

GEORGE

As a public servant, I am trying to feed hungry mouths. As an individual—I'm not so sure of my direction or goal.

HENG-SHEN

And what of your family—the Wangs in America? Where are they going? You haven't told me much about that.

GEORGE

We don't think in America of families going anywhere—it's more the individual.

HENG-SHEN

Oh, yes, I have heard that in America (it is the same in Europe, is it not?) the family means only the man and his wife and their children. When the man or woman dies, or they part, that is the end of the family. It seems very strange. Can it possibly be like that?

GEORGE

I'm afraid it is.

HENG-SHEN

It is very precarious for the children.

GEORGE

I know many a woman living alone, bringing up her children.

HENG-SHEN

With no man? What of her father-in-law? What of her brothers-in-law? And her father and brothers and uncles?

GEORGE

They don't seem to be around. They don't seem to take much responsibility.

HENG-SHEN

With us it is very different. The Chinese family is buttressed against misfortunes that happen to individuals in the family. There is continuity. The family includes the dead, the living, and those not yet born. The land and other property belong to the family, not to individuals. At the core of the Chinese family is the father and son.

FU

(*Returning.*) Ch'in has done your washing, Father. It has been put away in your bedroom.

HENG-SHEN

Good, good. The tie between the husband and wife is not so close as the tie between the parents and their son. A marriage is as much the parents taking a daughter-in-law as the son taking a wife.

FU

More so.

HENG-SHEN

Her first duties are to her husband's parents.

FU

Yes.

HENG-SHEN

But in return they are responsible for her. She is expected to produce sons.

FU

She comes into her own when she has daughters-in-law.

HENG-SHEN

(*Slyly*.) Whom she can manage as she has been managed all her life up until then.

FU

Yes.

HENG-SHEN

Like Fu's wife, Ch'in. (*A baby begins to mutter, but her sounds don't make words yet.*)

FU

What are you doing wandering around all by yourself, baby? (*The baby replies with a murmur.*)

GEORGE

Who is this?

FU

Hsiao-mair, my eldest boy's first child, my first grandchild.

HENG-SHEN

And my great-grandchild. Only it's a girl.

GEORGE

A very pretty child though.

FU

I think I had better take you back to your mother, Hsiao-mair. (*He leaves.*)

HENG-SHEN

There is a second great-grandchild coming soon.

GEORGE

In your family there doesn't seem to be the isolation between generations that plagues us, Uncle Heng-shen. In my world the children, adults, and old people lead different lives. Of course, in a society rooted to the land the work keeps you all together. But in the shifting industrial and commercial society in our cities there is a terrible isolation. I feel my children are strangers to me; and my father is a stranger. It is easier to grow old here than in America.

HENG-SHEN

Everywhere with age there come aches and pains.

GEORGE

But for the old men of China there are compensations: respect from the young, obedience. When I think of my father—I wish I could do something for him.

HENG-SHEN

Can you not?

[MUSIC]

GEORGE

This association with the old patriarch Hengshen made me think a lot about my father. He was not as old as Heng-shen, but already he was a cast-off; there was no place for him in our family. He was alone; all his children had set up establishments of their own, and my mother had died in 1939. It used to hurt me, his gratitude whenever we invited him over for a meal or suggested that he stay for the night.

FATHER

You are sure it will not put you out too much? You are sure it won't inconvenience you? I don't want to be any trouble. I—I can't stay longer than the one night. I must go tomorrow —business. I wish I could stay longer, but business—You're sure I won't be in the way?

DORIS

No, of course not, Dad. I'll get the bed made up for you.

FATHER

You are very good to me, Doris.

GEORGE

He knew he was not welcome, except for short visits. He stifled his pride and came. But I couldn't stifle my sense of shame, or the touch of contempt I felt for my wife's selfishness, the time I suggested he come for a longer visit.

[MUSIC]

DORIS

Why should we look after him?

GEORGE

You won't have to look after him, Doris; he can look after himself. You know he'll contribute more than his share.

DORIS

But he'll be in the way. If I can't have my household to myself—

GEORGE

I think it's the least we can do.

DORIS

Why? George, you know it wouldn't work. It hasn't worked with any of the families I know. I'm doing your father a favor by avoiding bad feeling later on.

GEORGE

That's a neat argument, I must say.

DORIS

We have nothing in common with him; you know that. What can we talk to him about? The things that we're interested in would just bore him stiff. And our friends—what has he got to say to them? It'd be uncomfortable all round. Be sensible!

GEORGE

Doris, I owe my father a great deal. He didn't have to give me as much schooling as he did.

DORIS

Pay him back some other way. I want my own house to myself.

GEORGE

All right, have the house to yourself, then.

DORIS

It's no reflection on your father. I like him, and I want you to do something for him. But having him live with us for a while just wouldn't work.

GEORGE

But that's all he cares about—the family, the kids.

DORIS

All right, invite him to come and live with us; but I won't be responsible if it doesn't work.

GEORGE

That's a fine basis on which to invite him. No thanks.

DORIS

Suit yourself.

[MUSIC]

GEORGE

I think I've got a good wife; we've had a pretty good life together. But the stand she's always taken toward my father bothers me. Like all American husbands, I have felt that the wishes of my wife have had to take precedence over the wishes of my father. With Fu in Nantao, the wishes of his father came first. (*With a sense of personal defeat.*) The wishes of my children too come before mine—and before my wife's.

(*Dissonant jive crashes in on the radio, and a teen-aged girl hums in accompaniment.*)

GEORGE

Turn that radio down. Turn it off, Janet. Nothing but noise.

JANET

Don't you know what that is, Pop? Hottest combo in town. (*Laughs.*) Razor sharp, that playin'.

GEORGE

I've heard better music from a squeaking wagon wheel. Turn it off. I'm trying to read a report here, but with that ashcan clatter—

(*Janet turns the radio off.*)

GEORGE

Whew, like the silence after an artillery bombardment.

JANET

(*Complaining slightly.*) I can study listening to that.

GEORGE

That's because you're a good deal smarter than your father. I suppose you'll be able to study while watching television too, if we ever get a set.

JANET

Sure.

GEORGE
I don't doubt it.

JIMMY
(*Enters. He is also teen-aged.*) Hey, Pop, we're playin' a game of ball tonight over in the east end, and we need another car to take the team over. Jerry McNie's old man had to go outa town 'safternoon suddenly. We were bankin' on his car.

GEORGE
No, Jimmy, you can't have the car.

JIMMY
But we're on a spot. We'll forefeit the game if we're more'n half an hour late.

GEORGE
I told you, Jimmy, when you got that last ticket for speeding, no car till next month, and I meant it.

JIMMY
I'm paying for it outa my allowance.

GEORGE
There's more than just you to consider; there's the public. You won't be so smart-alecky next time. You can't resist showing off when you've got a crowd around.

JIMMY
If we lose this game we'll be outa the running for the play-offs.

GEORGE
That important?

JIMMY
It's crucial.

GEORGE
Well, it's against all my principles.

JIMMY
You'll lemme have it?

GEORGE
I'm thinking of the rest of your team, not you.

JIMMY
Thanks, Pop. (*He starts to go.*) I'll strike out eleven batters for you.

JANET
Will you give me a lift then down to Columbus Avenue, Jimmy?

JIMMY
(*From outside.*) Yeah, if you're coming right away!

GEORGE
What're you going down there for, Janet?

JANET
Meeting Arnie.

GEORGE
(*With a sigh.*) Why can't he come here and fetch you?

JANET
He doesn't finish at the drugstore till seven.

GEORGE
I thought your mother said she didn't like your going out with him.

JANET
Oh, Mom and her ideas of who I should associate with. I don't know why I can't pick my own friends.

DORIS
(*Comes in.*) George, did you give Jimmy permission to take the car?

GEORGE
Yes. It's for his baseball team, Doris.

DORIS
You discipline the boy one minute and give in the next. He won't be happy till he's had an accident.
(*An urgent horn sounds outside.*)

JANET
Oh, I gotta go! Jimmy'll be going without me!

DORIS
(*Calling after her.*) Janet, I think it'd be better if you stayed at home!

JANET
(*From outside.*) Why should I? (*The door slams behind her.*)

DORIS
Janet! I should go and order her to come back.

GEORGE
I have these reports I have to get through tonight. Let her go. Have a bit of peace and quiet.

DORIS

You always let those kids have their way. And I have to do all the worrying.

GEORGE

I wish I knew the right answer.

DORIS

The children pay no more attention any more to me than a—

GEORGE

(*Now absorbed in his work. Mumbles.*) Twelve and a half per cent of 348 is—

DORIS

And neither do you.

GEORGE

What?

DORIS

The children have got their friends; you've got your work. But here I sit.

GEORGE

Doris, you can do anything you want to.

DORIS

What, alone? (*Forlorn.*) Yes, that's a great stimulus for doing something, isn't it?

[MUSIC]

GEORGE

I was tempted to say to Doris: "Well, this is the loneliness that goes with the kind of independence you've always wanted." But I never have said it. Who am I? Doris's predicament is no different from that of a lot of American wives and mothers I know. On the other hand Fu's wife's situation—at the age when Doris was beginning to feel that her life was over, Fu's wife was coming into her own.

CH'IN

I am a grandmother. (*The baby enters jabbering.*) Oh, listen to this talkative one, Hsiaomair! This one made me a grandmother, and in a few days I shall be twice a grandmother. But this time to a boy—I have been to a fortune teller.

[MUSIC]

FU

(*Entering.*) You are looking over the family shrine again, George?

GEORGE

Yes; and comparing your family and mine, Cousin Fu. Yours has a more solid foundation. You've more rigid traditions and customs defining the relationship of all the members of your family; this seems to make life run more smoothly for you day to day. And the peak in your lives, especially of your women, comes not in the middle years, but well along in life—something to look forward to. And there's this sense, wonderful sense of continuity: your life is not isolated, but bound to the past and to the future. Every age has links with every other age.

FU

George, we have our difficulties too.

GEORGE

Oh, I'm sure; but they can't be any greater than ours. The American family is restless these days. We ask: What do we want? How should it be, the family? Where are we going? I like the quiet, settled atmosphere around here.

FU

It was, it was—but it's changing. We listen with great intensity now to how other people do things; we wonder how we would like it.

[MUSIC]

GEORGE

My dream began to fade. Nantao, the mythical place in my heart, all-good, all-sense, all-harmony, began to be replaced by the Nantao of reality.

[MUSIC]

FU

Ah, the old fool, the old fool!

GEORGE

(*Comes in casually.*) Well, you sound upset, Fu. What's up?

FU

He does not know Asia is on the march!

GEORGE

Who?

FU

Heng-shen, my revered father.

GEORGE

You have had a quarrel with him?

FU

No, I am a dutiful son, but I may not be dutiful forever.

GEORGE

Why, what's wrong, Fu?

FU

The inoculation measures against disease you suggested to me for our cattle he will have nothing to do with. Unnatural, he said— it will not work, it will kill all our cattle. With every suggestion I make, it is the same; if he has not done it that way in the past, then it is no good. We had the same argument a month ago over a gasoline pump I wanted to install. In America you do not have to wait for the greybeards, do you? If the younger generation wishes to make a change, progress, they go ahead?

GEORGE

Yes. Frequently.

FU

There is a part of me that is not Chinese, not the old Chinese. I do not wish to wait until I am a greybeard—though I am close to it— before I improve things around here. I cannot wait for the slow advance my father is content with. Sometimes I almost feel I do not fear disobedience to my father. If my ancestors were alive today, they might well do what I want to do themselves!

[MUSIC]

CH'IN

(*Entering.*) Oh, it is over, it is over, it is over.

GEORGE

What is over, Cousin Ch'in?

CH'IN

Don't you know? Where have you been?

GEORGE

To the other end of the village.

CH'IN

My daughter-in-law has had her baby.

GEORGE

But I thought—

CH'IN

Yes, it is early. Another girl. Fu is so disappointed he wants to name her Hsiao Tseuh.

GEORGE

Little Mistake? A terrible name to go through life with.

CH'IN

What is her mother called but Hsia To— Little Too-Many. It is not good to be born a girl.

GEORGE

You seem to be thriving under it, Cousin Ch'in.

CH'IN

Now, maybe now. I am a grandmother. But all those years in between! You begin life knowing you are a disappointment to your father and mother. You are betrothed, and then marry, and move in among strangers. In a quarrel with your in-laws, your husband sides with his parents. You are all alone. You must not show too much affection for your husband, as they tell me women do in those moving pictures that come from Europe and America. You must obey your husband and his father and his mother and his grandfather and grandmother—with a bowed head, always submissive. You are nothing, always you must say to yourself, you are nothing—or you would get wrong thoughts about your husband's family.

[MUSIC]

GEORGE

Every day, Don, I became aware of more and more stress and strain in my Nantao family; it was there when I looked for it. By the time I was ready to leave, my family setup back home in San Francisco didn't look quite so bad. The Nantao family had the kind of long-term stability we sometimes yearn for—but at the expense of a lot of elbow room for the younger people, and for the women, and for the individual generally. If I came from Mars I don't know which kind of family setup I'd prefer; they both have advantages and drawbacks. But being American, and having grown into the American mold, I guess I'm for the American model, Don, with all the stresses and strains peculiar to it. I need elbow room more than stability.

DON
I guess I do too. So I'm stuck with it, eh?

GEORGE
Yes, what you gain one way you lose another.

DON
How's your family situation now, George?

GEORGE
Eased off a bit. Time, just the passage of time, is a great cure.

DON
If you can survive long enough.

[FINALE]

8. ETHICS

For people to live together, there must be rules. Every culture provides a set of regulations by which the people normally govern their conduct, one with the other. These regulations exist so that an orderly life may be preserved—so that each person has knowledge of his own rights and duties, and a set of expectations regarding the conduct of others.

Some of these regulations may be called tabus or proscriptions. We have tabus against certain types of marriages, against nudity, against the eating of certain foods. Other regulations may be called laws. These are established regulations for which specified modes of punishment are provided. Property laws, marriage laws, criminal laws, and a great deal of special legislation all serve to channel behavior in most modern countries. Other peoples also have legal systems of their own.

Underlying the laws and proscriptions of each society is a system of ethics. Ethics may be defined as the basic standards for proper conduct, the principles that govern the specific laws. Every society has such an ethical code, though not all societies have given so much explicit attention to it as our own. Ethics establishes the good and the bad; it distinguishes propriety from impropriety, right from wrong, as these are interpreted by the culture. These ethical assumptions are a part of the cultural heritage of each people.

Society may be viewed as a compromise—a compromise between the personal ends of each individual and the necessary subordination of these ends to the body politic, the society. If each individual were permitted absolute freedom to choose his own conduct, only chaos would result. There could be no such thing as property, as marriage, as organized effort. Even in a culture where all people are strongly motivated to a common set of values, there would still be conflict over the attainment of ends if there were no guides to the conduct of the individuals.

Anthropologists have perhaps given too little attention to the comparative study of ethics. This has been regarded as the proper province of the philosopher, and the philosopher rarely goes further from Western civilization than India or China. The anthropologist, on the other hand, has been content largely with the statement of specific tabus and regulations. The variety of such regulations seems infinite: cover this portion of the body, or that; do not scratch yourself while ritually unclean; do not eat venison and salmon at the same time; you may not marry the child of your mother's sister, but you may marry the child of your mother's brother. Thus on and on. The laws and regulations vary from one culture to the next. Some variations seem of no greater importance than custom, as, for instance, whether to drive on the right or the left side of the road. But even here, custom is important for orderly procedure.

There are insufficient studies to show if any elements in ethics are found in all cultures. One possible universal principle is the one known in our law as the "general-welfare principle"—that a person may not take any action considered inimical to the general welfare of the community. For instance, our culture gives great importance to the private ownership of property and the free rights of the owner; but these rights are curtailed under this principle by zoning regulations and condemnation proceedings. The Eskimo, on the other hand, feels that any person in need may take tools or food freely from some other person, but that he must not destroy food or engage in acts that endanger the welfare of others. This general-welfare principle may be abrogated by dictatorial rulers—though probably not for long. Whether or not such a principle is universal, it is certainly found in many primitive societies.

The general-welfare concept applies primarily to one's own group: the ethical code that limits murder and recognizes property rights stops at a border. That border delimits the society. Beyond that border, regulations may also apply—international covenants of warfare, mutual pacts of friendship, trade agreements. These, too, are based upon ethical principles, and form the basis for enlarging the scope of the society. Indeed, in the course of human cultural development there has been a gradual though faltering progression toward enlarging the area brought within a single ethical system. The logical (and undoubtedly necessary) end of such an evolutionary process is the establishment of a world community and the permanent elimination of borders that limit the application of basic ethical codes.

⋙⋙⋙

The development of a universal ethical system faces a major obstacle: it requires tolerance. Tolerance in esthetic tastes, in customs, and even in religious practices has been achieved from time to time, though with difficulty. But tolerance—let alone real understanding and appreciation—of varying ethical codes is far more difficult to achieve. There are three reasons for this. First, ethical assumptions lie deeply imbedded in our attitudes and behavior; they are rarely made explicit. Thus we act in terms of ethical assumptions that we find ourselves powerless to question. When circumstances bring these assumptions to the surface, they seem so self-evident that we call them God-given, or instinctive, or natural, or necessary. The second point is that ethics must be evaluative; they cannot be neutral. We must distinguish the rightness and wrongness in behavior, and we must feel strongly about the distinction. Finally, to question the validity of our ethical assumptions is to undermine the very foundations of our behavior. It takes a strong man to recognize the validity of alternative ethical assumptions, and yet live—as he must—strictly by his own ethical principles. It would take an even stronger society to make it possible for all of its members to recognize the rightness of other codes, and yet adhere to their own.

Yet the fact remains that different cultures do make different ethical assumptions. Let us examine one of our own—that it is right to be truthful. There can be no question of this; to us it is almost a tautology. Yet in some African cultures this assumption is replaced by another—that it is right to tell a person what he wants to hear. We know this rule, for we apply it frequently to women's hats and the boss's idea. The white lie is socially excusable in our culture though as a principle of conduct it is morally reprehensible. But to certain Africans a statement that gives offense to the listener is morally wrong.

This is a dramatic case, but others are perhaps even more important. For instance, work is for us a moral good, industriousness a virtue. "Idleness," we say, "is the devil's workshop." This attitude is found among the Achomawi Indians of northeast California and among the Yurok Indians (whose ethical code is the subject of "The Case of the Sea-Lion Flippers"). But in other cultures—such as in our own antebellum South or in ancient Greece—work was not a virtue.

The Yurok Indians considered it ethical to exact full compensation for any wrong, however slight it might seem to us. They had an elaborate legal code, which defined the manner in which a person who has been wronged should go about getting his repayment. Any Yurok who failed to make such a demand was not merely "soft," but wrong. The proper adjudication of all disputes is necessary to maintain equilibrium in the society, or as the Yurok Indians put it, to keep the disk of the world from turning over. The Hopi Indians, as shown in "Desert Soliloquy" (Chapter 4), have almost the opposite code: their ethical system demands the subordination of the individual interest, a giving in to the other fellow.

There is, of course, no clear and sharp distinction between ethics and values. We may think of values as the "desired" way of doing and acting, while ethics convey more the sense of "ought." Ethics are hortative. Values are approved and desired; ethics are expected and enforced.

If ethics are enforced, it stands to reason that there must be modes of coercion. No people are so filled with virtue (as their culture defines virtue) that they all live up to the full dictates of their culture. In all societies there are people who are crude, who are disrespectful, or who break the laws. Ethical systems are enforced in two ways. One is in the realm of belief—religion, ritual, the supernatural. All ethical codes are rooted in convictions of a broadly theological nature. They are given substance in ritual, in myth, and in the threat of divine or supernatural punishment. Our own ethical code rests upon Mosaic law and Biblical injunction; the Hopi child is referred to the Katchina spirits; the Yurok Indian saw the sins accumulate and threaten, as an enveloping miasma, to destroy the world.

The other aspect of coercion lies in secular power. Every social system provides some means for the punishment of wrongdoers. We have law courts and the police to provide us with this service. The Hopi have Katchina impersonators. The Tlingit Indians place power in the clan heads to maintain order within the clan (in the manner of the father of a family), and solve their inter-clan problems by the threat of force between them—a sort of regulated feud. While the Yurok Indians had no direct vested authority, except within the family, they did have an orderly means of allowing a wronged person to bring action against the wrongdoer.

The Yurok Indians dwelt on the northernmost coast of California. They lived entirely by hunting, gathering, and fishing; but the richness of their environment made possible permanent and rather large villages. They wove fine baskets, made dugout boats of cedar, and constructed substantial houses of hand-hewn cedar planks. The men slept in the sweathouse, a carefully constructed cellar-like excavation roofed with cedar planks. Sweating was a daily ritual of all proper Yurok men. They remained in the superheated structure as long as they could and then plunged into the icy stream—an act that was partly religious ritual, partly the daily bath.

The Yurok had a culture as interesting as it was rich. They had no officials, but the wealthy tended to control matters within a clearly defined legal code. They owned not only money and ceremonial goods, but also fishing, hunting, and gathering places. A proper Yurok was expected to accumulate property; to show great self-control in eating and sexual habits; to be industrious and frugal; and to sweat himself regularly. He was also supposed to protect his own interests with an almost Yankee shrewdness, as well as hard bargaining in any legal dispute. Any real or fancied wrong (and there were a host of specific restrictions) was the subject of lengthy litigation, mediated by a go-between, who might be any mutually agreed-upon person neutral to the dispute. If no settlement was reached, there would be bloodshed; feud was the final arbiter. Without officials, there was no government; the Yurok had a *laissez-faire* society. They believed, like Adam Smith, that society was best served if each person served his own self-interest—within the established ethical code and the value system of the culture. The emphasis upon wealth, the *laissez-faire* system, the importance of self-interest and bargaining give this culture a flavor similar to our own, despite the great difference in level of material achievements.

The Case of the Sea-Lion Flippers

LISTER SINCLAIR

"The Case of the Sea-Lion Flippers," a true case, was described in two versions, by Robert Spott (a Yurok) and by A. L. Kroeber. This legal case took place shortly after the first contact with Europeans. The two stories conflict only in legal details that do not appear in this story. The narrator was the stepfather of Robert Spott. The other characters are:

MINOT	*A man of about 50, well-to-do but weak by Yurok standards.*
WOMAN	*A relative of* MINOT.
OMEN	*Two relatives of* MINOT *who*
HIPUR	*live in a near-by village.*
PEKWON	*The go-between.*
YOUNG LAYEK	*Son of the murdered man.*
LAYEK	*The murdered man.*
SISTER	*Sister of the murdered man.*

The Yurok do not wish names of the dead to be used. Here all names, except that of Spott, are based on Yurok place names.

SPOTT

Now all this happened back around 1860, but we Yurok Indians are not going to forget it. It should be a lesson to everybody, the terrible things that happen when people don't do the right thing. I know all about it. I was the fellow who sat all night by the old man's body on the beach. I pulled the knife out of his head and watched his sister heat the stones and drop them in the blood and sand, and cook them up and make the curse—that's the kind of thing I mean! That's not the right thing, not at all.

But I'll give it to you from the start. We Yurok Indians live up in northern California right where the Klamath River runs out into the Pacific Ocean—where all the big redwood trees grow. Salmon and acorns we used to live on mostly in those days; and everyone had his own special places to fish and gather acorns, and it was up to him to look after his rights, and if someone came along and took away his rights, then you make the other fellow pay you something.

Now one of these special rights was in case a sea lion was killed anywhere along a special stretch of coast. The fellow that killed it got most of the meat, but old Minot of Rekwa had the rights to the sea-lion flippers. They're something we Yurok really like to eat. But of course that had nothing to do with it, really; it was a question of rights, property rights. Only important people owned such flipper rights. The rights belonged to Minot, and of course people should respect other people's rights.

So one day, Minot was sitting in front of his sweathouse, thinking about money, when he heard the shouting down at the mouth of the river.

(*Shouts of pleasure are heard from the distance.*)

MINOT

What's all that shouting and hollering down at the mouth of the river? Looks like old man Layek's harpooned him a sea lion. I guess I'd better roll down to the beach, and pick up my flippers. It's a comforting thing for a man to know he's independent and has property.

SPOTT

So old Minot started off downstream, and soon turned up at the beach.

MINOT

Hello.

WOMAN

Hello, Minot.

MINOT

Where is everybody? There was a whole crowd of people here. I thought someone harpooned a sea lion.

WOMAN

Yeah. Old man Layek got one just inside the rock where the falcon lives.

MINOT

He did, eh? Then where are my flippers?

WOMAN

Minot, he took them away.

MINOT

He couldn't have. That's my right. I'll tell you how I got it.

WOMAN

Don't bother telling me. I know it's your right. But Layek can be stubborn. He just hauled off the flippers with the rest of it. You'll have to do something about it. You'll have to make a claim. Taking away a man's rights is very bad.

SPOTT

Very bad. Old man Layek should have known that would lead to trouble. But he was a terrible fellow, right up to the day he got killed. So that was the first bad thing. Now here's the next: old Minot went back and sat in front of his sweathouse, and started to think.

MINOT

Well, perhaps they were pretty hungry over in Layek's house. Perhaps they couldn't even spare those little sea-lion flippers. Perhaps the sea lion was so small they couldn't divide it round the whole village. Perhaps he'll send a woman over to explain. Perhaps he'll come over himself. Perhaps I'll wait and see.

SPOTT

How about that, eh? Wait and see! When a man's rights have been trampled on, he's got to put in a claim. Otherwise, what kind of a man is he? How would people live if they didn't look after themselves? So that was the second bad thing: Old Minot fooled around and didn't make a claim.

So sure enough a few days later along came the third bad thing. (*Shouts are again heard coming from the shore.*)

MINOT

They've got another sea lion—just about where they got the other one. Now for sure, Layek'll come up with my flippers. I'll go and sit in the sweathouse, and think about money, and obsidian blades and woodpecker scalps, and get myself in the proper frame of mind for talking to Layek about my rights. If a man doesn't have his rights, what has he got?

SPOTT

Well, old Minot knew what to think, but he didn't know what to do. So he sat in the sweathouse until he got sick of waiting. Then he came out again and started downstream to the beach:

WOMAN

Hello, Minot.

MINOT

You've got a basket of meat!

WOMAN

Sure. Layek just killed a sea lion.

MINOT

Has he got my flippers for me?

WOMAN

Minot, I told you to make a claim last time this happened.

MINOT

You mean it's happened again?

WOMAN

What did you expect? If you don't do the right thing, anything can happen! You should have done something the first time.

MINOT

Well, never mind; Layek's going to regret this. I'll do something this time—I'll figure out something, I'll—just you wait and see! I feel as if I'm being trampled on. Why should this happen to me? I've tried to lead a good life. I've never made a pig of myself at meals, or chased after women. Everywhere I go, I try to keep my mind on higher things, spiritual things, money. And now that old man takes away my sea-lion flipper rights. I feel as if they're trampling on me.

SPOTT

Well, that's all very well, but a man ought to have some self-control and not act up like a child or a woman. But not old Minot. First he didn't do enough; now he does too much. He goes right back to his house, gets his bow and arrow, takes it over to his sweathouse, and starts getting it into shape. His wife was dead, and his sons had no idea how hard he was taking all this. Next thing, here he is half-sheltered behind the special board that protects the sweathouse door. Across the little creek in Rekwa, old man Layek comes out of his sweathouse and sits down on the stone platform overlooking the river. He's about fifty yards away. Old man Minot has got all his tackle fixed up and he leans out of the doorway just enough to get one knee on the ground and steady his aim. Then he lets fly at old Layek!

(*Minot lets fly an arrow,* and in the distance *Layek, hit, cries out.*)

MINOT

That'll teach you to go around taking other people's rights away—trampling on them!

SPOTT

And then he just beats it, as fast as he can go, up the coast to the village of Omen-hipur; I guess that's about five miles away, and Minot has friends there.

MINOT

(*Coming up,* winded.) Help! Help! Help!

OMEN

Sit down, Minot. Here, sit on the sweathouse bench.

HIPUR

What's the matter, fellow? You run all the way from Rekwa or something?

MINOT

Yeah. (*Still gasping for breath.*)

OMEN

Minot, you look about finished. Take it easy, now, take it easy. You're among friends. He really has run all the way from Rekwa.

HIPUR

All right now, Minot. Just breathe slow and easy. Rest, relax, don't get excited. Don't you know that's not the right thing to do? Relax. Try and settle your mind. Think of money— big dentalium shells. Try and think of a dentalium shell big as a salmon. That'll calm you down.

MINOT

Thanks. Feel better now.

OMEN

What's happened?

MINOT

I don't know whether I've killed a man.

HIPUR

Killed a man!

MINOT

Yeah, with an arrow.

OMEN

That's real trouble! That's serious, killing a man. That can run you into money!

HIPUR

Who was it?

MINOT

Old Layek.

HIPUR

Layek, eh! (*He turns to Omen.*) Sea-lion flippers.

OMEN

(*Quietly to Hipur*) Here we go! (*Pause.*) Minot, are your children and grandchildren at home?

MINOT

I think so. Where else would they be?

OMEN

You must be crazy. Layek's house will start killing them. We'd better get back.

HIPUR

Wait a minute. Are you sure he's dead?

MINOT

No, I'm not sure. I just hit him through the

upper arm. I think the arrow got to his ribs. Then I just dropped everything and lit out.

PEKWON

Well, where's Minot?

OMEN

You must be crazy. What kind of way is that to act? Come on, let's get everybody and get back to Rekwa!

HIPUR

We left him back at Omen-hipur. Lay . . . Is he dead?

SPOTT

When the fellows turned up from Omen-hipur, there was an awful gang of people hanging around with bows and arrows, and all the women screaming and chattering at each other like a lot of jays. (*The crowd talks in a confused babble*.) Layek wasn't dead after all, and he'd sent upriver for an intermediary to come along and help settle things between the two of them. People who were related to both parties just hung around and tried to sound intelligent without committing themselves. But they were all certainly waiting for the outfit from Omen-hipur.

PEKWON

Dead? Not him! Just a bit of a thump in the ribs. But that's not what's important. Minot tried to kill him, you know.

PEKWON

Know how it started?

WOMAN

Layek stole the sea-lion flippers.

PEKWON

Shut up!

HIPUR

That's what happened. Minot has the sea-lion flipper rights along this stretch of beach, and Layek stole them.

WOMAN

I don't care what you say—it's Layek's fault.

PEKWON

That's bad. Did Minot bring a claim?

WOMAN

I told him to bring a claim.

PEKWON

Shut up, all you women! Here are the men from Omen-hipur. Now shut up, you women, while we talk to them.

PEKWON

Shut up.

HIPUR

No, he didn't.

WOMAN

Layek stole the sea-lion flippers.

PEKWON

That's bad, too.

PEKWON

Shut up!

OMEN

But Layek took away his rights twice.

WOMAN

Twice! (*To which Pekwon gives a roar of disgust.*) I saw him do it!

PEKWON

Well, that's tough all right. Maybe there's something to say for Minot after all. (*To himself.*) I might have done the same in his position.

PEKWON

Get away, you screeching jays, you bother me! Now then—you fellows just got here from Omen-hipur?

WOMAN

Sometimes old Minot was kind. He wasn't greedy for food. Sometimes he would take only one of his flippers.

OMEN

That's right.

PEKWON

I see you brought your bows and arrows.

PEKWON

Well, what are we going to do? Layek sent for me to be intermediary. Where is he?

HIPUR

Yeah.

YOUNG LAYEK
He's in his house. He's too sick to come out, but I'm his oldest son.

PEKWON
Well, does he want to settle, or what?

YOUNG LAYEK
I don't know. I've no right to say what the old man will do.

PEKWON
Then what's the use of my coming all the way downriver?
(*The wrangling starts again.*)

SPOTT
The intermediary was pretty cross. He'd got his arms bare so that he could see the marks on his forearm where standard sizes of dentalium shells were tattooed. But before there could be fresh trouble with the intermediary, a rumor started running through the place.

VOICES
Here's Minot. Minot's here.

PEKWON
What's that? Someone say Minot's around?

WOMAN
That's right, he's just—

PEKWON
Shut up. Where is he? Is he behind all those women? Where is Minot?

OMEN
I guess she knows where he is.

PEKWON
All right, then, don't just stand there. Where is he?

WOMAN
In the brush just back of the creek.

PEKWON
All right, tell him to come out!

SPOTT
So Minot came out, surrounded by the women, in case there was any trouble. His weapons were all ready, and he had the blue clay on his face and body so that you could hardly recognize him. He had his hair tied up, and he was wearing the special bone hairpins with both ends sharpened, so that no one can grab you by the hair if there's a fight. Minot put down his weapons, but most of the men from both the houses stayed up in the creek bed, ready—in case anything was going to happen.

PEKWON
Hello, Minot.

MINOT
Hello.

PEKWON
I want to hear why you did it.

MINOT
He was trampling on me.

PEKWON
You've got the blue clay on. Maybe you've already made medicine for Layek to die.

MINOT
No, I haven't. I haven't done that.

PEKWON
Looks to me as though Layek was pretty much at fault.

MINOT
Yes, he was; but who cares about me? I'm getting old. Throw me into the river.

PEKWON
Now take it easy, Minot.

OMEN
Remember your grandchildren.

MINOT
That's right; I didn't think of them.

YOUNG LAYEK
I just ran back and saw my father. He says he's going to get well. He says he's to blame. He says he doesn't want to make trouble. He doesn't want any payment.

PEKWON
Maybe, if there's going to be payment, he's afraid he'd have to pay Minot even more for stealing the sea-lion flipper rights than he'd get for being shot. What do you say, Minot?

MINOT
If old Layek really means it—wants to end up the whole thing without payment—well, I won't bear any grudge. We'll be friends.

PEKWON

If Minot pays, Layek will have to pay still more. All the same, I think there should be a payment.

MINOT

No, no, that's all right.

YOUNG LAYEK

He says he doesn't want a payment.

PEKWON

Well, if that's the way you all want it—but this isn't the right thing. Every time there's an injury, there ought to be a payment. Things ought to be done the right way; otherwise there's bound to be more trouble. We'd better go over to Layek's house and shake hands and speak again.

YOUNG LAYEK

He says he can't do that today, because he isn't feeling right. But he'll shake hands and make friends as soon as he gets over the wound.

PEKWON

Oh. That all right with you, Minot?

MINOT

Sure.

PEKWON

Well, that's it; but this isn't being done the right way. There's going to be more trouble.

SPOTT

That intermediary fellow from upstream sure knew what he was talking about. A few days later, Minot had sweated and washed himself in the creek and was sitting in front of his sweathouse. Suddenly out came old Layek from his own sweathouse, with his arm in a sling. He spread out his fingers and cursed.

LAYEK

Minot, I mention the name of your dead father! May your family become dead as he is dead!

SPOTT

Minot said nothing. But now there was new trouble on top of all the old—especially when a week or two later Minot's grandson got sick and died.

MINOT

That was why old Layek wanted to settle without proper payment. He wanted to curse my family, and make prayers against them at the sacred cursing rocks. From this time, my family will not speak to Layek's; nor will my friends and relatives up the coast at Omenhipur!

SPOTT

From then on people began to think about the world-renewal ceremony, because there was so much sin to get rid of in the world. Everybody tried to do what was right—denied himself food and water, thought about money all the time he was gathering sweathouse wood, and generally tried to get himself in shape for some sort of big trouble. And it came soon enough. Old Layek was hardly better from his wound than off he went up the beach, away from his household, up to Omenhipur, where all Minot's friends and relatives lived. And he took his weapons with him.

OMEN

Look! See who's on the beach!

HIPUR

Old Layek!

OMEN

He's got his bow and arrow with him. He cursed Minot's grandson to death. Who's he meaning to kill now?

HIPUR

I don't know, but let's fix him. My bow's right here.

OMEN

Fine! We'll fix him all right—teach him to take away people's rights and curse people to death! Allow for the crosswind; there's a light wind blowing downbeach.

HIPUR

I know it. I'm waiting till he gets by that white rock. (*Pause.*) Now! (*Omen shoots, and Layek yells in pain.*)

OMEN

Watch out! You didn't kill him! He's shooting back! (*An arrow comes in at Hipur.*)

HIPUR

(*Yelps.*) He's hit me!

OMEN

Badly?

HIPUR

Just in the wrist.

OMEN

He's fallen down on the sand!

HIPUR

Get your knife, then. Let's run and finish him off!

SPOTT

They finished him off, all right—cut his throat, then stabbed him in the head with the big two-edged iron knife with the cross guard. They couldn't get it out; so they left Layek's dead body lying there on the beach with the knife sticking in his forehead.

OMEN

Let's send someone to Rekwa, quick, to tell them about this.

HIPUR

Why? He's a bad man—deserved to be killed.

OMEN

Sure, but if we leave him lying on the beach, his family will be able to claim extra compensation. And, this time, the claims are going to have to be paid properly. Things have got to be done right. We'll drag the body above the high-tide mark; then we'll get the cripple woman to go down to Rekwa and tell them about it.

SPOTT

Next thing, of course, all the people from Rekwa turned up—all the men with raccoon skin quivers full of arrows, and in full fighting equipment; and the women trailing long behind in their maple-bark dresses, and carrying branches of fir trees just in case they might come in handy. In front of everybody was old Layek's sister; and as soon as she saw the body she ran and fell on it, howling and crying. (*The wail is a high-pitched keening, very sing-song.*)

PEKWON

All right, now, take it easy! It's very bad, and a sad thing, but you must control yourself. There are people who depend on you. They'll settle for it; the cripple woman said so. They'll settle for it, all right. That'll be all right, huh? Ah, now, come on. We know he was your brother; but they're going to settle. Don't just kick the sand—agree to the settlement, and let's get all this fixed up. There's been enough trouble. What do you say?

SISTER

All right then. I agree. I agree to a settlement. But make it quick.

OMEN

We'll settle tomorrow.

PEKWON

Can't make it today?

HIPUR

We'll need to get obsidian blades, and woodpecker scalps, and maybe some white deerskins. This is going to take real wealth. We've got to try and raise it.

PEKWON

I guess so. They'll settle tomorrow, first thing. They need the time to get the things and make all the arrangements. That all right?

SISTER

Tell them to hurry up.

PEKWON

Sure, I'll tell them. They're hurrying, doing the best they can. They want to get this thing all cleaned up too.

SISTER

Don't let them wait too long.

PEKWON

Now what are you going to do with the body?

SISTER

I'll stay by it all night.

PEKWON

Why don't you come up behind the village?

꙳꙳꙳

SISTER

I'll stay here. He was my brother. One of the men from Rekwa can stay with me. Will you do it?

SPOTT

She was looking at me! What could I say? I couldn't refuse. In the morning, we'd take the body home in a boat. In the meantime everybody cleared off, and Layek's sister and myself, we built a fire and sat for the night by the body. Soon it was dark and she was up to something strange.

(*Waves are lapping at the beach; the seagull's sharp cry is interrupted by an occasional call from the loon.*)

SPOTT

What are you doing?

SISTER

Gathering my brother's blood. All the sand that the blood soaked into, I'm putting in this acorn basket.

SPOTT

What for?

SISTER

What for? I'm going to boil it. I've got stones in the fire to boil up that blood. You'll see.

SPOTT

Now, look here; don't forget you've promised to accept a proper settlement.

SISTER

I don't forget anything. We're a good family; always have been. Did you ever know a man deny himself things like my brother? Of course you didn't. He was a good man, a fine man, and no one's going to murder him and get away with it.

SPOTT

Well, you promised to accept a settlement, and that was the right thing to do.

SISTER

I don't want to hear about that. What I want from you is to pull out that knife from his head.

SPOTT

Now, take it easy.

SISTER

Pull out the knife, will you? Do I have to pull the knife out of my own brother's skull?

SPOTT

Okay, I'll try. But it won't come. It's stuck in tight.

SISTER

Push with your foot.

SPOTT

Still won't come.

SISTER

Kneel on it with both knees and pull hard.

SPOTT

There! There you are! Here's the knife. Now are you happy?

SISTER

Thank you.

SPOTT

Watch out now, be careful; you'll cut that body.

SISTER

I want to cut it. I want to gash it open—like this and this and this. Give me two arrows.

SPOTT

This is no kind of settlement.

SISTER

Thank you.

SPOTT

What do you want with the arrows?

SISTER

I want to break them. Then, I put them into the body. Now pass me the basket with the blood and sand in it.

SPOTT

Help me with it. It's all hot—pretty well boiling.

SISTER

That's the way it should be.

SPOTT

What are you going to do with it?

SISTER

Pour it into the body.

SPOTT

Now, wait a minute. This isn't the right thing at all—not at all it isn't!

SISTER

They killed my brother. I don't care what I do. Hold tight on that side while I pour out the basket.
(*The body of Layek gives out a deep groan.*)

SPOTT

Oh! Did you hear that? The corpse made that noise! Let's get out of here.

SISTER

Don't be a fool. It was the heat of the stones, wasn't it, Brother? I am glad you answered. You will eat them all, those who killed you. Kill their friends. Kill their relations—old people or children, kill the lot of them. No doctor will be able to suck out their pains. Their pains will be along their spines, as these broken arrows are along your spine, Brother. And, Brother, do not forget to let some of the sickness strike them in their feet and be incurable. All right, let go of the basket.

SPOTT

You said you'd take a settlement.

SISTER

I'm going to take a settlement. I didn't say I wouldn't curse them as well. Give me the other basket.

SPOTT

Now what are you going to do?

SISTER

Throw them in the sea. I give you these baskets, waters of the ocean, so that you will help me too, and prevent them from ever being cured. Now let us wait till dawn.

SPOTT

I hope I never spend another night like that one. By the time the boat came in the morning to take the body back, Layek's sister had prayed death on just about everybody she could think of; and when she got back home she spent the next five nights in the cemetery praying. I did my best to keep my thoughts on ideas of wealth and valuables. But it doesn't matter how much a fellow works on self-denial and self-discipline—there comes a time when even thoughts of money aren't enough to keep his mind serene. And the night Layek's sister made death magic on the beach with her brother's body—well, that was enough for me. After the days of mourning, the negotiations for settlement started, and this time the intermediary wasn't going to put up with any nonsense.

PEKWON

This time there's going to be a real settlement, in valuables. Then we'll all know where we are.

OMEN

We've brought along the stuff.

PEKWON

Spread out the double deerskin blanket, and let's all have a look at it. Now we all know Layek did wrong about the sea-lion flipper

rights; but you fellows at Omen-hipur did wrong killing Layek. So each of you owes the other something.

OMEN

I know, but we've agreed this settlement is just going to be the difference.

PEKWON

What? That's still not right. Both of you ought to pay the full amount.

OMEN

We've agreed to pay the difference.

PEKWON

It still isn't right. But let's get on.

HIPUR

All right. Here's a really good woodpecker-scalp headband, as used in the world-renewal ceremony.

PEKWON

Yeah, that's a very nice one. Do you see it?

SISTER

I see it.

OMEN

And here's a red obsidian, used in the deer-skin dance up the river. And we'll throw in the box for it, too.

PEKWON

Good. Excellent. See it?

SISTER

I see it.

HIPUR

And we also offer all these dentalium shells. Largest size: middle-finger length.

PEKWON

Wait till I roll up my sleeve and check these

shells against my tattoo marks. Yes, those seem fine. See them?

SISTER

Yes, I see them.

PEKWON

One woodpecker-scalp headband; one red obsidian; and all these dentalium shells, largest size. This is what they will pay.

SISTER

I don't want them.

PEKWON

Now, listen! I've had enough of people doing things, and then not having to pay the settlement. That's how things have got in this mess. Besides, you said you'd accept a settlement.

SISTER

I will accept a settlement.

PEKWON

What?

SISTER

The sea-lion flipper rights.

PEKWON

The sea-lion—But that's impossible!

SISTER

Why?

PEKWON

It's never been done before.

SISTER

I want the sea-lion flipper rights. Layek was killed for them. I want them.

PEKWON

Look. You may not realize it, but there are proper ways of doing things; and this isn't the proper way at all.

SISTER

I want the sea-lion flipper rights.

OMEN

Anyway, they belong to Minot.

PEKWON

They're offering enough. All this stuff—look at it. You ought to take it. How about it?

SISTER

No.

OMEN

I'll give you my sister as well.

PEKWON

How about that?

SISTER

I want the sea-lion flipper rights, because that's what he got killed over.

MINOT

Wait a minute.

PEKWON

What is it, Minot?

MINOT

I'm sick of everyone getting in a mess. We're all doing wrong. You're doing wrong asking for my sea-lion flipper rights.

SISTER

I'm doing wrong! What about—

PEKWON

Shut up. Go on, Minot.

MINOT

But I want to see this stopped. I don't want to see any more of my grandchildren killed. I'll give up the sea-lion flipper rights, and then maybe we can have some peace. I'm sick of being trampled on. Life like this is misery. I feel as if the disk of the world was going to turn over any minute. I give up the rights, and let's complete the settlement.

SPOTT

So he did. And if you can call that a settlement —well, then they had a settlement. But I don't call it a real settlement. Everyone was very unhappy after it and felt they'd been denying themselves for nothing. You see, the real trouble was this: from first to last, things weren't done properly, the Yurok way. First one man would do something wrong, then another, and so it went on. One bad thing after another. In this world, you have to do the right thing. Two blacks don't make a white, and never did and never will. And that, I guess, is what it all boils down to—do the right thing, everything goes fine; do the wrong thing, everything's in a mess.

9. AUTHORITY

>>>->>>

Man must live by rules. In all societies some means must be found to maintain order among men. Some power must be recognized which will enforce the rules, punish the miscreant, sanction propriety; there must be authority. Authority is the constituted power, resting in the hands of one or more persons, to make decisions, render judgments, and enforce conformity to the established regulations. Such power must exist in some form or other in all societies. But the manner in which authority is exercised—how those in authority are chosen, the manner in which they may then enforce their rules, and the restraints to which they are subjected by those over whom they exercise authority—these differ from one culture to another.

The world of today is much concerned with authority. Whereas once religious beliefs set man against man, competing political ideologies today constitute the divisive element. The narrowing circle of the world—as its modes of communication become more effective—makes the differences more immediate and of great concern to all. But the problem is not really a new one; it is an old problem cloaked in new forms, involved with new urgencies, and broadened into world-wide scope.

There are two aspects of authority in a society: internal and external. *Internal authority* involves modes of leadership, adjudication, and ordering within a group which recognizes its own unity and homogeneity: the parent's authority over the family, the boss's authority over the employee, the chief's powers in the tribe, the government's powers in the nation. These are constituted powers, established by custom, law, or fiat.

External authority involves the nature of power between separate social entities—adjudication between neighbors, trade agreements between corporations, tribal disputes or international amity. The *external* authority among one type of group may well be ordered by the *internal* authority of some larger entity—the family by the tribe; the corporation by the nation.

We may well view the broad history of human societies as the gradual expansion of the scope of internal authority—the orderly enveloping of minor sovereignties within the greater sovereign entity. Some family unit, with parental authority over the children, must have characterized early human societies, as it does those of man's near relatives, the apes. And, indeed, the simplest organization of known primitive tribes either rests all internal authority fundamentally on the family or places power in the hands of a few elders. In such societies the scope of internal authority is often quite narrow, extending to but a few dozen individuals. Many more advanced primitive peoples have built their political systems on the basis of the family ties by extending the family itself. This is done by creating a super-family—a clan—to include hundreds of people who believe themselves to be descended from some real or mythical common ancestor, and thereby related by ties of blood. These families may be spread over fairly wide areas, but always they are interspersed with other clans, each with their own internal authority.

The external authority between such separate sovereign entities may be no more than an agreed-upon amity, a live-and-let-live arrangement resting upon the threat of force should one group overstep the bounds. Such was the case among the Tlingit, whose clans were such sovereign entities, although they agreed to rules by which calamitous wars could be avoided, as shown in "Stand-in for a Murderer" (Chapter 1). In some societies that have clans there is also an authority above them, to which each clan is subordinate in matters that go beyond its confines, so that a political system establishes a larger order of internal authority for the adjudication of grievances.

Such systems may be viewed as holding the seeds of nationality. For nationality involves the recognition of a higher constituted authority to whose will the lesser entities are subordinate, in so far as events extend beyond that lesser group and engulf the interests of those outside. Nationality—which has come into being at various times and places in the world—is thus an expansion of the scope of sovereignty.

The Iroquois, whose social system is described in the "Legend of the Long House," were a people making an effort to expand their scope of sovereignty. The League of the Iroquois, an organization of sovereign tribes and sovereign clans, combined into a single unit a wide area and a large population. It was a government of limited scope, being little more than a means of preserving internal peace among the separate nations, and channeling their warring activities against outsiders to the mutual benefit of the member tribes. Indeed, the League was more nearly comparable to the United Nations than to the United States. It had no armies, no taxing powers, and no public works. Its ruling body of sachems, appointed from the separate tribes, served as their representatives. All decisions required unanimity. The League was a remarkable instrument for preserving external authority among separate social and political units, but it fell short of being a true nation.

Authority is necessary in any social system; but authority is tricky. To fulfill the creative capacity that man is endowed with, people must work in harmony. And in order to work together, they must recognize leadership and authority. Yet, by placing power or leadership in someone's hands, each individual gives up a measure of his own self-determination, a measure of his freedom to act. This is true whether we speak of a small social clique—and these, as shown in "You Are Not Alone" (Chapter 6), also have a form of government—or whether we speak of the possibilities of world government.

The giving up of powers for the accomplishment of greater ends is a good bargain, so long as these powers are not abused by those to whom authority is given. Men have long tried to solve the problem of giving authority in a manner that will not let its powers be used to the detriment of those governed—and perhaps nowhere more conscientiously than among the framers of the Constitution of the United States. For the Iroquois, the problem was relatively simple, for the several tribes were related by ties of clan and had a homogeneous culture supported by a common religion.

But for modern states the problem is complicated by the wide diversity of cultural backgrounds. To organize such variety into a homogeneous pattern without burdening the population with repressive laws requires great skill and constant vigilance. A few principles seem clear, however. The first of these is that the rules should be formulated by others than those placed in power to enforce them. Where societies emerge with rules that are the ethical formulations of a cultural heritage, the problem does not arise; but where nations are created or severely altered to meet changed conditions, it is of primary importance. The second is that institutional means should be established for the orderly selection of leaders to whom authority is given. The third is that means should be available to review the actions of the leaders, to recall and replace them when they exceed their powers.

In the realm of authority, there are two dangers. A society that fails to allocate powers finds itself weak in leadership and unable to take necessary and decisive action in time of crisis. A society that does not provide adequate restraints upon those in power will find its leaders serving their own interests at the expense of the general welfare. In such circumstances the necessary allocation of authority degenerates into authoritarianism.

Legend of the Long House

LISTER SINCLAIR

The Iroquois were living in and around New York State when the Europeans arrived. At that time the separate tribes were bound together in the League, which lasted until the American Revolution. Disagreements and the encroaching European civilization caused it to dissolve. The League was a fabric woven of two elements— the separate tribes, which occupied distinct but adjacent territories; and the separate clans, social units whose members considered themselves related by blood to one another. The clans extended across tribal boundaries, and thus served to unify the territories and give strength to the League.

The Iroquois have their own legends about the origin of the League. They believe it to have been the creation of two leaders—culture heroes—of the sixteenth century, Dekanawida and Hiawatha. The present legend—which is not an Iroquois one at all—accepts their deification. The time, therefore, is "in the beginning."

[MUSIC]

DEKANAWIDA

For his bones, I take the birches;
For his flesh, the salmon and the stag;
The black bear's hide shall be his hair,
And the good red clay his skin.
The dark of deep waters shall shine in the
  shadow of his eyes.
His private spirit shall be strong magic and
  great medicine.
His nature shall be noble, fiery, heaven-bent,
  and proud.
And in the book of the world, his name shall
  be written: Man.

[MUSIC]

NARRATOR

This is not an Indian legend, but a legend about Indians. Some of it is the truth of legends, and some of it is only the truth of fact; we shall try and tell you which is which. The legend is all about the Iroquois, the Six Nations, the Long House people, the Indian tribes who once lived near the Great Lakes under a very remarkable system of authority. The League of the Iroquois really existed; it existed in one form or another for some hundreds of years, and the Iroquois themselves had many legends about how their League was formed, and how the Six Tribes were brought together.

But this is not an Indian legend. It is a legend we have made up about the Indians, to show how the League worked. How authority was given, and how authority was checked. For wherever men live together, there must be some kind of authority; and wherever there is authority, two things are important— how it is given, and how it is checked.

[MUSIC]

NARRATOR

Now once upon a time, there were no Six Tribes—none at all. There was only the great chief Dekanawida, who was so great as to be almost a god; and his friend the chief Hiawatha, who was nearly so great as to be nearly almost a god. And these two sat by the Great Lakes one afternoon, smoking their pipes, and finishing off the job of creating the earth, which they had been ordered to do by the Great Spirit.

DEKANAWIDA

Have you finished the insects yet, Hiawatha?

HIAWATHA

They are all finished. My brush is loaded with the blood of the dove, for I am marking in the spots in the throat of the lily.

DEKANAWIDA
Did you make the lilies all red, orange, and yellow?

HIAWATHA
(*Sadly*) Yes.

DEKANAWIDA
Why be sad? These are the colors of the lilies.

HIAWATHA
I should so much have liked to make a blue lily. If we have the power to make the forests and all that goes in them, why do we not have the power to make them as we please?

DEKANAWIDA
Because power is always given, and then it is always checked. Things must be made in the nature of things; that is the check upon our power. How do you like this plant?

HIAWATHA
It looks glossy and prosperous. What is its name?

DEKANAWIDA
Poison ivy—the check upon man's authority over the plants. The quiet dumb vegetables will be respected the more because of this shiny creeping fellow, feeding on the sun and standing with his feet in his grave like all the other plants.

HIAWATHA
But who is going to respect him, Dekanawida? The skunks will roll in him; the chickadees will eat his fruit.

DEKANAWIDA
There is one more task to do. We must make man; and he will respect poison ivy, just as he will respect mosquito and rattlesnake; for things must be made in the nature of things. Now sprinkle tobacco on the fire, and let us concentrate while I make the master to finish off the house.

[MUSIC]

For his bones, I take the birches;
For his flesh, the salmon and the stag;
The black bear's hide shall be his hair,
And the good red clay his skin.

The dark of deep waters shall shine in the shadow of his eyes.
His private spirit shall be strong magic, and great medicine.
His nature shall be noble, fiery, heaven-bent, and proud.
And in the book of the world, his name shall be written: Man.

[MUSIC]

DEKANAWIDA
Greetings, Friend. Welcome to the world.

MAN
What am I?

DEKANAWIDA
You are man.

MAN
Man. What is that? Is that good?

DEKANAWIDA
Very good. Man is the highest form of life—as yet.

MAN
Are there other forms?

DEKANAWIDA
Many, many other forms.

MAN
Who is the leader?

DEKANAWIDA
I don't understand.

MAN
Am I in charge of the other things, or is one of them in charge of me?

DEKANAWIDA
You are all in charge of each other.

HIAWATHA
And poison ivy, mosquito, and rattlesnake will remind you of the rights of the smaller creatures.

DEKANAWIDA
The forests are yours, and the beasts of the forests; the lakes and streams are yours and in them the fish. Be brave, be noble, fiery, heaven-bent, and proud.

MAN
I take my destiny! Nothing in the world shall be as ambitious as man!

HIAWATHA
Enter into your domain. Enjoy yourself, and raise a family.

MAN
Thank you, I will. But how?

HIAWATHA
How? Dekanawida, have we forgotten something?

DEKANAWIDA
You have forgotten woman, to live with man and be his comrade and his comforter, his mistress and his wife, his toiler and his autocrat, his chattel and his choice.

[MUSIC]

For her bones I take the slim white clouds;
For her flesh, the dove and the doe;
The blackbird's gloss shall glitter in her hair,
And sweet fruit ripen in her skin.
The black tears of the pinetree shall be melted in her eyes.
Her private spirit shall be great medicine and strong magic.
Her nature shall be yielding, unpredictable, resilient, and bright.
And in the book of the world, her name shall be written: Woman.

HIAWATHA
Very nice, indeed. Greetings, my dear.

WOMAN
I suppose so. Who am I?

DEKANAWIDA
You are woman; you are the wife of this person here, who is man.

MAN
Everything you see is under my protection. Everything you see is my property. Come along. I have my destiny to attend to.

WOMAN
What about my destiny?

MAN
Your destiny is to attend to my destiny. I have no time to lose. Hurry!

WOMAN
Very well; but I can see we shall have to talk about destiny. Where shall we go?

DEKANAWIDA
Tell them, Hiawatha.

HIAWATHA
Decide between you.

DEKANAWIDA
Is that your best answer?

HIAWATHA
Certainly. And a very good answer it is.

DEKANAWIDA
If you think so. Well, then, decide between you. Farewell.

WOMAN
Farewell.

MAN
Farewell. I am monarch of all I survey.

DEKANAWIDA
Oh, just one thing!

MAN
What's that?

DEKANAWIDA
Watch out for the poison ivy.

[MUSIC]

HIAWATHA
Dekanawida.

DEKANAWIDA
Yes, Hiawatha?

HIAWATHA
Many years have passed since you and I sat and smoked on the shores of Onondaga Lake and made the first man and the first woman. I wonder how many children they have.

DEKANAWIDA
A great many, I expect.

HIAWATHA
They will be very happy.

DEKANAWIDA
Oh?

HIAWATHA
Let them decide for themselves—that was my policy.

DEKANAWIDA
I remember.

HIAWATHA
You can't go wrong. Peace, perfect peace.

(*A man runs in, howling and crying.*) What was that?

DEKANAWIDA
Peace, perfect peace.

HIAWATHA
Someone's in trouble.

DEKANAWIDA
I thought they would be, sooner or later.

HIAWATHA
Why?

DEKANAWIDA
They didn't understand authority. (*Calling to Man.*) Stop! You! Don't throw that rock at your wife!

MAN
She'll hit me with a club if I don't!

DEKANAWIDA
No, she won't. Both of you, come here! Now, then, what's all this about?

MAN
Ask her.

HIAWATHA
This isn't the man we created, is it?

MAN
Yes, it is.

HIAWATHA
I can't recognize him.

DEKANAWIDA
His face is swollen.

HIAWATHA
What happened?

WOMAN
Poison ivy. I told him to make our lodge by the river—but, no, he always knows best. He camped in the biggest patch of poison ivy I ever saw.

MAN
All right, shut up. Any man's entitled to make a mistake.

DEKANAWIDA
Of course he is. Is this enough to make you take a club to your husband? Surely he is punished enough as it is?

WOMAN
(*Sadly.*) We always take clubs to each other. For years we've been doing it. And the children, too. I dread it when anything has to be decided. First we all scream at each other; then the fighting starts.

MAN
Sometimes I think our children do not kill us only because we are stronger than they are.

WOMAN
For the time being.

DEKANAWIDA
There is something you must learn.

MAN
What?

DEKANAWIDA
How to decide. If people live together, they must learn how to decide. They must know what is allowed, and what is not allowed.

WOMAN
Teach us how to decide. What is the way?

DEKANAWIDA
There is not one way; there are as many ways as there are stars. But I will give you a way for you and your husband on the shores of Onondaga Lake. Let us sit by the fire and take up the pipe and consider. How do you build your lodge?

MAN
Of wood—a long house, with the door to the west and the fire at the other end. Down each side, there are seats.

DEKANAWIDA
That is a good house. Now you and your wife, and all parents, must sit on one side of this Long House of yours; and your children and all children must sit on the other side. The father side must have authority over the son side; but only so far as the son's own good is concerned. The son side must owe obedience to the father side; but only so far as the father asks what he is entitled to ask. Outside the lodge, the man shall be master; for you will be the master of the forest. Inside the lodge,

-»»

the woman will be mistress; for you will be mistress of the home. This is your authority toward each other, and how far it goes. And this is your authority toward your children, and how far it goes. And whenever you enter your lodge and sit down in the Long House, the parents on the one side, and the children on the other, you will remember, and know that each has authority, and each has responsibility. Now go, my children, and be happy.

[MUSIC]

NARRATOR

So far, so good. The League of the Iroquois did, in fact, base its authority in the family on the principle of the Long House. And you notice that the woman was given a certain amount of authority. Women in the Six Tribes had more authority than perhaps in any other society except our own. The Iroquois were one of those societies (there are quite a few of them) that trace descent in the female line, and not in the male line. Their argument is that it's much easier to be sure of a child's mother than of its father. There is a good deal to be said for this point of view.

Authority, then, in the League of the Iroquois began in the family and was bound up with the idea of the Long House. Now for some more legend.

[MUSIC]

DEKANAWIDA

Hiawatha, I have created many more men and women. In fact, I have created a number of families—a tribe.

HIAWATHA

Have you thought of a name for them?

DEKANAWIDA

Well, I created them on these hills.

HIAWATHA

Then they shall be called the Onondaga, the People of the Hills.

DEKANAWIDA

(*Mildly.*) That is just what I was going to suggest.

HIAWATHA

Good! Glad to hear it. It was a very good suggestion.

DEKANAWIDA

These people are coming to be told how to live together. Would you like to tell them how to do it?

HIAWATHA

Nothing could be simpler. Let them decide for themselves—though, of course, they'll have to be taught how to decide.

DEKANAWIDA

I think they will.

HIAWATHA

Now let me consider the proper way for a tribe to decide.

DEKANAWIDA

There are as many proper ways as there are stars in the sky. All you need do is teach them one way. Then that will be the Onondaga way, and they will all live happily.

HIAWATHA

Nothing could be simpler. All right, Dekanawida, bring out this Onondaga tribe of yours, and let's begin!

HIAWATHA

(*Addressing the tribe over the commotion.*) Let all you people be silent! (*There is silence.*) Open your ears and shut your mouths. I am going to tell you something important. My colleague has created you people to be a tribe. You will be called the People of the Hills, the Onondagas, and you will live in the Long Houses, according to the Long House rules.

Now, my colleague and I, thinking of your happiness, have given you the forests and the streams, and everything necessary for a happy life. Among your dogs, you will find some white ones; and if at the New Year you sacrifice some white dogs, they will take away all your sins, providing you feel really sorry.

But my colleague and I think you will be much happier if you try not to commit any sins at all.

Now, then, has every family got a husband and a wife? (*Assent from the crowd.*) Did we remember to create a mother and a father for every child? (*Assent.*) Very well, then, go and be happy! Hunt the deer and the grouse, and fish the lakes and the rivers; plant your crops and enjoy the growth of the earth. But remember when it comes to crops that the Spirit of the Corn, the Spirit of the Beans, and the Spirit of the Squash are sisters; and these three young ladies don't like to be separated. So plant corn, beans, and squash all together; the three spirits will be happier, and you'll have much more to eat.

Thank you for your confidence in my creating you, and your patience in listening to me. Go and be happy.

(*The crowd begins to disperse.*)

DEKANAWIDA

(*To Hiawatha.*) Who's in charge?

HIAWATHA

What?

DEKANAWIDA

You have forgotten to teach them how to decide. Remember what happened in the family.

HIAWATHA

Oh, yes. (*He calls to the crowd that is leaving.*) Stop! Come back! Again, open your ears and shut your mouths. My colleague has just told me that he forgot something. I must teach you how to decide as a tribe. Now let me see, authority must go to somebody. What is your name?

TO-DO-DA-HO

My name is To-do-da-ho.

HIAWATHA

Then, To-do-da-ho, you shall have the authority of the tribe. Whatever you say, shall be done. Do you all hear?

CROWD

We all hear.

DEKANAWIDA

Is that all?

HIAWATHA

What else is there? I have now given the authority; nothing else remains.

DEKANAWIDA

Just you wait and see.

HIAWATHA

My colleague expresses his appreciation of the arrangements. Thank you very much, and good-bye, People of the Hills, and your commander, To-do-da-ho.

[MUSIC]

DEKANAWIDA

Well, Hiawatha, how is To-do-da-ho? Is he satisfactory as leader of the Onondagas?

HIAWATHA

Naturally. Give a wise, responsible, well-intentioned man all the authority, and the job is as good as done.

DEKANAWIDA

No complaints?

HIAWATHA

None whatsoever. Indeed, it's been several months since I've heard a word from any of them one way or the other. When people are happy and industrious, they're always wrapped up in their own affairs. (*Pause.*) Have you heard anything?

DEKANAWIDA

Not up to the present. But who is this running through the forest?

HIAWATHA

To-do-da-ho! And he looks like a man running for his life!

TO-DO-DA-HO

(*Comes on yelling and flings himself at their feet.*)

Help! Help! Help! Hiawatha, Dekanawida! Help me, protect me!

(*Loud shouts of anger are heard from the crowd in the distance, approaching.*)

HIAWATHA

What's happened? Why is the leader of the Onondagas doubling through the forest like a hunted deer?

TO-DO-DA-HO

Ask the tribe. A man could as soon bring order to a pack of wolves as lead those surly, cruel cutthroats.

DEKANAWIDA

I did not create the people in the form of wolves, To-do-da-ho; I only created them men.

TO-DO-DA-HO

Then that is bad enough!

ONONDAGA ONE

(*Calling from a distance.*) There he is! There he is!

OTHERS

(*Getting closer.*) Kill him! Kill! Kill! Kill!

DEKANAWIDA

Silence! (*The crowd falls silent.*)

TO-DO-DA-HO

(*Bitterly.*) There are the Onondagas, there is the tribe that you created! Only created them men!

DEKANAWIDA

Why are you trying to kill your leader?

ONONDAGA ONE

He ordered us to leap off the bluffs into the river to test our bravery. Some of us would be killed; all would be injured. We will not kill ourselves for him.

DEKANAWIDA

You would kill him instead?

ONONDAGA ONE

If there is no other choice.

DEKANAWIDA

Probably we can find another choice. Why did you do this?

TO-DO-DA-HO

I thought it for the best.

DEKANAWIDA

And yet they want to kill you for it?

TO-DO-DA-HO

I had the authority to order them to do it. He gave it to me.

DEKANAWIDA

So he did. Did you give him the authority to kill off the tribe if he felt like it?

HIAWATHA

Well, no. I—

DEKANAWIDA

You see now what you have done. You gave the authority; that is good. But you forgot to check it. You forgot to say how much authority. Authority must be given and it must be checked. Now we will forget this leadership affair, and restore this poor fellow to the tribe again; and I will ask you for another suggestion. Now you have learned that good intentions are not enough. We must have a way of protecting ourselves, against the authority we have had to give. (*Pause.*) Well?

HIAWATHA

If men are always going to behave foolishly, perhaps the authority had better not be with men at all.

DEKANAWIDA

(*In blank amazement.*) What on earth do you mean by that?

HIAWATHA

(*Uneasily.*) Perhaps some oracle, a talking tree, a talking rock, something—

DEKANAWIDA

My dear Hiawatha, do not make up stories. The ax of authority must rest in the hands of men; but men being what they are, the shield of safeguard must rest there too. Now, every person here lives in a Long House? (*The crowd murmurs assent.*) And in that house, parents face their children and remember their rights and responsibilities? (*Again assent.*) Then I set in authority over you fourteen wise men, or sachems; and these men will meet in a Long House like their home, to be a remembrance to them of rights and responsibilities. Also, I set limit to their authority in this way: these sachems shall be chosen by you yourselves, they shall be elected by all of you; they shall say what is to be done, and shall do it; and they shall judge between one man and his neighbor, if there is a quarrel. But, again, there shall be a check on this authority; every one of you shall watch the sachems carefully, and since they shall all be men, let the women do the best part of the watching. Then, if a sachem does badly, or does not do what you feel is for the general good, you may recall him, and choose another man to be raised up as sachem in his place. Also, before anything is done, every single sachem shall agree. This will be the government of the People of the Hills; so much authority is given, and in such way that authority is checked. Go now, Onondagas, and peace go with you! (*The crowd disperses.*)

[MUSIC]

NARRATOR

How or when or why the government of the tribes of the Iroquois was set up, we don't know. But we do know how they worked. They worked as we have just heard: each tribe was governed by the unanimous vote of a group of wise men, sachems, chosen by everybody, and subject to recall if they misbehaved. And the family structure of the Long House was carried over to the council of the tribe. And again the women had a good deal of say in things. The Onondagas had fourteen sachems. As for the other tribes—well, we shall find out about them in a moment, for here is Dekanawida hard at work creating them.

[MUSIC]

(*A creation chant by Dekanawida brings forth the several tribes.*)

DEKANAWIDA

You shall be the lighters of the sacred fires; and you shall be called the People of the Flint, the Mohawks!

[MUSIC]

DEKANAWIDA

You, created on this mountain, shall be called the People of the Great Hill, the Senecas!

[MUSIC]

DEKANAWIDA

You, created in the land of the glittering rocks, shall be called the People of the Granite, the Oneidas!

[MUSIC]

DEKANAWIDA

You, created among the swamps and lakes and the standing water, shall be called the People of the Marshes, the Cayugas!

[MUSIC]

DEKANAWIDA

And you, who come into this land as exiles from a far place, wearing your own peculiar buckskin shirts, you shall be the sixth tribe, and be known as the People of the Shirt, the Tuscaroras!

[MUSIC]

DEKANAWIDA

So now the land is peopled. Every place has its proper tribe; shall we go now and leave them in peace?

HIAWATHA

Not if we want them to remain at peace. As you say, they must learn how to decide. This morning I saw some young men from the Mohawks meet some young Cayugas on the trail of a deer. For a moment there was death in the air; and I do not think it was the death of the deer.

DEKANAWIDA

You are quite right. These tribes cannot live next to each other in peace without some giving up of authority. I have asked them all here tonight to this spot on Onondaga Lake where we first began, to tell them how to rule themselves. But what shall we say? Each tribe is ruled well enough by its sachems: the Onondagas have their fourteen, the Mohawks nine, the Cayugas ten, and so forth. Each has a number suitable to the size of the tribe, and each council of sachems sits in its Long House. But—

HIAWATHA

Then let all the sachems come together. Let this grand council make the Six Tribes into a League; let the council of the League meet in a Long House. Which are the strongest tribes?

DEKANAWIDA

The Mohawks, the Onondagas, and the Senecas.

HIAWATHA

Then let their sachems sit on the parent side of the Long House of the League; and let the Oneidas, the Cayugas, and the Tuscaroras sit on the child side. Then each man may continue to remember his rights and responsibilities concerning those who are sitting opposite him.

DEKANAWIDA

You know, Hiawatha, I think that by this idea that you redeem yourself.

HIAWATHA

Well, we must all learn, and I flatter myself that I learn faster than most people. I think I understand the way men operate.

DEKANAWIDA

Perhaps—because all men operate alike. But all the same there are as many ways of giving and checking authority as there are leaves in the forest. This is only one of them.

HIAWATHA

I understand that quite well, and I flatter myself—

DEKANAWIDA

(*Smiling.*) No, don't; let me flatter you instead. You have made a very good suggestion. There is only one thing that worries me; and you may have a suggestion for that too.

HIAWATHA

Anything I can suggest, I certainly will.

DEKANAWIDA

You certainly will, indeed! Now come along with me!

[MUSIC]

DEKANAWIDA

(*Very confidentially.*) Look through the trees there.

HIAWATHA

Yes.

DEKANAWIDA

What do you see?

HIAWATHA

A Cayuga in war paint, with his quiver full of arrows. He is crouching behind a tree and looking across the river.

DEKANAWIDA

That river divides the land of the Cayugas from the land of the Onondagas. Let us go across the river!

[MUSIC]

DEKANAWIDA

(*Still in a whisper.*) Look behind those rocks there.

HIAWATHA

Yes.

DEKANAWIDA

What do you see?

HIAWATHA

An Onondaga in war paint with his quiver full of arrows. He is crouching behind a boulder, and he too, is looking across the river.

DEKANAWIDA

That river indeed divides the land of the Cayugas from the Onondagas. Let us ask him why he is on guard. (*He addresses the warrior.*) Greetings, friend.

ONONDAGA ONE

Greetings, Dekanawida.

HIAWATHA

Greetings.

ONONDAGA ONE

Hiawatha, greetings.

DEKANAWIDA

Why are you wearing your war paint? Why are you watching across the river? Is there some dreadful enemy approaching?

ONONDAGA ONE

I'm on duty watching the Cayugas. Just a precaution. We want to know what they're doing.

DEKANAWIDA

I can tell you that. Do you see the pine tree between the two sugar maples?

ONONDAGA ONE

Yes.

DEKANAWIDA

Behind that tree there is a Cayuga brave, also in war paint, and also carrying his weapons.

ONONDAGA ONE

(*Through clenched teeth.*) There is? Then we were right to watch them!

DEKANAWIDA

You are each watching the other.

ONONDAGA ONE

They have nothing to fear from us. But who knows what we have to fear from them? Thank you for telling me. I shall report it to our council of sachems at once.

DEKANAWIDA

You yourself are surely one of the sachems?

ONONDAGA ONE

I am.

DEKANAWIDA

Surely if you were all to meet in one Long House, there would be no need for this suspicion? Think of the land, indeed, the whole land, as a great Long House.

ONONDAGA ONE

Perhaps so. But we live in our territory, we're the people of the hills; and they live in theirs, they're the people of the swamp. We don't mix much, and I think we'd feel safer just keeping a good lookout all the same—though, certainly, we'd always be happy to talk things over.

[MUSIC]

HIAWATHA

Now what are you going to do? Those two tribes are just huddled up behind their boundaries glaring at each other. It's going to take a very wise council to make those two relax.

DEKANAWIDA

Don't think it's just those two. Wherever two tribes meet, you will find the sentries peering at each other suspiciously.

HIAWATHA

Ridiculous!

DEKANAWIDA

Not at all. You will not understand men, Hiawatha, if you think that everything that you wouldn't do is ridiculous. What they are doing is dangerous, and may be disastrous; but it is not ridiculous. You see, each tribe loves its own land so much, it is so proud and delighted with the country where it lives, that it thinks that all the other tribes must necessarily feel envious and suspicious.

HIAWATHA

How else can it be done?

DEKANAWIDA

How else, indeed? But I think I have an idea. Tonight, when I have told the people about the grand council of the League, I will tell them what else they must do so that the Six Tribes may live together in peace.

[MUSIC]

(*A natural clearing with a large crowd of Iroquois; a meeting is going on.*)

DEKANAWIDA

. . . and therefore the Grand Council of the League shall be made up of the fifty sachems of the tribes, who will sit together in the Long House of the Council, as I have told you. Every decision must be unanimous, so that any sachem may veto what is wished by the others. This will help to check the authority of the Council. But remember this. The Council is not to be a battleground for arguing sachems. The best sachem is not the one who argues best and who persuades most people to his own point of view. It is rather the one in whose presence men find it easiest to arrive at the truth.

So much then for the Council of the League. Now open your ears and close your mouths, for I am going to tell you something else very important. Every person belongs to a tribe; everyone is a Mohawk, or a Seneca, or whatever. Everyone loves his tribe and its territory, and is anxious to defend it to the death, so that those who belong to a tribe are drawn together by a bond. Now I say to you that every man shall belong not only to a tribe but to a clan;

and the clan shall be the family made larger and spread wider and, like the family, taken from the mother's side. There shall be eight clans: the Wolf, the Bear, the Beaver, the Turtle, the Deer, the Snipe, the Heron, the Hawk. Each clan will extend across all Six Tribes; and each tribe will extend across all eight clans; thus a Mohawk may also be a Beaver and find brother Beavers in every other tribe. This then will be another bond; just as strong as the bond of the tribe. You will be drawn together one way by your tribe, by being for instance a Mohawk; and the other way by your clan, by being for instance a Beaver. The clan shall be a check upon the tribe: the tribe shall be a check upon the clan.

Now you are all a warlike people, though you will never war upon each other; and what is to be done about those chiefs who are not sachems, but who become proud and important in war? These chiefs you will also make part of the Council, to check their authority, and for fear that they will destroy it if they are left outside it. But they will not be elected, nor will they have a vote, but they will be joined to the Council by the choice of the Council itself.

NARRATOR

Dekanawida must have taken all night to explain his League. We don't have time to describe all the refinements and details; in addition to the ones you've just heard—the vertical division into tribes, and the horizontal division into clans.

All we have time to say, once again, is that the League of the Iroquois, which really existed, is one of the most remarkable examples of the organization of primitive authority. Our legend about the League has tried to make clear the two points about authority: First, whenever men live together, authority has to be allocated. Second, good will is not enough to prevent abuses; authority must not only be given, but also marked out and checked.

[FINALE]

10. STATUS AND ROLE

A position of authority is one kind of position to be found in any society. There are many others. In our society we have the positions of president, judge, voter; of boss, foreman, member of the board, janitor; of mother, father, uncle, stepchild; of priest, elder, member of the congregation; of fraternity brother, member of the gang, clubwoman; of scientist, scholar, pupil; of old man, adult, debutante, infant. All societies recognize certain positions in their society, and these positions define for the individual his relation to other persons with respect to some phase of social life. One person may hold many such positions: the judge may at the same time be a member of the board, a father, a church elder, a scholar, an old man. In the simpler societies the number of positions may be more limited, but even there a person will hold several positions.

These positions are related to what the sociologists call *statuses*. Some positions carry more prestige or more influence than others. The way different statuses vary with respect to prestige is of great interest to the sociologist—as it is to the people in the society itself. Therefore, the sociologist often speaks of a person as having "high status," or even of having "more status," when he means that the position is one that confers greater prestige. The confusion between position and status is a natural one, for all positions involve relative amounts of prestige, and a person's prestige status is compounded of the various particular statuses that he has.

All societies confer prestige; all societies make distinctions between high and low status. But they confer prestige for different things and in different ways. And in some cultures the people give greater importance to prestige than in others. Needless to say, the way in which status is viewed depends upon the values of the culture. In a culture where artistic accomplishment is highly valued, status is conferred upon the artist. In a society where business acumen is highly valued, more prestige is granted to the successful businessman—though in a society as complex as our own, where different values are recognized, the very successful businessman will often enhance his prestige by becoming a patron of the arts.

The relation between values and status works to establish the particular "genius" of a society—as it is sometimes called. The point was made in the discussion of "When Greek Meets Greek" (Chapter 5), but it bears repeating. If a people set great store by certain things—if these things are prime values in a culture—the people who have these things tend to be given high status. This is what took place in ancient Athens in the realm of philosophy and arts; what took place among the Pueblo Indians in the realm of religion and ceremony; what took place in nineteenth-century Germany in the realm of science and music; and what has taken place in the United States in the realm of invention and technological improvements. Of course, this point doesn't explain why a culture emphasizes certain values in the first place, though sometimes we can get a clue as to why.

Status may be conferred chiefly either upon circumstances of birth or upon individual accomplishments. Sociologists call the first of these "ascribed status;" the second "achieved status." The status a person has because of his age, or because of his sex, or because his parents were nobility, or Brahmans in India, or Negroes in modern America is ascribed status. There is nothing he can do to change this status, so long as the culture attaches certain meanings to it. The status a person has because he has made a lot of money, has created works of art, has been a military leader among the Plains Indians (or in the United States) is achieved status. Some societies emphasize ascribed status, as among the Hindus of India (or anywhere that a caste system prevails); others emphasize achieved status, as among us. Probably no society is concerned purely with one or the other. The Tlingit Indians in "Stand-in for a Murderer" (Chapter 1) were very conscious of status. Each warrior was thought of as being born to his particular status; and yet they thought more of a man if he was a brave fighter and if he had given generous potlatches.

In the United States we believe that status should be a matter of individual accomplishment, and we disapprove of societies where status is a matter of birth. But even here we still tend to recognize birth as a basis for status. Many people feel that race automatically confers status, and in some communities the old residents have more status than the *nouveaux riches*, even when they have less wealth or fewer accomplishments. John P. Marquand, in *Point of No Return*, showed the ascribed status in the social system of the important families in the old city of Newburyport, Massachusetts, as contrasted with the achieved status of the bankers in Boston. In general in the United States, we feel that achieved status is important and tell our sons: "You can be President."

Meanwhile, we must not forget that there are other aspects to status besides the aspect of prestige; status refers to the position that a person has in relation to other persons in his society. And for each position the culture provides appropriate modes of behavior, proper conduct, and attitudes toward others. This the sociologists call "role." The term is very appropriate, for it is much like a part in a play, where the attitudes and action are provided but where the actor must interpret the part.

All of us have at some time or other had the experience of suddenly becoming aware of our role—usually when we have just acquired a new one. The roles of the new supervisor, of the bride, of the confidante must be learned if the person is to meet his obligations. The important thing about role is not only that a person feels he must perform in a certain way, but also that other people expect him to. When we meet a situation where somebody fails to fulfill his role—for instance, a doctor who won't take seriously a patient's aches and pains—we find the situation upsetting. It undermines the whole pattern of expected action.

Just as all societies recognize status, all societies provide each status with its appropriate role. The person must learn the role that is required of him whenever he takes on a new status. Our own society, because of its great diversity and its rapidly changing character, sometimes does not adequately train people for the roles they are to assume, and this often leads to difficulties. Another point about our society, which is less likely to be true of primitive societies, is "role conflict." Role conflict appears when a person with two different roles finds he must play both at once, though they are not mutually appropriate. Think of a judge, whose role is characterized by dignity and authority, confronted at court by his children demanding a "piggy-back" ride. Or a young person whose friends (among whom perhaps he is a leader in escapades) are visiting his sedate parents. These role conflicts arise in our society where we can have several separate groups of associates—

whereas in a small community or in a primitive tribe all the people one knows are also known to one another.

In every society the culture provides for differences in status, though the basis for determining status varies widely. And in every society the culture establishes the appropriate role that persons in a given status must enact to the best of their abilities. Though we may find a comparable status in two societies, the role will not necessarily be the same.

All the World's a Stage

LISTER SINCLAIR

⋘-⋘

HERE and THERE take examples from various parts of the world to make their point about the nature of status and role.

HERE

In every society, at every moment, a man has a certain position. It may be because of the work he does, or the amount of property he owns, or the color of his skin. It may vary from time to time. Your position as a father is different from your position as a son, and both are different from your position as an uncle or as a brother. You may have one kind of position at your work, another in your family, and another down at the club where you're bowling champion. Each of these positions is called a *status*.

THERE

And different societies have different ways of placing a man on the ladder of status—higher or lower. For instance, among the Chuckchee Indians of Siberia, if you can throw epileptic fits, it greatly improves your status; it makes you a magician and a curer.

HERE

In our society some of the different jobs and ways of life that give a man status are listed in the old children's fortunetelling rhyme.

RHYME

Tinker, tailor,
Soldier, sailor,
Rich man, poor man, beggar man, thief,
Doctor, lawyer, Indian chief.

HERE

All these things have different status in our society; and from each particular status particular behavior is expected. We expect the doctor to behave differently from the poor man; and we expect the lawyer to behave differently from the thief. If you're a landlord, your outlook on rent controls is different from your outlook if you're a tenant. Every society, in fact, expects from each particular status a particular way of behaving—a particular *role*.

THERE

Status and role. A man's status is the place he has at any given moment on the ladder of his society; a man's role is the behavior his society expects from that particular status.

HERE

In other words, Shakespeare told us all about it, long ago.

SHAKESPEARE

All the world's a stage
And all the men and women merely players:
They have their exits and their entrances;
And one man in his time plays many parts.

[MUSIC]

HERE

Wherever we go, we hear phrases that show how conscious people are of status:

ONE

They come from across the tracks.

TWO

She's one of the First Families of Virginia.

THREE

Of course, they say he has royal blood in him.

FOUR

Sure he's a big shot; look at his low license plate.

FIVE

I'm afraid we can't give you a raise, but we can give you a desk nearer the window.

SIX

Listen to this: "Reforestation Praised by Well-Known Movie Actress." Gee! Her!

[MUSIC]

THERE

It's the same all over the world. In New Guinea, among the Mundugumor.

MUNDUGUMOR

He's an important man: he has seven wives.

THERE

In New Zealand, among the Maori.

MAORI

Very sacred person: first-born son of a chief.

THERE

In India, among the Hindus.

HIND

He is a very high-caste man: thrice-born. A Brahmin.

THERE

Or among the Mohammedans.

MOH

See his red-dyed beard? He is a Hajji; he has made the pilgrimage to Mecca.

[MUSIC]

HERE

Similarly, we hear all round us phrases showing that we are all conscious of role—the part we ought to play.

ONE

Well, here's how I see it from where I sit.

TWO

Well, at least I can give you the woman's point of view.

THREE

Speaking as your lawyer, I feel I ought to say this.

FOUR

Oh, it was nothing at all really. Anyone could do the same—any crack golfer at all.

FIVE

The experts can say what they like, but I want to speak as a layman.

SIX

I'm sorry, Johnnie, I just couldn't; but I am willing to be a sister to you.

[MUSIC]

THERE

One of the best public examples of how a man's behavior, his role, can change with his status was Admiral Darlan's attitude toward the French fleet. When he was just an admiral, he wanted to get the fleet to the Allies; when he was promoted to Minister of Marine, he felt he ought to keep the fleet in France. Here's what Winston Churchill says about it in his memoirs. One day Darlan had said he would order the French fleet to Allied harbors.

READER

The next day General George met him in the afternoon and asked him what had happened. Darlan replied that he had changed his mind. When asked why, he answered simply, "I am now Minister of Marine." This did not mean that he had changed his mind in order to become Minister of Marine, but that, being Minister of Marine, he now had a different point of view.

THERE

Admiral Darlan's status had changed, and with that came a change in role. As admiral his role was to save the fleet, as Minister of Marine it was to remain loyal to France. Darlan understood that every status requires its proper role. Status, then, is a man's part in society; role is the way he is expected to play that part.

[MUSIC]

THERE

Every society has its own ways of defining status. But roughly speaking, there are two main kinds. First, the kind of status you are born to.

HERE

Like being a king, or an eldest son, or in New Guinea being born with the umbilical cord wrapped round your neck, which gets you the high status of being an artist.

THERE

The other kind, is the kind of status you earn through your own exertions.

HERE

Like being elected President of the United

States, or becoming a doctor, or getting a million dollars, or learning to write symphonies.

THERE

We'll take this one at a time. First the kind of status you're born to.

HERE

To be a nobleman or a commoner, a man or a woman; to be a native citizen of a certain nation—all these things a person has to be born to, and all of them may give him more or less status.

THERE

Here's an example of the status given by citizenship. When the Apostle Paul was preaching in Jerusalem, he was taken prisoner by some of his enemies.

ENEMY

Away with such a fellow from the earth—for it is not fit that he should live! (*The crowd murmurs its support.*)

THERE

(*Continuing to narrate, but now solemnly.*) And as they cried out and cast off their clothes and threw dust into the air, the chief captain gave them an order.

CHIEF CAPTAIN

Bring him into the castle and there let him be examined by scourging, so that he might know wherefore we cry against him!

THERE

And as they bound him with thongs, Paul spoke unto the centurion that stood by.

PAUL

Is it lawful for you to scourge a man that is a Roman, and uncondemned? (*At this information the crowd becomes agitated and appalled, repeating the fact that Paul is a Roman citizen.*)

THERE

When the centurion heard that, he went and told the chief captain.

CENTURION

Take heed what thou doest, for this man is a Roman.

THERE

Then the chief captain came and spoke unto Paul.

CHIEF CAPTAIN

Tell me, art thou a Roman?

PAUL

Yea.

CHIEF CAPTAIN

With a great sum obtained I this freedom.

PAUL

But I was free born!

THERE

Then straightway they departed from him which should have examined him; and the chief captain also was afraid, after he knew that he was a Roman, and because he had bound him!

[MUSIC]

HERE

The chief captain had acquired his valuable status, the freedom of a naturalized Roman citizen, "with a great sum." But Paul was a Roman citizen, "free born"; and in ancient days that gave a great deal of status.

THERE

Another example of status that you are born to—the caste system in India. Among the Hindus, there are four prime castes; and outside them there are the people with no caste, the so-called untouchables. If you are a Hindu, you are born into your caste, and there is absolutely no way of changing it.

BRAHMIN

Excuse me, not strictly true. We Hindus believe that a person cannot change his caste in this life; but if he has lived properly in this incarnation, he will be reborn next time into a higher caste.

THERE

What caste do you belong to?

BRAHMIN

There are four castes: Brahmana, the teachers; Kshatriya, the guardians; Vaishya, the feeders; and Shudra, the servants. There are also those

Hindus who are born without caste, who are therefore known as untouchables.

THERE

And which are you?

BRAHMIN

I am myself a Brahmin; this is the highest caste.

THERE

Then you are a sort of nobleman—a sort of aristocrat?

BRAHMIN

Not at all, no. I am only a very humble clerk; but I am very high caste. My employer is a very wealthy man, very rich and very important; but he is not so high caste as I am, not at all. I must be careful while I am eating that he does not come along; for then my dinner will have been ceremonially polluted. Of course, I would not pollute his dinner, because I am higher caste; but then of course I would not get near him, because he is a very rich man, and eats in very expensive places where I would not go anyway.

THERE

Then caste among the Hindus gives you a special status, quite apart from what you do or what you earn?

BRAHMIN

Exactly. The Hindu law book of Manu says that though Brahmins occupy themselves in all sorts of mean occupations, they must be honored in every way; for each of them is a very great deity. So you see caste is a very important thing for an orthodox Hindu: it is above all the one thing that he is born with, and which nothing can take away from him. You may think of Hindu caste as giving a man a fixed status. But we think of it, on the contrary, as marking what progress the man has made in his journey through successive reincarnations.

[MUSIC]

HERE

In our own society, status is not nowadays regulated by what a man is born to—though the doctrine of the divine right of kings is a Western one. But many of us regard the color of a man's skin as something that should help in fixing his status; and to this extent we too have set up a caste system in our society.

THERE

Still another kind of status we are born to is the status of sex. In all societies men have a different status from women—sometimes higher, sometimes lower, sometimes only different. Listen to what the Chinese poet Fu Hsüan said about woman's status in China about 1700 years ago; and notice how the poem tells us of the role expected from a woman at that place and at that time.

[MUSIC]

WOMAN

How sad it is to be framed in woman's form!
Nothing on earth is held so cheap.
A boy that comes to a home
Drops to earth like a god that chooses to be
    born.
His bold heart braves the Four Oceans,
The wind and dust of a thousand miles.
No one is glad when a girl is born;
By her the family sets no store.
When she grows up, she hides in her room
Afraid to look a man in the face.
No one cries when she leaves her home
(Sudden as clouds when the rain stops).
She bows her head and composes her face;
Her teeth are pressed on her red lips.
She bows and kneels countless times;
She must humble herself even to the servants.

THERE

But in Tibet, where there are more men than women, women have the higher status, and sometimes a woman will be the head of a household of several husbands.

HERE

Indeed, in our own society, some people think that the head of the household is nowadays the wife.

THERE

Age is another basis for status; but it may mean different things in different places. In China, the high status went to old people. In China, people wanted to seem old, for much respect was paid to age.

HERE

But in our society people want to seem young, for the future belongs to youth!

THERE

Some societies have combined the two; the Plains Indians of North America often gave status to both the very old and the very young. On the other hand, the BaThonga of Africa gave the very old and the very young as little status as possible. Elsewhere in Africa, the Zulus gave the status to the old. But, on the other hand, the Akikuyu, from Kenya, give the high status to the young, and in fact make a great deal of the young men taking over from the old ones.

HERE

Thus status is often determined by age, or the lack of it: and this is something you cannot really do much about. If you live long enough, you will either lose status, or gain it, depending on what society you happen to be living in. And of course every society prescribes the role, the appropriate behavior, for every different age.

THERE

It's worth pointing out right now that high status is not necessarily entirely comfortable. For every status, there is an appropriate role; and the role appropriate to high status may not be an easy one.

HERE

In our society, we have often heard of the loneliness of greatness. A job that carries one of the highest statuses in the world, that of President of the United States, has a role so exacting that it has been called a man-killing job.

THERE

In other societies, things may be even more uncomfortable. On the west coast of Africa there lives a tribe governed by the great and mighty priest-king Kukulu. Nobody has higher status than this king; but in his society the role expected from the king is so arduous that nobody has a more miserable time.

AFRICAN TRIBESMAN

Why should he be comfortable? The great king Kukulu is responsible for the safety of our whole tribe.

HERE

You mean he is a commander-in-chief?

AFRICAN TRIBESMAN

No, he regulates the storms and the state of the atmosphere.

HERE

How?

AFRICAN TRIBESMAN

Just by sitting in his chair.

HERE

All the time?

AFRICAN TRIBESMAN

Certainly, all the time! If he lay down, no wind would arise and navigation would be stopped.

HERE

Does he sleep in his chair?

AFRICAN TRIBESMAN

Of course. If he lay down, the wind would stop and all the boats would be in trouble.

HERE

What does his wife think of this?

AFRICAN TRIBESMAN

The great king is not allowed to have a wife.

HERE

What if he wants to leave his house?

AFRICAN TRIBESMAN

He is not allowed to leave his house.

HERE

So his advisors go to him?

AFRICAN TRIBESMAN

He has no advisors. He lives alone, in his

house, in the woods, and all the time he sits still in his chair. He is a very important man indeed.

[MUSIC]

HERE

This may seem very hard, but people of high status have always had to live up to very stiff roles. For instance, take the ancient kings of Ireland. Take the king of Leinster. If he followed the rules, he could expect to live to the age of ninety without the decay of old age; moreover there would be no epidemic while he was reigning, and the earth would be fruitful. On the other hand, if he failed to obey the rules, the people of Leinster would be visited with plague, famine, and bad weather.

THERE

And what were the rules?

HERE

They were all things he mustn't do. The king of Leinster might not go round Tuagh Laighean left-hand-wise on a Wednesday, nor sleep between the Dodder and the Liffey with his head leaning to one side, nor encamp for nine days on the plains of Cualann, nor travel the Dublin road on Monday, nor ride a dirty black-heeled horse across Magh Maistean.

THERE

Can you bring it up to date?

HERE

Certainly. Nowadays people don't have much status if they don't have a television set. But they may not be able to afford one—so some of them just put up the antenna without the set. The number of dummy antennas seems to be about one in twenty. If you work in the office, you usually have higher status than if you work in the plant; but you have to pay for it. You can't carry a lunch pail any more; and a lot of people carry their lunch to work in briefcases. And in the special society of Hollywood, your status may depend on your going to the right hairdresser, the right dressmaker, the right restaurants, and living in the

right neighborhood; so a promotion may mean you have to spend so much money keeping up appearances that you end up worse off than you were before.

THERE

This is true not only in Hollywood. The point, I think, is clear: everything isn't necessarily lovely for people of high status. The role that their society expects from that status may make them do things they don't like doing, and it may stop them from doing things they want to do. But, of course, we think high status well worth the price we have to pay for it.

HERE

There's another point to bring out here, too. The status of the late King George VI in England and the status of the priest-king Kukulu in West Africa was roughly the same, each in his own society. But the role expected from the status of king was very different. The same status in a different society may mean a very different role.

THERE

So much then for the different roles expected from a given status; for the discomforts of status; and for the kind of a status a man is born to.

[MUSIC]

THERE

Now let's consider the different ways a status can be earned.

HERE

There are two principal ways: by doing things, and by getting things—that is to say, you can get status through skill, or through property. The skill may be that of doing without things: ascetism has always given high status in Christian and some Near Eastern societies. Similarly, the property may be no property: deliberate vows of poverty have sometimes given high status, especially in societies where wealth is very much respected.

THERE

But in most societies it is very often the useful

skills that give the status. Consider the Eskimo, for instance, living under conditions that demand the very utmost for mere existence. In this society, hunting was important for a man, and household skills for a woman.

ESKIMO

My father and my mother were both very respected people. My father was the greatest seal-hunter among many families. Nobody was better than my father at crawling along the ice while the seal was resting. Then he lay perfectly still and quiet while the seal lifted its head and looked around; but he began to crawl again, as the seal lowered its head. Thus my father nearly always drew close enough to kill the animal at once with the beautiful harpoons he used to make himself. So we always had plenty of meat; and my father was very skillful at cutting out the snow blocks for the igloo where we sat in the evening, while my mother worked. She was much respected for the sealskin and caribouskin clothes she made; she was specially skillful at sewing the seams with sinews so that they were waterproof. Moreover, her teeth were worn down almost to the gums through chewing my father's boots to thaw them out in the morning and make them comfortable to wear while he was hunting. You could tell just by looking at my mother's teeth that she was an expert and hardworking housekeeper. These things made my father and mother very important, and it was very fine to be one of the children of such people.

HERE

Our society too, attaches status to the husband's being a good provider and the wife's being good around the house.

GOSSIP

I will say this for him: everything he touches turns to money. He's one of the smartest operators I ever heard about, and handy around the house too; and his wife and children get anything they want. Of course, she keeps them looking beautiful (they live right next door, you know), and she still has time to put up all kinds of fruit and vegetables, and I don't know what else. You know I don't loaf about in bed much myself, especially on washing day. Well, I can tell you it's very few Mondays that she hasn't got her things all out on the line before anyone else. Sometimes I think she must almost do her wash on Sunday evening!

[MUSIC]

HERE

We too give status to the men and women who have domestic skills. But these are not the only things that give status. Being a football star, or being able to play the violin very well, or being able to tell stories—all these things can give a man status in our society.

THERE

And in other societies as well. Take musical skill, for example. Well, the people of Bali are probably the most musical people in the world.

BALINESE

Even little children of four or five are playing in the orchestras. Night and day, the island is full of music; little gongs and chimes, beautiful small bells, and stringed instruments are sounding through the trees. Even their names sound like the instruments: the Kenong, the Gambang, the Rebab, and the Chelempung. In our society of Bali, it is a very great and splendid thing to be a musician; so much so that even our princes used to envy the people who played together so happily in the orchestras—which they could not do because of their high rank. So they would solemnly divest themselves of the princely status they were born with, so that they might earn the status of a musician—only resuming their royalty after the performance was over.

HERE

So much then for status acquired through some kind of skill. Of course for every status acquired in every society there is an appropriate role.

THERE

Come over here. I'll show you a skill you'd forgotten about. And I'll show you a role too that might surprise you. Look!

[MUSIC]

(*We are on a beach watching a boy and girl talking in the distance.*)

HERE

Where are we?

THERE

This is Samoa. Look at the young man talking to the girl.

HERE

Ah! The art of courtship!

SAMOAN YOUTH

See the lovely presents I've brought for you!

(*The girl giggles shyly, from time to time.*) Look at those fish! I just told them you were going to be eating them, and they practically jumped out of the water of their own accord. Let me have the hibiscus from your hair! Please! That's better! Tonight there will be a moon; but after the moon has set, why don't you come down to the beach, where the three cocoanut palms lean out over the fishing pool. By midnight it should be quite dark: and there will be no wind. Only the scent of the flowers. And of course you will have eaten well—all this fish, and this nice chicken, too. The chicken practically died of joy when he heard you were going to eat him. But you must have many fine meals like this, because of your innumerable flocks of lovers. There must be an endless procession of wonderful young men eager to throw themselves at your feet and shower you with rich gifts!

HERE

It's quite true: skill in courtship gives status in Samoa just as it does in many other places.

THERE

Not in every place but, as you say, in many.

HERE

But Samoa seems to ask a suitor to play very much the same role as we ask. I only feel sorry for that young man way over under the trees, who looks so forlorn. Has he no girl friend?

THERE

Samoa does not ask a suitor to play the same role as we ask. That forlorn young man you mentioned is the suitor—as prescribed by Samoan society.

HERE

Then who's this making all the sweet talk?

THERE

That is the suitor's friend. It's his job to make the girl look kindly at the young man. If you watch closely, you'll see her glancing at him every now and again. So it looks as if he may be successful.

HERE

Remember what Priscilla said to John Alden.

PRISCILLA

Why don't you speak for yourself, John?

THERE

This is a question not asked in Samoa, because of the role demanded of Samoan suitors. So you see, even where the status is much the same, in a different society, the expected role may be vastly different.

[MUSIC]

HERE

In most societies, you can acquire status by doing something; and you can also acquire it by owning something. In our own society, perhaps this is the highest kind of status. We often feel that a man would not own a great deal unless he were able to do a great many good and useful things. Consequently we feel that the status to be got by ownership may well include all the other kinds of status and thus is to be counted best of all.

THERE

And what about the role?

HERE

The role? We all like to act as if we had a little more money than we really do. And that is the role—except, of course, for very rich men indeed, who are so rich that they can pretend to be poor if they want to.

THERE

Ours is not the only society that gives status to wealth; but what constitutes wealth differs from one place to another. In Africa among the Ba-Ila, we hear this:

BA-ILA

I am a very wealthy man. I possess numerous cattle.

THERE

But among the Manus of New Guinea, we hear:

MANUS

I am a strong man, for I possess many dog's teeth, and pay high taxes.

THERE

And the Indians of the Pacific coast of both Canada and the United States pay great attention to property. In the south, in California, there are the Yurok, who say:

YUROK

A good Yurok stands up for his rights, and keeps his mind on spiritual things like money: dentalium shells, obsidian blades, and woodpecker scalps.

THERE

But further north on the Pacific Coast live the Tlingit Indians. They too attach great importance to property. A man shows his status, however, not by keeping his property, but by giving it away—in the right sort of way, of course.

HERE

A man in our society might try to improve his status by giving large, conspicuous tips, and spending money lavishly on things that are not really useful and that he buys only for the purpose of impressing the neighbors.

TLINGIT

Ah, that was how it was with us Tlingit in the old days. That was how it was when we could give a potlatch!

THERE

What was a potlatch?

TLINGIT

A potlatch was a feast; a feast in which a man built a great fire, and invited everybody to come.

THERE

All his friends?

TLINGIT

And his enemies. A potlatch was to show what a big man he was. He built the fire, and then he threw on it blankets and copper shields, and allowed precious oil to pour on it through special spouts. Loudly he would point out how rich he was, and how much valuable material he could afford to destroy. And the oil would sizzle in the flames and blaze up splendidly! And he would give away all kinds of presents to his guests—as much as he could afford.

THERE

But of course they would have to give him presents in exchange?

TLINGIT

They might try, but he would hope that they wouldn't be able to repay him; then they would all lose face. His family would applaud him and encourage him, but his enemies and the men he wanted to impress would pretend to ignore it, and pretend not to notice that anything special was happening. Occasionally the fire would blaze so mightily that the other people would get burned, and sometimes one or two were killed, for they would much rather die than retreat from the flames.

THERE

Why?

TLINGIT

Why? Because then, of course, they would be acknowledging that they had noticed something, that the display had made an impression on them—and then they would lose face. Far better be burned to death and make the other man lose face! Oh, a potlatch was a glorious thing!

[MUSIC]

THERE

So there it is. Every society is marked off into different kinds of status. Every society has its own way of arriving at status, and (you've probably noticed) its own way of rewarding people who have achieved high status.

Furthermore, every society expects from each status a particular kind of behavior, a particular role. Each society has its own rules for determining status, and its own rules for determining role. But everywhere there is some sort of status and role.

SHAKESPEARE

All the world's a stage
And all the men and women merely players:
They have their exits and their entrances;
And one man in his time plays many parts.

[FINALE]

11. ARTS

Everywhere the anthropologist goes, he finds people singing, dancing, telling stories, adorning themselves, and devoting special care to decorating and shaping things to their own taste. When he digs up remains of ancient cultures, he finds not only tools and weapons but evidences of an effort to make things beautiful. Even as far back as the Old Stone Age there were decorated objects, statuettes, and elaborately colored cave paintings. We do not know how far back such efforts go, but we are reasonably certain they are as old as our species. Culture everywhere produces art.

Art is not easy to define. People generally "know what they like"; they know what art is for them. But they react differently to other people's art. Philosophers have tried to define the nature of art and to establish universal principles of esthetics, but with little success. Perhaps it is adequate to say that art is the product of human imagination and creativity done for its own sake, for the pleasure in the doing. All peoples derive pleasure from such activity—though there is much variety in the form it takes, the importance it has, and the meaning they give to it.

We do not know what the oldest art form is. We do know that all peoples have dancing, all peoples decorate themselves, all peoples have vocal music and some form of instrumental accompaniment, if only the beating of sticks. We know, too, that all people tell stories, and have a sense of style—of artistry—in the telling. While the making of pictures is not found everywhere, the decoration and special shaping of objects is. These last are the oldest forms of art we know about, because they are the ones that remain after the people are gone.

We do not know what makes art universal—what there is about the human animal that makes him want to create things, and in the creation to form them in a way that gives special satisfaction to the eye or ear. But perhaps we can say that it is this talent more than any other that makes man a special creature—differing not only in capacities from other animals, but in spirit as well. In this way man has altered the environment not only to suit his needs but also to suit his tastes.

Esthetic judgment is a product of culture. What we see as beautiful, what we do that is satisfying to our senses, is established as a part of a cultural pattern. In part, this is habituation. But art also reflects the spirit of a culture. Perhaps the most dramatic example of such a relation was seen in Nazi Germany, where the thunderous and martial music of Wagner had official sanction. Another example comes from the island of Bali. Here the people are devoted to music—and indeed to all the arts. The music consists of highly elaborated orchestration of gongs, xylophones, and stringed instruments. Balinese symphonies are the product of many hands, each doing simple things but the whole forming a complex unit. This form of music reflects the sense of unity in the village life, and the subordination of individual action to the general interest, so typical of Balinese culture. The music also reflects the Balinese world outlook, for it is elaborate in detail and delicate in tone, but lacking in dramatic climax—to the point of monotony to Western ears. The Balinese, similarly, tend to avoid dramatic displays of emotion in their daily life, though they are meticulously careful about protocol.

Again, we may notice the relation of art to culture in the differences between European and Chinese painting. The Europeans, especially since the Renaissance, have emphasized portraiture and the individual object, just as European culture places emphasis upon individual accomplishment and personal differences. Chinese art tends to emphasize landscapes, where a few small figures may be seen as minor elements in a greater whole. Even in portraits of their emperors, the Chinese artists give elaborate treatment of the garments and reduce the faces almost to a mask. Chinese culture does not emphasize the individual but sees him as one element among many in the world. Art, like language, reflects culture.

Art moreover influences culture. It is often an active force not only expressing but also supporting action. The clearest examples are those artistic expressions that reinforce the sense of unity among men, such as national anthems and military music. It is true also of such ceremonies as the British coronation of a new monarch, in which the nation expresses its unity. Similarly, the elaborate ceremonials of the Hopi Indians express their group unity. It is not surprising, when we know the culture of these Indians, to learn that very small children toddle along with the dancers as best they can, included in the ceremonial unity as they are in the social unity.

In the United States, we too have our songs of unity. There is no fraternity or college campus in America that does not have its songs, and the singing together is as important in the expression of unity as are the sentiments in the lyrics.

Literature is doubtless the most influential of the arts because of its versatility. The literature of a people expresses values, creates models for behavior, re-enforces group sentiments, inspires action, according to the demands of the people's culture.

The arts are the dividend in culture. Other animals are themselves beautiful, and some by instinct sing or dance or build nests. But man is unique in his creative capacities, and in devoting the time he can spare to the creation of works of esthetic satisfaction.

But I Know What I Like

LISTER SINCLAIR

HERE *and* THERE, *the two narrators, again show us through the world—this time to demonstrate the universality of art and its social uses.*
[MUSIC]

HERE

Art is universal. Every society has some kind of art: every society has literature; every society has music; and every society has its own special arts as well. Art is what we do for its own sake. Books must be written to tell us things; but that they should be beautifully written is the work of the art of literature. Houses must be built to shelter us; but that they should be beautifully built gives rise to the art of architecture. As the fellow from New England fully realized when he said:

NEW ENGLANDER

I'm building my house myself. Doing it with

my own hands, and the wife, of course, helping with the heavy work. Then when it's all finished, nailed up tight ready to go, I'll bring down a fellow from Boston to put on the architecture.
[MUSIC]

HERE

All societies, then, have some sort of art. All societies look for the beautiful.

THERE

But they don't all look in the same place. The Japanese consider flower arranging one of the fine arts, and also the ceremony of tea drinking, which is an elaborate social occasion as well.

HERE

In our own society we consider gardening one of the arts—though our ideas are very different from what the seventeenth century considered one of the high spots of the art of gardening, Cardinal Richelieu's celebrated water-garden at Ruel, in France.

JOHN EVELYN

The garden has in its midst divers noble brass statues, perpetually spouting water into an ample basin, with other figures of the same metal. On one of the walks, within a square of tall trees, is a basilisk of copper, which, managed by the fountaineer, casts water near sixty feet high, and will of itself move round so swiftly that one can hardly escape a wetting. At the further part of this walk is a plentiful, though artificial, cascade, which rolls down a very steep declivity, and over the marble steps and basins with an astonishing noise and fury. In the middle stands a marble table, on which a fountain plays in divers forms of glasses, cups, crosses, fans, crowns, et cetera. Then the fountaineer represented a shower of rain from the top, met by small jets from below. And at going out, two extravagant musketeers shot us with a stream of water from their musket barrels.
[MUSIC]

HERE

The water-garden was an art in seventeenth-century France. The same country also made cookery into an art, so that the great chef Brillat-Savarin could say in his *Anatomy of Taste:*

BRILLAT-SAVARIN

Architecture is a branch of cookery.

THERE

A useful reminder when you meet a cook who thinks cookery is a branch of chemistry. Every society has its special arts; and very often the form of the art has risen out of the nature of the society. Consider, for example, the case of the Grecian urn:

KEATS

O Attic shape! Fair attitude! with brede
Of marble men and maidens overwrought,
With forest branches and the trodden weed;
Thou, silent form, dost tease us out of thought
As doth eternity: Cold Pastoral!
When old age shall this generation waste,
Thou shalt remain, in midst of other woe
Than ours, a friend to man, to whom thou
    say'st,
"Beauty is truth, truth beauty,"—that is all
Ye know on earth, and all ye need to know.

THERE

Keats's "Ode on a Grecian Urn" is one of the glories of our art of literature; and, by the way, it expresses the attitude of the artist in all societies. But the Grecian urn itself is a piece of art that springs from the very roots of ancient Greek society. Let us call up from the past a citizen of ancient Athens.

[MUSIC]
(*Greek shepherd's pipe.*)

GREEK

Ancient Athens was a city on the sea, locked in by the barren rocky hills of Attica, upon whose stony sun-baked slopes only one tree would grow with ease; and that was the olive. The flocks were pastured between the olive groves, and—Pardon, sir, what music is that I hear?

THERE

Something to try and make you feel at home, old Greek. It is a Greek shepherd playing upon a clarinet-like pipe that he has made with his own hands.

GREEK

In two thousand years that sound has hardly changed. (*Pause.*) I know the tune. It came into Greece at the dawn of the Golden Age, at the time of the Persian wars; and the Greek shepherd on the hill remembers it still upon his homemade pipes. (*Pause.*)

THERE

(*Giving a gentle reminder.*) The Grecian urn?

GREEK

Pardon. Athens, as I have said, had two things only: the sea before her, and the olive trees behind her. Clearly she had to trade, and by sea. She became a great maritime nation, in her day the queen of the ocean. But her chief treasure, her commodity, the thing she could exchange in trade was the olive, and the pre-

cious sweet oil that comes from the olive. Now this oil must be placed in something; and so we took the clay of the Athenian hills and

made it into pots and jars and urns to hold the olive oil. So much was for commerce, which said that urns must be made for olive oil; then the potter's art arose and said that they must be beautifully made. And so they were.

READER

(*Very softly.*) Thou still unravish'd bride of quietness,
Thou foster-child of silence and slow time,
Sylvan historian, who canst thus express
A flowery tale more sweetly than our rhyme.

HERE

(*Starting on a new point.*) Art then often arises from the circumstances of society—the Grecian urn from the olive-oil trade; the Navaho blanket from the chill nights of the southwest desert; and the paintings of the cave man from the attempt to make magic to guarantee good hunting.

THERE

This talk of pictures makes it worth mentioning that not every society has such things as pictures.

HERE

Indeed?

MOSLEM

Very much indeed. You Christians do not, it

seems, know your own Ten Commandments. But we Mohammedans, who revere Moses as a great prophet, always remember the words of the Second Commandment: "Thou shalt

not make unto thee any graven image, or any likeness of anything that is in heaven above, or that is in the earth beneath, or that is in the water under the earth." The Hebrews of the olden time respected this commandment; and Islam, the faith of Mohammed, respects it to this day. Nowhere in Islam will you find a picture of anything whatever made by one of the faithful. But alas, we are all human, and this is not the only commandment broken of men.

[MUSIC]

THERE

So it appears that not every art is universal—though certainly many are. The art of adorning the human body, for example.

HERE

We do it by clothes, by dressing our hair, and by coloring our faces and shaping our bodies. The Chinese used to shape their feet; the North American Indians used to shape their heads; we usually shape the parts in between. We wear clothes for warmth and for modesty—though improved heating changes the first, and fashion changes the second. Nonetheless, added to these necessary uses, there is the art of the tailor, the dressmaker, and the hairdresser.

THERE

Though nowadays we do not go quite as far as the eighteenth century, when a lady's hair was cemented up with false hair and frameworks, and then left for weeks, while madam slept with her neck resting on a wooden collar.

HERE

We do not have time to go into the many things that human beings have made the object of art of one kind or another: tattooing, telling stories, making wine, breeding goldfish, striking coins, decorating boomerangs, designing clocks, catching foxes, making pictures out of corn pollen or butterfly wings, spinning ropes, carving statues—all these things and many more have been fine arts to somebody, sometime, somewhere.

THERE

Art is universal. Every society has forms of art, and the nature of the society gives rise to the nature of the art. Art in fact is a part of society. This is true of every art, but we'll show you how it works for the art of music. (After all, we can't make a noise like a Rembrandt.)

[MUSIC]
(*"Music, Music, Music."*)

HERE

Music. Music is found in every society. And every society says the same thing about other people's music.

OPINIONATED

Call that music! It's just a lot of noise.

THERE

Not just about other people's music! People say that about their own music. Archeology has yet to discover the oldest inscription ever set down by the hand of man; but when it turns up we can make a pretty good guess what it will say.

OLDEST INSCRIPTION

Set down, by Me, in the Year Dot, the following, namely: What in the world is the modern generation coming to, and as for all this new music; so-called—it's nothing but a lot of noise.

THERE

Age cannot wither it, nor custom stale the same old story. What we say about Stravinsky, people said about Mozart.

HERE

But it all comes to the same thing. In music, as in all arts, there are many different styles. Here, for example, is some of the vigorous, highly ornamented music of Arabia, basically unchanged through the 1400 years since Mohammed, except to add fresh subtleties to its buoyant, exuberant expression.

[MUSIC]
(*Arabian folksong.*)

THERE

The Arabians have a style of music quite different from ours, but—

HERE

But questions of musical taste are something else again. Different societies have different kinds of music (some of which we'll be hearing), and even the same society has different kinds of music. But what we're after is music as a part of society—the way we use music without really paying attention to questions of musical taste. Consider these two fellows. (*We find ourselves in the midst of revelry.*) They're at a New Year's party. One of them is wearing an admiral's hat made of green crepe paper; the other one is holding a thing that unwinds when you blow into it and tickles someone's nose with a feather. They are discussing fundamental questions of musical taste.

WILSON

Look, Jack! These days, who cares about Bach? He's dead.

JACK

He's dead; but his stuff isn't. As long as music exists, you've got Johann Sebastian Bach.

WILSON

That stuff sounds like a sewing machine.

JACK

What! (*He is inarticulate with indignation.*)

WILSON

Music never got off the ground until it got clear of all these old-fashioned boys. The whole thing was dying on its feet. Why, right now, there wouldn't even be any music if it hadn't been for Dizzy Gillespie. Say what you like about him—I know his stuff sounds old-fashioned. Modern bop has left him far behind; but his stuff was the real primeval dawn, he was the pioneer.

JACK

Do you call that stuff music? I could get more melodies by shutting a tomcat's tail in a rusty escalator. What's the matter with those guys— got all their sheet music upside down?

WILSON

(*With elaborate dignity.*) They don't ever use printed music at all.

JACK

(*Triumphantly.*) I thought it was something like that.

WILSON

(*Cross and disgusted.*) Listen! Bop's a real art form. Take a figure like this: (*He begins to hum to illustrate his point.*)

JACK

Don't conduct yourself into my drink! What about the Brandenburg concertos? There's Bach at his best. (*He begins to hum a few bars from a Brandenburg concerto.*)

VOICE

Hey, everybody! (*They stop, and the party falls quiet.*) It's twelve o'clock! Happy New Year!

(*The midnight hour begins to strike and everybody shouts New Year's greetings.*)

JACK

Happy New Year, boy!

WILSON

Same to you, fellow—many of 'em!

BOTH

(*Starting to sing; the crowd joining in.*) Should auld acquaintance be forgot
And never brought to mind!

Should Auld acquaintance be forgot,
And days of Auld Lang Syne!

[MUSIC]
(*"Auld Lang Syne."*)

HERE

Bach versus bop is a matter of esthetics—of musical taste and judgment. But singing "Auld Lang Syne" at New Year's has nothing to do with whether you like the tune or not. It's simply the proper ceremony in our society when the New Year comes around.

THERE

Similarly, the Chinese hold processions in the streets and let off firecrackers. The Chinese are particularly scrupulous about celebrating the New Year. Indeed, they have been scrupulous about almost every ceremony and rite. In the ancient and complex society of Confucius, there was an important social function belonging to music—an importance and significance which even extended to precise musical instruments.

[MUSIC]
(*Classical Chinese music.*)

MASTER

What does the Emperor think of when he hears the clear and resonant note of the bell?

PUPIL

The note of the bell creates an impression of majesty, and this inspires a sense of the military power. Therefore, the Emperor thinks of the military officials.

MASTER

What does the Emperor think of when he hears the sharp and clear-cut note of the musical stone?

PUPIL

This music fosters the sense of decision and makes it easy for generals to die in battle. Therefore he thinks of his military officers who die in battle at the border.

MASTER

What when he hears the plaintive quality of stringed instruments?

PUPIL

These cleanse the soul and make for a sense of righteousness. Therefore he thinks of his righteous ministers.

MASTER

And when he hears the floating quality of bamboo flutes?

PUPIL

He thinks how the sound floats everywhere and brings together the masses of the people. Therefore the sovereign thinks of the ministers of the interior.

MASTER

It is seen, therefore, that in hearing music the Emperor hears not only the sounds of instruments, but also the significance proper to the different sounds.

HERE

It is the same with us. Certain instruments have certain strong associations.

GREEK

And in ancient Greece it was the same with us. A good education was based on two things: gymnastics and music. We took the view that music had two functions—first, the accompaniment of the noble words of the poets; second, the accompaniment of dances and other exercises of the limbs. Many philosophers thought children should hear only firm, traditional music—proud and brave for the boys, modest and pure for the girls. Innovations might destroy the spirit of the constitution; and sweet, flaccid music is fit only for slaves. Like the Chinese, we Greeks felt that music, being an important part of society, should be an important part of education.

HERE

We do not feel that, though a superficial knowledge of music has long been listed among young ladies' accomplishments. All the same, our society has very strong associations for different kinds of music. Some of the ways we think of musical instruments were described by the poet Dryden.

[MUSIC]

DRYDEN

The trumpet's loud clangor
Excites us to Arms
With shrill notes of Anger
And Mortal Alarms.
The double double double beat
Of the thund'ring Drum
Crys, Hark the Foes come:
Charge, charge, 'tis too late to retreat.

The soft complaining Flute
In dying Notes discovers
The Woes of hopeless Lovers,
Whose Dirge is whisper'd by the warbling Lute.

Sharp violins proclaim
Their jealous pangs and Desperation,
Fury, frantic Indignation,
Depth of Pains and Height of Passion,
For the fair, Disdainful Dame.

But oh! What Art can teach
What human voice can reach
The sacred Organ's praise?
Notes inspiring holy Love,
Notes that wing their heavenly Ways
To mend the Choires above.
When to the Organ vocal Breath was given,
An Angel hear'd and straight appear'd
Mistaking Earth for Heaven.

[MUSIC]

HERE

Perhaps the best way to think of the social uses of music is to think of all the tunes that we use on special occasions: Chopin's Funeral March, "Happy Birthday to You," "For He's a Jolly Good Fellow," "Hail to the Chief," and dozens of others. And most striking of all, perhaps, is the national anthem.

THERE

Nowadays two of the signs of a civilized country are a national debt and a national anthem. Why do we stand up when we hear the national anthem played? Certainly not because we like the tune.

HERE

As a sign of respect.

THERE

To the music?

HERE

Not to the music, no. The music symbolizes the country; we stand up as a sign of respect to the country.

THERE

A national anthem, in fact, is a really fine example of a social use of music. And some kind of tune that is specially revered is characteristic of very many societies. We all know our own national anthem; and we probably know the tunes of half a dozen others besides. But what do we make of this?

[MUSIC]
(*Royal Watusi drums.*)

THERE

This is African music, marked as usual by

complicated and subtle rhythms. These are the royal Watusi drums, the sacred drums that everywhere accompany the King of the Ruanda in the forests of the Belgian Congo. These drums are playing at the royal court at

Kigali, and the King himself and the provincial chiefs are playing the drums.

HERE

The royal Watusi drums are respected as the symbol of the King. In our societies we carry national anthems still further: they are respected when the chief of state is not even present in person. But the point comes out again: music, like all the arts, has not only an esthetic value, but also a social value.

THERE

The social value is very often expressed with the voice. We have shown you some instrumental music, but the truth is that in most societies the human voice is the heart of music.

HERE

In our own society, almost every piece of popular music is a song.

THERE

And of the many societies that love to sing, many love to hear voices alone. On the island of Tahiti, for instance—the Pearl of the Pacific, as it calls itself—the first European explorers found elaborate music sung in two and three parts. Sometimes the Tahitians used coconut-shell drums; but sometimes the girls would just get together and let their unaccompanied voices carry the spirit of Tahiti.

[MUSIC]
(*Tahiti vocal chorus.*)

THERE

The human voice may be the heart of music. But the ancient Greek told us of their two uses of music.

GREEK

First, the accompaniment of the noble words of the poets; second, the accompaniment of dances and other exercises of the limbs.

HERE

And we are very well aware how closely music is connected with the dance.

DAPHNE

But, Daddy! I've got to go to the dance on

Saturday night! Everybody will be there! A girl's got to go to an important dance like this one, or her social life's just jellified: how's she ever going to meet any boys?

[MUSIC]
(*American dance music.*)

HERE

Ours is not the only society in which young people meet each other at dances. There was a time, in fact, when one special dance was particularly important. It was called the coming-out dance; and it was a polite way of advertising that the debutante was available for marriage, and that her family was ready, willing, and anxious to get her safely off their hands.

THERE

Anthropologists call that sort of social hint about getting married a girl's puberty ceremony. Such ceremonies are very frequently closely connected with music—music as a social function.

[MUSIC]
(*Navaho Squaw Dance.*)

THERE

This is the Squaw Dance of the Navaho Indians of the Arizona desert. Sometimes this dance is called Enemy Way, for it was the ceremony of purification for those Navaho who had been polluted by contact with the enemy. Nowadays, it's a ceremony to cure Navahos whose sickness seems to be the result of meeting strangers. But the main attraction is that the Squaw Dance is also the debutante's coming-out party. The boys and girls turn up for the dance separately, but it's the girls who choose their partners—often with their mothers doing the coaching in the background.

The social use of music as a puberty ceremony is very common in many societies; indeed, you might say hardly any ceremony is complete without music.

HERE

Or any job, either. Take work songs, for in-stance. Work songs are songs to help you get something done. Sea chanties are work songs. So are marching songs—and lullabies. So are the Scottish songs for stretching cloth. So is American dance music—modern industrial studies show that factory workers keep up a better output if they're able to hear music from time to time.

THERE

You might not call that real work music, in the sense that the work isn't actually being done in time with the music—with the music actually acting as a mechanical aid to doing the job. But here's a piece of real work music,

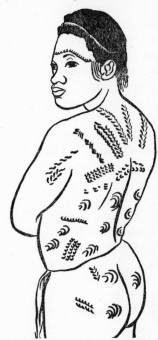

a song to help a lot of girls pound bananas for cooking. You can hear the sound of the pestles going.

[MUSIC]
(*Bongili Work Song.*)

THERE

These girls live in the great forest of central Africa—the Bongili of French Equatorial Africa. They spend several hours a day beating out bananas, both the fruit and the skin, into a paste for cooking; it's a great delicacy. This song is a typical African work song, with the soloist improvising on the delights of beaten-out banana, while the chorus never changes.

HERE

Work songs are another example of the social use of music. In almost every society nearly any kind of ceremony has appropriate music—from a funeral to a wedding. In our society, in fact, wedding music is so firmly established and rigidly dictated that a girl can get some horrible surprises.

DAPHNE

But, mother! If your great-grandmother died before Mendelssohn was even born, there wasn't even a Wedding March! We've got an ancestor who wasn't properly married!

[MUSIC]
(*The Wedding March.*)

HERE

To say nothing of *Lohengrin*, and "I Love You Truly," and "Because." Music at weddings is rigidly prescribed; in our society, it has an important social use.

THERE

And in other societies. Music, for example, is often connected with religion. Religious songs are common. Religious dances are less common in societies familiar to our own—though King David is reported as dancing before the Ark of the Covenant; and in the Greek Orthodox Church part of the wedding ceremony consists of a highly formalized and very stately religious dance.

HERE

In our society, music and church are so closely connected that Alexander Pope could say:

POPE

  Some to church repair
Not for the doctrine but the music there.

HERE

And music in church is perhaps only an extension of the feeling of our society that, of all the arts, it is music that properly belongs in heaven. We all hope that painters, sculptors, and poets may be there, and in quantity. But we all know that when they get there, they'll be singing in the heavenly choirs. For we regard music as above all the heavenly art. In our view music is not only an important part of life in this world, but an important part of life in the next. Dryden, for instance, fittingly concludes his great song for Saint Cecilia's Day with the triumphal declaration of what music will do on the day of judgment.

[MUSIC: *from The Messiah.*]

DRYDEN

As from the Pow'r of Sacred Lays
The Spheres began to move,
And sung the great Creator's Praise
To all the Bless'd above;
So, when the last and dreadful Hour
This crumbling Pageant shall devour,
The Trumpet shall be heard on high,
The dead shall live, the living die,
And Music shall untune the Sky!

12. RELIGION

Mankind has everywhere found it necessary to create a broader world of understanding. For man, despite his sagacity and his creativity, despite his constant probing of nature in attempts to influence it in his own behalf, is nevertheless subject to forces beyond his knowing and outside his direct control. Wherever we find man, we find also efforts at understanding these forces, and at understanding his own place in relation to them, and we find also attempts to make them accede to his demands. Everywhere men have religion.

Belief, faith, accounts of origins, explanations of illness and death, the source and ultimate end of man himself are all part of religion. They are the ideas that are found in the culture—each culture with its own set of ideas. Rituals, incantations, divination, the manipulation of spirits for good or evil, supplications for aid are also part of religion; they are the various efforts man makes to alter these larger unseen forces to which he is subject. Both the system of ideas and the efforts at influence are found among all peoples, no matter how primitive or how civilized they may be. But the particular ideas and the specific efforts to control the world vary from one culture to another.

Some persons feel that term *religion* should be limited to the great religious system of Asia and Europe. Some, indeed, see religion only as what they themselves believe. These people would reduce the religious beliefs of primitive peoples to something less than religion to "animism" or "totemism." But these animistic and totemistic beliefs are to primitive cultures what the great religions are to more developed societies. As anthropologists we are concerned with the relation of religious beliefs to the social organization and other aspects of the culture.

Everywhere religion attempts to account for the universe. It offers an explanation for the origin of the world and of those elements in the world that appear important to the people. Needless to say, religion accounts also for the beginnings of man and frequently, if not always, for the beginnings of many of his cultural forms. Religion also endeavors to explain the culturally approved relations among individuals in the society. The proper roles and statuses, from the mother-in-law avoidance to the divine right of kings, are given religious sanction. The orderly fulfillment of the social system has religious sanction. Even a society devoted to the pursuit of scientific truth does not fail to assume the sanctity of the family and the divine support of its political institutions. The ideas about the deities and spirits are often a direct reflection of the social system itself—just as among the Arunta of Central Australia the pre-human world of the spirits is organized along the totemic lines of the Arunta themselves.

And if religion gives meaning to the relations among men, it also must give meaning to the nature of men. In one form or other every society recognizes the soul. It may be considered immortal (as among ourselves); it may be thought to have come into being before men existed (as among the Arunta); it may be conceived as one with the body or separate from it. It may manifest itself in dreams, in the human shadow, or in man's works.

The concept of the soul may be viewed as the cultural explanation of what makes an individual what he is. In some societies the soul has special power. The Indians of the Great Lakes region called it *Arenda*. The Melanesians called it *Mana*, and anthropology has adopted this word. Mana is not equally distributed among men. The Mana a man or thing has is shown by his actual accomplishments. In other societies the individual seeks an external power, a guardian spirit, to give him the strength to act. The Plains Indians sought such spirits by fasting and hardships. Mana or guardian spirit are each efforts to explain the manifest differences among men—just as the idea of instincts or the psychiatrist's hypothesis of subconscious motivations and repressions are efforts at such explanation.

Religion supplies a world view. The religious beliefs of cosmography—as the theologians and early anthropologists expressed it—provide a topography of the supernatural world. Often such ideas, stemming as they do from limited experience of the world, seem quaint and inadequate. But so does the Ptolemaic view of the universe as seen by modern astronomy. World views provide more than a geography of the universe; they provide also an understanding of space, time, and causation. This point was suggested in "A Word in Your Ear" (Chapter 2). The Navaho see the universe largely in terms of forces at work, whereas we tend to see agents. This concept affects their religion, just as it affects their politics. Our religious literature is replete with agents of good and evil, which we see as self-propelled actors. We also view ourselves as self-propelled actors. To us, man is a free agent, building bridges and damming streams, but also free to establish his virtue or fault, free to make of himself what he will.

Of course, there is not a complete antithesis here. No people see the world all one way or all the other. Like the Navaho, we recognize unseen forces; like us, the Navaho engage in ceremonies to alter events. By some means the peoples of all parts of the world endeavor to shape fate, to bend the supernatural forces to their own ends. When this is done to evil intent—to harm others—it is sorcery, witchcraft, the black arts. But most of man's energies are devoted to the beneficent manipulation of a sometimes harsh universe: the Hopi snake-dance to bring rain, the health ceremonies of the Navaho or the Australian Arunta, the ceremonials of harvest and of fertility in the spring, the prayers for peace among men.

One aspect of religion is inadequately treated here—as perhaps it is in the literature of anthropology as a whole. That is religion as a personal experience. In our scientific culture we tend to separate understanding from feeling; the scientist slights the subjective aspects of experience. But the emotions are deeply involved in all religions. This personal aspect of religion is better left to the student of psychology, except in so far as such experience has important consequences for social behavior.

The religious experiences of the individual influence his emotional reaction to the events in his world, particularly to those events that relate him to other persons in his environment. Ceremonies of initiation, tribal rites, the religious pageants of all peoples certainly give the individual a strong sense of his own involvement with his group, and thus strengthen the emotional bonds within the group. In this way, religion re-enforces the internal unity of the society and gives it the necessary strength to accomplish as a group what its members could not do as individuals.

Religion, then, has many faces. But it always tries to provide man with the answers to recurrent questions about the origin and nature of the universe, about the character of the social world in which he lives, about himself and his relation to society and the universe. It gives him also a means of facing—if not always of meeting—the challenges that his environment presents.

Sticks and Stones

LEN PETERSON

➤➤-➤➤

The Arunta lived in the great Australian Outback—a nomadic stone-age people in an inhospitable desert. Among the most primitive peoples known to modern anthropology, they knew no agriculture nor domestic animals, save the half-wild dog that followed them about as they wandered in search of food. Though poor in material things, they tracked game on clues that would escape our most intrepid woodsmen, and obtained water where we would die of thirst. Their houses were brush huts, and they went about naked.

Two aspects of Arunta culture were elaborately developed: social organization and religious life. The Arunta social organization was built upon various groupings: bonds that shared economic resources, totem groups that were religious units, and "subsections" that governed marriage. The regulation of marriage was strict and complex, as indicated by the fact that a man had to find a bride who was, by Arunta reckoning of kinship, his mother's mother's brother's daughter's daughter.

The religion had many ramifications, but only three need be mentioned: totemic beliefs, ritual initiations, and shamanism. Totemism is the belief that each group of persons is spiritually related to a particular species of plant or animal. The totemic group and the animal species were considered to be descended from a common set of spirits who dwelt in a golden age before man was created. These spirits still inhabited the sacred grove of the totem, and from time to time one entered the body of a passing woman to become for a while a human being who belonged, thereby, to that particular totem.

The totem group was in charge of many elaborate rituals. Among these rituals were a series of initiations, by which the individual was raised to ever higher planes of ritual and social participation. These rites involved elaborate bloodletting; they also involved the indoctrination and inculcation of youth into the beliefs and mysteries of the Arunta world. It was only after a man had gone through each successive initiation that he became an elder and could help to govern his small band. It was only then also that he might see his sacred Churinga, the large flat ovals of stone, decorated with intricate geometric patterns, which had been made at the time of his birth and which held a part of his own spirit.

Shamanism rests upon the belief that spirits cause sickness and death. These spirits can be manipulated by special medicine men (shamans), both by sending them into the body of the foe, and by extracting them from the dead. Together with an elaborate mythology these beliefs and practices related the Arunta not only to the world of nature and to the further unseen world of the spirit but also to his fellow men.

"Sticks and Stones" shows the Arunta answers to the eternal questions of man.

[MUSIC]

YOUNG MAN

How was it, I wonder, before I came?

ANTHROPOLOGIST

Everywhere in the world men wonder about the unknown and the unknowable. Sometimes it is idle wondering, like the play of children. Sometimes it is forced upon men by the heavy burden of necessity. Even among the most primitive of peoples this wondering goes on. Take the Arunta, a stone-age people in central Australia.

YOUNG MAN

How was it, I wonder, before my father came?

ANTHROPOLOGIST

The Arunta cultivate no crops and keep no herds. They live on the plants, animals, reptiles, and insects they find in their wanderings about the countryside; they even eat pounded anthill clay. They wear no clothes. They have few implements—only stone knives, axes, and

A Churinga

picks, digging sticks and wooden troughs in which they carry food, water, seed, and babies. They have few weapons—only boomerangs, shields, clubs, spears, and spear-throwers, grooved sticks that increase the leverage of the throwing arm. Yet the Arunta wonder about many things.

YOUNG MAN

How was it, I wonder, before anyone came?

OLD MAN

Out of nothing came Numbakulla. He is the greatest ancestor of the Arunta; all the others are less than he. He arose in the south at Lamburkna and traveled north, past here, creating rivers, mountains, flatlands, animals, and plants as he went.

ANTHROPOLOGIST

The young man who sought word of the beginning repeated what he had heard to others.

YOUNG MAN

(*In repeating the formula, he experiences it again.*) Out of nothing came Numbakulla. He arose in the south at Lamburkna and traveled north, past here, creating as he went.

ANTHROPOLOGIST

Each time it is said it becomes more true, until no one doubts it. And new details are added.

TALL MAN

Where did we of the Arunta tribe come from?

ANTHROPOLOGIST

If a question can be asked, there must be an answer.

WISE OLD MAN

Numbakulla created many spirits out of himself. And he made Churinga for the spirits to dwell in, sacred slabs of stone and wood. Dig into this cave and you will find some.

ANTHROPOLOGIST

The men who were the wise old men dug and found round and oval sticks and stones. Some were wrapped in bark, some in strings made of human hair. Many had simple designs on them.

TALL MAN

These were put here by the great Numbakulla?

WISE OLD MAN

Some were put here by the men of the Arunta. But in the beginning Numbakulla traveled about the country burying Churinga. And as he went he made the landscape. Look out along the horizon. There he put his foot down and made a hill, and farther along another hill. There he sat down, and the mountain range sank under his heavy weight. There he threw his yam-stick at a dog, and if you go there you will find a heap of white stones to mark the place. Farther along Numbakulla camped and made the ravine to sleep in.

ANTHROPOLOGIST

The wise old man pointed around the circle of the horizon, linking trees, hills, valleys, and stones with the exploits of Numbakulla or other great ancestors of long ago—Intwaili-uka, Alantunja, and Chitchurta.

WISE OLD MAN

And from the Churinga, from the sacred slabs of stone and wood made by Numbakulla, spirits came forth and became men. And each man was linked with an animal or plant or thing, his totem. From one Churinga came the first wildcat man, from another the first kangaroo man, from another the first Hakea-flower man, and from another the first witchetty-grub man. Ever since then the places where they came forth have been sacred totem centers, places where the totemic spirits dwell, and come forth in bodied form—one time as men, another time as creatures of the totem. The same spirit can become a kangaroo man or a kangaroo. And so it is with all the totemic spirits: the wildcat, the opossum, the frog, the lizard, the rock wallaby, and all the others.

[MUSIC]

ANTHROPOLOGIST

The explanation was passed down from generation to generation and became a hard truth that no one dared question. But other questions arose.

CHILD

Where did I come from, Mama?

MOTHER

From a Churinga, like all of us.

CHILD

How?

MOTHER

From a frog Churinga.

CHILD

But how?

MOTHER

Like all the other frog people.

CHILD

But how? How, Mama? How did I come from a frog Churinga, Mama?

MOTHER

I do not know, my little Kanjia. I have never

seen a Churinga. They are tabu to women and boys.

CHILD

How was I made, Mama?

MOTHER

One day I went for a drink of water near the bluffs, where the frog spirits dwell in the Churingas buried there and in the trees and rocks. I heard a voice crying "Mama, Mama." I ran away, but I did not run fast enough. A frog spirit entered me, and in time you were born, Kanjia. That is where you came from, and that is how you were made.

ANTHROPOLOGIST

Among the Arunta—so they believed—the men had little to do with the conceiving of the children; they might prepare the way, but it was the spirits' entrance into the women when they went too near the totem centers that gave them babies.

[MUSIC]

MOTHER

(*Musing.*) I shall not be able to care for this

new baby; it has followed too closely the last one. I went too near the hill where the lizard spirits stay right after the birth of my little Arria-iga. But if I—

ANTHROPOLOGIST

Sometimes beliefs can make acceptable the terrible deeds that man must do in order to survive.

MOTHER

If I kill this baby, its spirit will go back to the hill, and wait awhile to be born again—when little Arria-iga will be older and I'll be able to feed and carry this baby around.

ANTHROPOLOGIST

For how can one woman nurse and carry two babies while wandering over the desert in daily search for food?

[MUSIC]

SHORT MAN

We have been long without rain.

HEAD MAN

Yes, and the plants are scarce and the animals are scarce.

OLD MAN

The time of rain should be near.

SHORT MAN

And we shall have some witchetty grubs to eat.

HEAD MAN

But the witchetty grubs do not last long.

OLD MAN

Last time after the rains the kangaroo did not come. There should be some way of making the kangaroo abundant. Is there not some way?

ANTHROPOLOGIST

Another question posed.

HEAD MAN

Oh, kangaroo men of our tribe, the time of rain is near, the time of the hunt. You are kin to the kangaroo, you are born of the same spirit—

VENERABLE MAN

(*With dignity.*) The kangaroo is the same as us.

HEAD MAN

We have grown lean in the long time without rain. We need a good hunt for our tribe.

VENERABLE MAN

We must talk to the kangaroo spirits, but I do not know what—

ANCIENT MAN

Long ago I was a great kangaroo. I set out for the place Okirilpa. On the way I came upon some wild dogs with their mother. They chased me, and though I hopped away very fast, they caught me on the Chulina plain and ripped me open. They chewed my liver and pulled off my skin and ate all the meat from my bones. Then they lay down. But I was not done with. My skin gathered up my bones, and I hopped away again. Again the dogs chased me and caught me and ripped me open. This time they did not eat my liver. A dark hill like a liver marks the spot. Once more my skin gathered up my bones and I hopped away. Again I was caught. And again. This fourth time they cut off my tail and buried it near here. It changed into a stone. Let us unearth it and through it speak to the kangaroo spirits.

[MUSIC]

ANTHROPOLOGIST

The men went to the spot where the sacred stone lay. The head man uncovered it. It was triangular in shape, like the tail of a kangaroo. Buried with it was a smaller flat stone. The leader rubbed the flat stone on the "kangaroo's tail." The other men watched solemnly.

[MUSIC]

ANTHROPOLOGIST

Then the "kangaroo's tail" was lifted up for all to see. The men crowded around to examine it and touch it. Many felt an emotion in their stomachs as they did so.

[MUSIC]

ANTHROPOLOGIST

The sacred stone was buried again.

ANCIENT MAN

Now come with me.

ANTHROPOLOGIST

They followed him past a watering hole,

>>>->>>

where they drunk, and then they moved around the base of a cliff.

ANCIENT MAN

Look up. See those two rocks sticking out from the cliff. One is an old kangaroo, the smaller one a woman kangaroo. Two of you climb up and rub them with stones.

[MUSIC]

ANTHROPOLOGIST

Two of the men did the ancient kangaroo man's bidding. The belief possessed them that what they were doing would increase the number of kangaroo in the land of the Arunta. The two who had gone up the cliff descended.

ANCIENT MAN

(*With more emotion.*) Now paint the rock edge. Paint it with red clay and white clay. Paint it in red stripes and white. Let the red stripes be the red fur of the kangaroo; let the white stripes be the bones. The youngest of you, climb on the ledge, cut your arms with flint stone, let the blood spurt out and run down over the sacred stone.

ANTHROPOLOGIST

They did as they were bid.

[MUSIC]
(*Singing chants.*)

ANTHROPOLOGIST

And the men remaining below them sang of the abundance of kangaroo that were sure to follow. There was faith in their words, faith in the manner in which they chanted. And it began to rain.

ANCIENT MAN

Young men, go now—go out on the rocks and the plains and hunt the kangaroo. Old men, return to camp and await the return of the young men with their bounty.

[MUSIC]
(*Australian singing chants.*)

ANTHROPOLOGIST

It became a ritual, repeated each year and essential to the hunt. When the hunt was small, the Arunta blamed not the ritual but hostile spiritual forces working against it. Rituals developed for the increase of the witchetty grub and the honey ant, and the wild turkey and the plum tree, and the Hakea flower—which, soaked in water, provided the Arunta with their favorite drink. Rituals developed for the increase of most of the totem animals and plants, even for flies and mosquitoes—not that these pests were desired, but that with them came valuable rainfall. And further instructions were added.

ANCIENT MAN

Man of the kangaroo totem, eat a little of the kangaroo that have been killed—or your power for the kangaroo ceremony next year will be gone and the kangaroo will not increase.

MAN

We get some kangaroo spirit that way.

ANCIENT MAN

Yes, but only eat a little. And the little you eat—let it not be a good part of the kangaroo. Give all the rest to those who are not kangaroo men.

ANTHROPOLOGIST

There was something wrong in eating the animal or plant born of the same spirit as oneself. Each totem group handed over its plant or animal to those outside. But the totem groups were mixed up. In every family and band there were members of several totem groups. They hunted their totem animals and gathered their totem insects and plants for one another. What each one hunted or gathered he gave to others; what the others hunted and gathered they gave in part to him. Beliefs led to rituals or ceremonies; beliefs led to special kinds of group relationships.

[MUSIC]

TALL MAN

Why do you keep falling behind, Ingapaila?

ANTHROPOLOGIST

The mystery of sickness and death. Imagine two men of the Arunta tribe walking along a trail, one clutching at his middle, moving with difficulty.

TALL MAN

It will be dark before we reach camp. We must move faster.

YOUNG MAN

(*Groans.*) I have a pain in my belly. I feel weak.

TALL MAN

What is it?

YOUNG MAN

It is like a sharp stick or stone. I cannot walk farther.

TALL MAN

Put your arm over my shoulder. Lean on me.

YOUNG MAN

No, let me lie down.

TALL MAN

What is hurting you, Ingapaila?

YOUNG MAN

(*Writhing with great pain.*) A sharp stick or stone in my belly.

TALL MAN

You have swallowed it?

YOUNG MAN

You know we have not eaten for two days.

TALL MAN

Then how did it get into you? When? (*The young man groans.*)

ANTHROPOLOGIST

A great mystery. And more questions. What has made the young man sick? What is this? What makes this hurt? What makes this weakness and wasting away?

TALL MAN

How did this stick or stone get in your belly, Ingapaila?

YOUNG MAN

(*In pain and anger.*) Agh! Avenge the one who put it there!

TALL MAN

Was it someone? Who?

YOUNG MAN

(*Still in great pain.*) I do not know!

ANTHROPOLOGIST

If men of the Arunta could with the help of spirits influence plants and animals and the wind and the rain, then why not one another? Why couldn't men, with the aid of these spirits, cause one another to grow weak and waste away? And so the Arunta used spirits and magic to cause the death of those they would destroy.

SHORT MAN

Ingeliba has stolen my wife. She is with him now.

MAN

He is better with the spear and the club than you.

SHORT MAN

Agh! I would fight him, but there are many men in his camp, many more than in ours. They would all come out to fight.

MAN

So you have lost your wife.

SHORT MAN

No, I am going to kill Ingeliba.

MAN

How? Ambush him? But he is clever.

SHORT MAN

Yes, and he will be very wary now that he has taken my woman. I have made something. I will fix him with this tiny spear and spear-thrower.

MAN

Ah, painted red with white, yellow, and black stripes—to make him sick.

SHORT MAN

And now I must charm it with an evil spirit. Come with me to the other side of those rocks where no one goes and help me sing over it.

ANTHROPOLOGIST

They climbed over the rocks to a secluded spot and set the miniature spear and spear-thrower down, pointed toward the camp where the wife-stealer was. They left it there for several days. Each day they came and sang over it.

SHORT MAN
Go straight; go straight and kill Ingeliba.

MAN
Go straight; go straight and kill Ingeliba.
(*The two men repeat the formula three times in unison.*)

ANTHROPOLOGIST
The last day, after singing over it, one of the men huddled down with his forehead touching the ground. The second, the injured husband, picked up the evil-laden weapon, and standing between the feet of his friend hurled it as far as he could toward his enemy. Then he too knelt down with his head between his friend's feet and waited to hear the evil spirit

speak. Several hours they waited motionless and silent. And then—they were sure they heard it.

BOY
(*Distant and strange.*) Where is he? Where is he?

ANTHROPOLOGIST
They returned to their camp, still silent, still listening. And there was a second sign. (*A crash and roll of thunder in the distance.*)

ANTHROPOLOGIST
A noise like thunder, which meant that their weapon, in the form of a great spear, had gone straight to their victim.

SHORT MAN
Oh, that cut through Ingeliba.

MAN
He is dead or badly hurt.

SHORT MAN
He will die.

ANTHROPOLOGIST
The device worked often enough to continue being used. Pointing sticks and bones also became popular. Like the tiny spear they were sung over—charmed—and pointed at the victim.

HEAD MAN
May your backbone be split open and your ribs torn apart. May your backbone be split open and your ribs torn apart.

ANTHROPOLOGIST
Real weapons were sometimes sung over, too, and the slightest blow or wound from such a weapon was fatal—particularly if the man so injured knew or suspected that the weapon had been charmed. The Arunta could not accept any human death as natural. To them, every illness and death was caused by someone using evil magic. Every death must be avenged: a life for a life.

Medicine men could sometimes overcome the evil magic. The patient lies on the ground. The medicine man rubs and sucks him (*he is heard sucking noisily*) where the pain is and occasionally spits out the supposed bits of bone, wood, or stone that are doing the damage. If this method does not work another one is tried.

MEDICINE MAN
The poor old fellow has a short barbed stick in him. That is why it is so hard to get out. (*The group reacts in dismay. The venerable man cries out in pain.*)

MEDICINE MAN
It has a string attached to it; it is the evil spirits pulling it that make the pain. Sit him up.

TALL MAN
He is too weak.

MEDICINE MAN
Then support him. Now give me room.

ANTHROPOLOGIST
The medicine man stands looking intently down at the patient. Great skill is required to

remove a barbed stick. He walks some distance away, bends forward a little and jerks his arms sidewise a number of times. (*The medicine man grunts, jerks about, and begins to run back and forth as he explains what is happening.*)

MEDICINE MAN

I have hurled some magic stones into his body to work against the evil spirits.

ANTHROPOLOGIST

Several times he runs back and forth, lifting his knees high, and hurls more stones into the patient. Then he comes up to the patient and examines him carefully with his hands, finally making a cutting motion with his stone knife.

MEDICINE MAN

I have cut the string on the barbed stick. (*The group reacts in satisfaction, while the medicine man starts again to suck noisily and spit violently.*)

MEDICINE MAN

Agh, the barbed stick is not coming out whole, but in bits. (*Pause.*) That is all. (*The group reacts—they are impressed.*) Now he will get better—unless I have been called in too late.

[MUSIC]

YOUNG MAN

What is death? What happens when a man dies?

ANTHROPOLOGIST

Among the Arunta, like everywhere else, the terrible question has been eternally asked.

WISE OLD MAN

Erpolingarinia is dead. His spirit has left his body. It has flown away as a little bird, the Chichurkna, to the cave where the Churinga are buried. It has joined its totem spirit.

HEAD MAN

Lift Erpolingarinia's legs up, bend them up against his chest, and then let us carry him to his grave.

ANTHROPOLOGIST

The grave is a round hole. The man's hair is cut off by one of his sons, and he is lowered into the grave in a sitting position facing toward the camp of his ancestors.

WISE OLD MAN

Erpolingarinia's spirit will come soon to protect his body.

HEAD MAN

Don't pile the earth so high on the side toward the camp; the spirit must be able to go in and come out.

WISE OLD MAN

Take the hair of Erpolingarinia and weave a girdle for his son.

HEAD MAN

Burn down Erpolingarinia's camp; destroy everything. Let his family take up a new site.

[MUSIC]

ANTHROPOLOGIST

A period of mourning follows. The dead man's name is never spoken except occasionally in a whisper when necessary; the dead man's spirit must not be disturbed by references to it. His widow smears white pipe clay over her body—white being the color of mourning among these dark-skinned people. For many months she does not speak but communicates with a sign language. After a year, or a year and a half, the mourning ends with a ceremony, "trampling the twigs on the grave."

[MUSIC]

OLD MAN

(*Vigorously.*) Ba-au! Drive the spirit down! Drive the spirit down!

[MUSIC]

ANTHROPOLOGIST

The mourners jump and dance wildly about on the grave, trampling the twigs that cover it. The widow and the younger sister of the dead man wear headpieces of ringneck-parrot feathers, human hair, and the bones of small animals, which they tear to pieces near the end of the ceremony and place in a hole they dig in the top of the grave.

[MUSIC]

ANTHROPOLOGIST

The men and then the women prostrate themselves on the grave. Then the widow, standing on the grave, rubs the white pipe clay from her body.

WIDOW

Ended is my mourning. But I shall wear a white band on my forehead. I still sorrow a little for Erpolingarinia. I do not wish to marry yet.

VENERABLE

Spirit of Erpolingarinia, from the bottom of the grave you have watched the ceremony in your honor. Your widow has been painted white all this time, and she has worn the headdress of bones; you have been properly mourned. The gay feathers of the ringneck parrot told you the mourning is over. With the headdress your widow has buried all our sorrow. The loud shouting—you know, spirit of Erpolingarinia, what that means; you attended many tramplings on the grave, before this one of yours. We do not wish to be frightened by you; we shall be angry if you do not rest. We want you to watch over us, spirit of Erpolingarinia, guard us from harm and visit us in our dreams; but you must not come in a way that will frighten us. Return to the wildcat Churinga. Return to the ancestral place of the wildcat totem. Wait for the time when you will be born again a wildcat or a wildcat man.

[MUSIC]

ANTHROPOLOGIST

Always with the Arunta there is a return to the Churinga, the sacred stone or wooden object that gives each individual a link with his ancestors and the past, a link with his world today, a link with the spiritual world, a link with his group, his totem, and his own hereafter. The Churinga provide a focal point for the Arunta tribe. Ceremonies connected with the Churinga bring the tribe together and provide means for passing on the culture of the tribe—a culture in which there is no division between religion, science, and medi-

cine. They are all one. The Churinga may be seen only by the initiated men of the tribe. The punishment for any woman or uninitiated boy who by chance sees a Churinga is death or blinding with a fire-stick. Great indeed is the day when a young man has become fully initiated.

HEAD MAN

My young man Erlkintera, you have gone through all the tests: that of being thrown up in the air and painted, that of being circumcised and cut a second time, and that of lying upon a fire. You have the strength, courage, and wisdom of a man. You have learned to obey the old men. And now you will be shown the sacred secrets of our tribe.

[MUSIC]

ANTHROPOLOGIST

The sacred secrets are linked with the Churinga and the totems. The Churinga are unearthed and unwrapped for the newly initiated. The ceremony is performed with patience and reverence, and frequently with deep emotion. Tears come to the eyes of some of the old men. Many associations well up for them as they caress these stones and pieces of wood. They know the power and sacredness inherent in them; they know that as long as they possess these Churinga the loved ones taken by death are not really lost to them. The old men have a great storehouse of truths, the Arunta religion, to pass on to the young men. And they have questions still unanswered.

WISE OLD MAN

Did Numbakulla make the white man too?

ANCIENT MAN

Why does the white man wear clothes?

HEAD MAN

What kind of Churinga does he have? One white man told me the only Churinga he knows are the clock Churinga and the pocketbook Churinga. But they must have more than just two. No? We have many, many.

13. SOCIETY: A Summing Up

Man is one, but cultures many. This is the basic lesson in understanding the ways of mankind. Since the last glacier retreated from Europe and Asia, the world has known only one species of man. He varies in skin color, in the texture and amount of his hair, in size, in and several other superficial features. We refer to these characteristics in describing the different races. But research has consistently shown that in the attributes that make man what he is, no important biological differences exist among the races. Man everywhere has the same senses, though in some cultures more importance may be attached to one than another. Man everywhere has hands capable of making and using delicate tools, though in one place he may create thimble-sized, feather-decorated baskets, in another machine tools with tolerances of .001 inch. All men, everywhere, imagine stories, wonder about the world's origin, fear the afterlife, and struggle with the problem of good and evil. And, of course, men everywhere tell these stories and discuss these problems in language; for all men speak. All men, too, are capable of laughter and the shedding of tears. No race or group is, by virtue of its biological inheritance, more religious, more artistic, or more righteous than any other. Thus it is that man is one.

But that is not to say that man is everywhere alike. Obviously not. For we vary in the cultures we are heir to. Peoples vary in the uses to which they put their talents. They have found different solutions to the problems of gaining a livelihood, of delineating good and evil, of facing death. So, too, with all other aspects of behavior that make up the diverse ways of mankind. Thus it is that, though man is one, cultures are many.

Common threads run through all cultures; this we have repeatedly shown. The unity in human behavior has two sources. The first of these sources may be thought of as biological—the qualities men share because they are animals. Some are so obvious that merely to mention them is enough. Man must eat. He must procreate. He must protect himself from the inclemency of weather by clothes or shelter. Others are perhaps just as obvious, but not so often thought of. They are the special endowments that make culture a possible and useful instrument for preserving the species.

Consider first the hand. It is the tool that makes all other tools possible. A delicate instrument capable of the most intricate embroidery and of the sensitive fingering of a violin, it is also gross and strong enough for lifting and throwing. With the tools man makes, he can master every environment; he can protect himself from snow and desert and the beasts of the forest; he can get food from the open sea and the good earth. In all this the eye is partner to the hand.

Consider man's language. Speech is his unique gift. Language makes possible the storing of knowledge. Someone invents fire, someone else string. Another person finds he can render grass seeds digestible by cooking, while another discovers how to leach poison from a particular food. And so for centuries the new discoveries and inventions that humans make are stored in the form of speech.

Stored and passed on—which is the second point about language. Each new generation does not have to start afresh, but can be told of the tricks that have been learned. A cat will show its young how to catch mice, a doe will communicate to the fawn the dangers in the smells of its predators. But they can do so only when mice or predators are about; they cannot, as man can, show or warn of what they do not experience in common. Language is necessary for culture.

Culture is behavior learned from one's fellows and shared with them. And there is so much to learn—where the dangers lie, what is food, how things are made, who are friends. In the simplest of societies the task is great and takes time. Therefore man's prolonged immaturity, his slow growth to independent adulthood, is a social advantage. All mammals and many other animals must be nurtured during the first part of their life. But no animal takes as long as man to grow up; even the elephant is self-sufficient in six or seven years. These years of dependence are necessary for the young to learn what must be learned. It keeps the child under the guidance of his parents; it makes him dependent, willing to subject himself to the long and arduous process of learning the skills that his culture provides. This prolonged immaturity is important to culture.

The unity in all human behavior has two sources. The one is biological: man's needs as an animal. The other is social. For, as we have seen, man is everywhere by his very nature committed to living in society. Long maturation requires it; the strength of co-operation gives it special virtue. The fact that man cannot live alone has further consequences: he must develop those features of organization that will preserve the system of co-operation we call society. One such feature is communication. Language is a special endowment already recognized; but this has been expanded and made more eloquent by gesture in intimate communication, and extended by the signal drum and the radio in more distant communication.

Each culture must also have groups. A society is itself a group, bounded by those psychological frontiers which distinguish member from outsider, friend from stranger. But it is constructed of myriads of lesser groups to do the more specific tasks: families to nurture children, work groups to accomplish tasks, religious groups, fighting groups, social groups.

Societies must also have rules. There must be regulations to channel behavior, define propriety, and give order to action. In the absence of rules there would be only chaos. Remember Alice's croquet game, with flamingo mallets and hedgehog balls: no rules, no game. Some of the rules of a society we call ethics, and all peoples have ethics. Some we call tabus, proscriptions ("Thou shalt not . . .") which are deeply felt because they are sanctioned by our religions. Some rules we call law. But whatever we call them, and however they may be formulated, all societies are governed by these rules.

Rules require sanctions. Most people, most of the time, obey most rules. Nevertheless, rules will not long retain their meaning unless there are means by which they can be enforced. Some system of authority is needed to remind people of the rules, to prevent them from breaking them, to maintain order. There must be some mode of settling the disputes that arise between men. Authority may be inherited; it may be a matter of election; it may go to the aged or to the wealthy; it may be formally established or informal. But ultimately, in any given place and time, for any particular purpose, someone must be responsible. This is true whether we speak of priests, presidents, or parliaments—whether we think of the family or the football team.

We may think of the person in charge as having a particular position—a status. In all societies there are such positions, and there are also other special statuses. We may think of the status of farmer, of father, or of fraternity brother. In every society there are many different statuses. These positions are recognized, and every person has a number of them. Usually, some positions are more desired and more desirable than others, so that when we use the word *status* we usually refer to differences in the degrees of prestige that the positions give. Such differences in status are found in all societies, but the same status is not necessarily given the same rating in different societies.

For each such status there is a proper part to play. The way a person is expected to act when he occupies a particular status is his *role*. The notion of proper role is often caught in some of our stereotyped jokes—for instance, about the absent-minded but erudite professor, or the mother-in-law, or the moon-faced lover. These are roles, or parts of roles, that we ascribe to certain statuses. The culture will specify the general behavior for each position; the person in the position is supposed to live up to this behavior pattern within the limits of his own ability.

Rules, status, and roles all suggest that people everywhere tend to place a value on persons and human behavior. All societies do have a measure by which the judge they behavior of their fellows. The members of each society share a feeling that some forms of behavior, some personal situations, and some material possessions have particular importance for them. These become goals, which the people hope to achieve by such means as the society provides. They may be called the values of the society. Values are a kind of lodestone—a magnet which orients the behavior and attitudes of a people. They are necessary to the unification of societies.

Societies share other features. Since culture is learned behavior, there must be means of teaching. Schools are a regular and important part of our own social system. Schools are not found everywhere, but some regular means of instruction are found in all human groups. Most important teaching is everywhere undertaken by the parents and the other family members of the young. But instruction may also be carried on by persons with special skills. Often religious ceremonies are used to instruct children in the attitudes and feelings of the culture.

Men regularly find esthetic expression. Art is universal, though arts vary. It is perhaps impossible to say that art is necessary to society, but it does appear to be necessary for man. For everywhere men have found special pleasure in creating things according to various established canons of taste. It is through art that man's creative ability has most enriched the world.

Men in all societies also have religion. Through religion they seek to explain the world about them, the sources of pleasure and grief, their own existence, and their own behavior. The efforts to answer such eternal questions, and their views of the forces in the world, together with their efforts to manipulate these forces, constitute their religion.

These universal imperatives operate on all men everywhere. Some stem chiefly from man's biological characteristics; others stem more directly from the needs for social organization. In the "Museum of Man" appear the displays that demonstrate these imperatives. But though these general features exist in all human life, various peoples in various parts of the world have found their own solutions to these universal problems.

Museum of Man

LISTER SINCLAIR

➤➤➤

The Museum of Man is the world itself, and its exhibits are the world's peoples. The only character is the speaker, who is our guide.

SPEAKER
"Dust as we are, the immortal spirit grows
Like harmony in music; there is a dark
Inscrutable workmanship that reconciles
Discordant elements, makes them cling
    together
In one society." So speaks the poet; but the philosopher says: "Man seeketh in Society comfort, use, and protection."
The lawgiver says: "Man was formed for society."
And the reformer: "Society was formed for man."

What *is* society?

The Museum of Man is at the very top of the building (at present). We enter through this dark and lifeless Pre-Cambrian basement. Press the button and wait for the automatic elevator.

You'll be glad to know the collection relating to Man is specially good. Indeed, Man himself *is* the collection, and all the exhibits show him to the life. Some say it's done by waxworks, or by statuary, or by mirrors; some say the specimens are stuffed. Don't believe it.

Everything you shall see here—the men and women, what they do, what they think and what they *are*—is real. They are in glass cases for the moment to avoid embarrassment. Here comes the elevator. (*The elevator door opens.*)
After you. Press the top button, please. Thank you.
(*The elevator doors close, and we start going up.*)
Sometime we must see the other floors.

You would like the hall of fishes, made from the old red Sandstone; and next to it the black polished mezzanine of the carboniferous, the coal story, with giant ferns like forest trees and lung-fishes pioneering on the land.

But now we are passing the second. Here you should see the marble hall of reptiles. It contains a hundred feet of Brontosaurus, with a brain no bigger than a kitten's—the brain in his head, that is. Brontosaurus had a rather larger extra brain in his rump—"to catch a fleeting afterthought."

Third floor; feel the atmosphere changing? Every scene is packed with birds and mammals here: Eocene, Oligocene, Miocene, and Pliocene. Some of the birds had teeth, some of the horses had claws, some of the tigers had tusks, some of the elephants had long shaggy hair. But the galleries of the third floor are making preparation for the fourth floor—the Museum of Man! (*The elevator stops and the doors open.*) (After you!)

What a piece of work is a man! How noble in reason! How infinite in faculty! in form, in moving, how express and admirable! in action, how like an angel! in apprehension, how like a god! the beauty of the world, the paragon of animals! And yet, to me, what is this quintessence of dust?

The Museum of Man. Admission: through pain and travail. Infants in arms only. Official closing time: three score and ten. Some go sooner. Others, by special permission, linger after hours a little while.

The Museum of Man. Everything you find here is characteristic of the societies of Man. Black, brown, yellow or pink; tall or short; smooth or hairy—Man is one single animal, with one blood and one nature. All the exhibits, laid out to the life in all their dazzling diversity, show us, nevertheless, the forces that move all men, in spite of differences. They are the strings that pull all cultures, the universal axioms that regulate us two-legged animals without feathers.

In this Museum of Man, there is no place for Orthodoxy, which is my doxy, or Heterodoxy, which is the other fellow's doxy. All are alike here; for all alike are governed by these same overriding postulates that together make Society.

Of which the first, undoubtedly, is that a man has to be born. And before that can happen, there are universal preliminaries—which is, no doubt, why this first gallery has inscribed above its door "Bees," and "Flowers," and "Marriage Bells." Every society must procreate children—or else of course it must soon disappear. Some societies are more anxious to have children than others; look over here, among the palm trees. Samoa, in the south seas, where the ideal for a girl is: before marriage, as many lovers as possible; after marriage, as many children as possible.

But over here a long row of children are shown being put to death—usually exposed on hillsides, and usually girls. This is the tally of those societies that do not want girl children, and do all they can to discourage their arrival and hasten their departure.

Procreation then is universal and so is birth. Man enters the world as one of the most helpless of animals.

And, after birth, man must eat. He must dig his grave with his teeth as soon as he has any teeth, and before that he must dig his grave with his gums; for if he stops eating, he will certainly die. Along this wall we have specimens of man's food laid out. Almost every living thing is eaten somewhere by man. Let us strike off a sample menu.

Soup from China, made from the nest of a small bird that mixes little bits of fish with its saliva and lets it harden into a basin. Bird's Nest Soup.

Entree from the Eskimos. Seal blubber, the skin of the white whale (as full of vitamin C as orange juice), and the vegetable contents of diving birds' stomachs.

Main course. Take a medium-sized sea creature, closely related to the spiders, boil it alive, and serve its muscles with the fermented milk of the cow. Lobster Thermidor.

Vegetables. From North America, fiddleheads—the tips of growing ferns. And also the lumps on the roots of a plant of the deadly-nightshade family that comes from the high Andes—potatoes.

Savory. Coagulated blood mixed with lumps of fat—the black pudding of northern England. Or fried witchetty grubs from the Australian desert.

Dessert. A cake made from ground-up grass seeds (wheat flour) plus the secretion from the insides of small flying insects (honey).

Fruit. Bananas, the staple food of much of Africa. The thickened and swollen stem of a relative of Spanish moss—the pineapple. And the dried flower cluster of a desert tree—the fig.

Nuts. All sizes, from poppy seed to the cocoanut.

Beverage. Something fermented—grapes or tree sap. Something distilled—barley or potatoes. Something stewed out of a plant—tea or coffee.

> Nothing to eat but food
> Nothing to do but work
> Nothing to wear but clothes
> To keep one from going nude.

After food, shelter. Man comes into the world bare naked. He needs clothes for comfort as well as modesty—from the warm fur parkas of the Eskimo to the ceremonial scars of the Australian bushman. In these racks are the infinite variety of the costumes of man. Look at that—a cloak of brilliantly colored feathers—from Peru.

But here are other human shelters: houses and huts, shacks and palaces. Look at those houses on stilts that seem to have stalked into the edge of the lake like herons. They belong to the Manus, a tribe that lives in Melanesia, near the coast of New Guinea. And over here, like luminous mushrooms, are the igloos of the Eskimos at night.

> Mid pleasures and palaces, though
> we may roam,
> Be it ever so humble, there's no
> place like home.

Just as all men need food, all men need shelter. Man is a mighty fine fellow, but he must still pay homage to the universe as a naked, hungry animal—in spite of the fact that he is a tool-making animal, as Benjamin Franklin said.

And here is a great gallery full of them—all the things man makes to help him do things. The plow, the wheel, the lever, the boomerang, the bulldozer, string. Pass on—quick! We freely acknowledge man is a tool-using animal as well, and turn the corner (*pause*) into this somber gallery.

[MUSIC]
(*Tibetan lament for the dead.*)
Hidden music as we cross the threshold. Tibetan lamas chanting the lament for the dead. And a great gallery filled with coffins, mummies, and the infinite ceremonies with which man faces his latter end.

See the darkness there illuminated by the dim flicker of flames as the burning Viking ship sails into the night with the body of the warrior chief on board. Look in this case here, and see the vultures sitting on the rim of the round fat Towers of Silence, waiting for the bodies to be placed on the grid for them to eat; the Towers of Silence belong to the Parsees in India. The Parsees still follow the Magus Zoroaster, and hold that the earth, the water, the air, and especially the fire are

sacred. The Parsee way to eternity lies through a vulture's gizzard—just as ours lies through an embalming room and a seepage-proof coffin.

It has been said men fear death as children fear to go in the dark; as that natural fear in children is increased with tales, so is the other. It is as natural to die as to be born, and to a little infant perhaps the one is as painful as the other.

Enough of this. Man must be mated; he must be born; he must feed; he must shelter; he must die and pay his final debt as an animal. All these things are common to all men and all society.

SOUND
—·—· ——— —— —— ··— —· ·· —·—· ·— — ·· ———
—·

SPEAKER
I beg your pardon?

SOUND
—·—· ——— —— —— ··— —· ·· —·—· ·— — ·· ———
—·

SPEAKER
"Communication"? Is that what the flying dots and dashes say? One rap for no—two raps for yes!

SOUND
(*Rap! Rap!*)
Yes! Communication! Man is a communicating animal. Nigerian talking drums, smoke signals, hieroglyphs, printing, and above all speech—man is the animal with language. Animals can communicate feeling: the wolf that howls on the track of his mate tells us what he is feeling there and then. But he cannot ask her for a date on Saturday next. Language extends a man's personality in both space and time: the past and the future it makes present; and the distant it makes near.

Language is so powerful a servant, indeed, that it may become the master. We begin by speaking as we think, and end by thinking as we speak. Here are the Navaho Indians, of the Arizona desert, whose language in its very form and structure, in its grain, in its patterning, is made by habits of thought—and in turn makes habits of thought quite different from ours.

And here is an exhibit of small children, misbehaving. Even as they correct them, their mothers teach them, through language, attitudes, and ways of thinking. "Be good," says the English speaker. "*Sois sage*," says the French. Be wise: a very different thing. "*Sei artig*," says the German. Get in line: very different again. "*Ble snil*," says the Norwegian. Be friendly.

The very words from the mother's lips turn the child's thoughts into its proper tracks. Be good, in English; but be wise, in French. Get in line, in German; but be friendly, in Scandinavian. As we think, so we speak; but as we speak, so we think. Man is a communicating animal.

And so we find ourselves in here. All these cases are full of groups, some small, some large. The ones down this side are groups that you belong to automatically by birth, perhaps, or age: the family, the nation. On the other side, are the groups that you join for some purpose: churches, political parties, model-railway clubs. Among these, you will notice many with little blinds over the glass cases.

Let's lift one up and peep in privately. See? It's a secret society. This particular one is the Biting Society, a secret society of the Kwakiutl Indians of the Pacific coast of Canada. Next to it is (let's peep again): the Freemasons.

All these are groups; for man feels himself bound to his fellow men in many different ways.

No man is born unto himself alone;
Who lives unto himself, he lives to
    none.

But what is this exhibit doing in the midst of groups? A man alone, a Crow Indian from the plains of North America. And yet, solitary as he is, he is surrounded by his society. He is looking for a vision, so that he may belong to the important group of men who have found their vision. Even the vision itself is apt to be a kind of adoption into a spiritual family—a joining, in other words, of another group. At his most lonely the plains Indian seeking his vision is still bound by the web of groups that all men live in, in which all men express their personalities, and through which all men act on the larger mass of their society.

But if groups are universal, if men universally assemble for different purposes, then it is universally necessary that men have rules to regulate their conduct, one toward another. This library here is the library of the rules of man, which he calls Ethics. Each society has its own book of rules; each society has its own Hoyle. But that they have such things as ethical rules is something they all have in common.

Draw one at random. The Yurok Indians of California. Rule 1: "A good Yurok should always fix his thoughts upon money." That rule sounds familiar. "The good Yurok should always stand up for his rights; if he doesn't do it, no one else will." That also sounds familiar.

What's this text here? "Never tell a man a thing he doesn't want to hear. Never mind if it's a lie. It would be inexcusable and unethical to tell a man something he did not want to hear solely because it was the truth." Whose book of rules is this—high-pressure salesmen? No, the Ba-Ila of Rhodesia, Africa.

Evidently there is some fascination in ethics. Not every society has the same standard of conduct as our own. But because there may be differences, we must not think that there are no ethics at all. For some sort of ethics, the rules by which man lives, is found in all societies.

Just turn into this gallery, whose door is guarded by the ballot box and the whip. Presiding, we see Justice, blindfold with her scales and sword; Rhadamanthus, dipping souls in the burning lake; and here (Oh, the pity of it!) Pharaoh laying his lashes on the toiling slaves. For this is the hall of authority. On one side are powers—the whip, the order, and the stake. On the other side are checks and balances—the vote, habeas corpus, and the indignant uprising of freemen. All constitutions are somewhere between the wall of powers and the wall of limitations. Here, for instance, is Czarist Russia with its label: "This constitution is absolutism moderated by assassination."

Here is the League of the Iroquois, like cloth on the loom. The web is the six tribes: Mohawk, Onondaga, Seneca, Cayuga, Oneida, and Tuscarora; and running across to make the fabric whole is the woof of the eight clans: the Bear, the Wolf, the Snipe, and so forth. Every Iroquois fits into this pattern; every man belongs to both a tribe and a clan. The tribe is the check on the clan, and the clan is the check on the tribe.

The hall of authority with its powers on one side (whips and scorpions) and its checks on the other (laws and ballot boxes) tells us that for men to live together authority must be given; but that good intentions are not enough. Authority must be not only given, but also marked out, also checked.

So saying, we step into the lobby of a theater. From considering the rulers and the ruled, we find ourselves considering status—a man's position in society. Right by the door is a first edition of Joe Miller's Joke Book. "Who was that lady I saw you with last night?" "That was no lady, that was my wife." Here, the difference between the lady and the wife is status.

The Admiral is the ditch-digger's employee. But which has the higher status?

Leaving the lobby, we move into the theater itself and onto the stage. For if status is a man's part in society, he must always act his part; in every society, at every moment, man has a status, and in that status he has a role to play. Out here on the stage, already I can feel my face itching for the grease paint.

Tut, I can counterfeit the deep tragedian,
Speak and look back, and peer on every side,
Tremble and start at wagging of a straw,
Intending deep suspicion.

What an actor! Performing the proper role is something every man does every minute in his life:

All the world's a stage,
And all the men and women merely players:
They have their exits and their entrances;
And one man in his time plays many parts.

Let's get out of here before I get carried away! I don't normally carry on like this. But surroundings exert a potent influence: we play the part our position demands. Our status changes from one situation to another; and our role is the way we play our status.

What's in here? Look at the inscription over the door? "How much is a man's death worth? How much is a man's life worth?"

This is the gallery of values. Here are the things that men have thought it worth dying for, worth living for, worth working for. These are the rewards that every society holds out to symbolize achievement. Here is a case of medals: the Congressional Medal of Honor, the Victoria Cross. Here is a case of diplomas and degrees: Doctor of Philosophy, Certified Master Mariner. Here are certificates of initiation, and privileges: fraternity pins, membership in African secret societies, puberty rites to certify that the boy is a man, the girl a woman.

All these are part of values. And you notice that the gallery of values is circular.

Values run in a circle: respect the values of your society and your society will respect you.

See, in the center, two Greek cities: Sparta and Athens. Two thousand years ago they fought a war of annihilation, one with the other. Sparta had those values of endurance and austerity that we still think of as Spartan. Athens had those values of inquiry and freedom of thought that we still think of as the liberal Greek inheritance. (In both cases only for citizens, of course; slaves did not count.) But in both cases boys were brought up looped in the circle of values that this circular room represents. Certain things are good; the men who have these things are great men; if you want to be a great man, you must learn to have the valuable things great men have. And these are not only virtues, but the things that symbolize the virtues: honors, public awards, and position.

Now we come to the hall of arts, the hall of religions—all these things societies have in common. The hall of education. Ah, but here's the exit. We might as well slip out and get some refreshment. Food and rest are part of our animal inheritance; every society must provide for them, just as it must provide for birth and shelter and death.

And every society, too, must provide a way for men to communicate with one another. Even Trappist monks, vowed to silence, have a language of signs. Every society, too, breaks down into groups—or, if you prefer, is built up from groups. For these are the bricks of society. And every society has its own system of ethics to tell its people what to do. And every society has its own system of authority to try and make sure that the people do it. And every society has levels and attitudes—different kinds of status, each with its appropriate behavior.

Finally, every society has its system of values—the aims and objects of its members, and the things by which the achievement of these aims and objects are symbolized.

The care of man's body, communication, groups, authority, ethics, status, and values—these are the great overriding demands, the *universal imperatives* of Society.

Indeed, these are Society.

14. WAYS OF AMERICANS

Anthropology had its beginning in curiosity. The increasingly detailed reports of travelers and missionaries in the nineteenth century gave rise to speculation about the nature of human differences and the origin of human culture. This speculation has been replaced by increasingly detailed study and the gradual improvement of theoretical formulations. Anthropology has become an implement of social action. As with other sciences, the curiosities of pioneer scholars have been turned to specific usefulness. Modern industrial relations, psychiatry, international relations, and the administration of native peoples have all benefited from the study of culture. Anthropology can today justify its existence in the same way that physics, chemistry, or biology can—they all offer tools for human betterment. These practical considerations are important in the development of a science and afford the basis for the growing support of research in anthropology.

But neither its satisfaction of human curiosity nor its social engineering is the truly important product of anthropology. More significant is the world view it fosters.

Anthropology helps us to understand the community of nations of which our society is a part. The cultures of the primitive people that the anthropologists have studied are perhaps not important in the modern world, for they represent small populations and little power. But the lessons derived from them can be applied to the great cultures as well, and anthropological understanding gives us a means of appreciating our neighbors on the planet. During World War II, detailed studies of Japanese and German culture enabled us to understand the motivations and actions of our enemies. What was important in war is doubly important in peace. Only through an appreciation of the values, the motivations, and the problems of other cultures can we learn to live in harmony with them. Russia, China, and India represent three divergent cultural systems, each with its own values, social organization, attitudes, and ideas. The differences between Americans, Russians, Chinese, and Indians are differences in culture. If a mode of co-existence is to be worked out with them and with the other nations of the modern world, it must be done through the mutual understanding of the cultural system of each.

The second important product of anthropological understanding is the new view it gives of ourselves. Anthropology and sociology have increasingly directed attention to modern America. Detailed studies of American communities and efforts at demonstrating the central tendencies of the American culture have already been made. Ultimately we come to understand the spirit of our own cultural system by means of contrast with other cultures. Through such self-awareness, and through an awareness of the forces that are responsible for our present culture, we learn to re-enforce the important strengths and eliminate the weaknesses in our cultural behavior. The anthropologist has substituted "cultural nature" for the popular conception of "human nature"; and we do know that this cultural nature can be changed. The ultimate value of anthropology is that it enables us to follow the dictum "Know thyself." The value of primitive societies is that they provide a "mirror for man."

The stories in this volume have made only limited and oblique reference to the American culture. Now and again a somewhat more direct glance at our own behavior has been taken, as in "Home, Sweet Home," and less fully in "A Word in Your Ear" and "Desert Soliloquy." But the reader of these plays cannot fail to think how things are similar or different among us. Comparison is implicit in each situation, and through these likenesses and contrasts there may emerge a picture of modern America. This is not the place to present a detailed analysis of the American cultural scene. But perhaps it will be worth while to draw attention to a few of the dominant motifs, as they emerge from reflection on each of the several stories presented in this series.

"Stand-in for a Murderer" raises the question: What groups would Americans generally be willing to die for? The nation itself, of course. Beyond that Americans would die only for groups of their own choosing—their own family, or perhaps certain buddies who command their complete loyalty. This is significant, for Americans cherish having full freedom of individual choice in their emotional ties and not permitting outside forces to determine these. Friends, neighbors, and, above all, marriage partners are usually chosen by the individual without duress. This is one clue to the character of the American culture.

The English language places great emphasis upon the noun, or the agent—just as in our culture we tend to see some person or thing as responsible for all acts. In our religion we speak of the "will of God" and also of men as having "free will." In our very language we have acquired the strong idea of man as a doer, and this has given support to our creative spirit, on the assumption that we can accomplish almost anything.

This view of man as the doer has in turn given support to the unique creativity of Western man, and especially to Americans, who pride themselves on their technological accomplishments. It is undoubtedly the importance we give to inventiveness that causes us to admire the Eskimo beyond all other primitive peoples. The engineer and the inventor are heroes among us. No other nation of comparable wealth so much admires work with the hands—witness our hobbies and the present fad for home workshops. The "hot rod," rather than the violin or the love sonnet, is the symbol of American youth.

This practical spirit appears in our educational system, which increasingly is concerned with the development of technical proficiency; the humanities are giving way before the sciences and the professional schools. Teaching is more often viewed as the transmission of techniques than as the inculcation of values; learning becomes an instrument. Even anthropology frequently rests its ultimate justification in such practical uses.

"When Greek Meets Greek" compares two sets of values, both of which have had an influence in modern America. The asceticism of Sparta is extreme; and yet the puritanical code of our New England forefathers was not so very different. The intellectualism of Athens seems a little precious; yet we too take pride in our intellectual and esthetic achievements.

In the American culture, values are symbolized by luxuries—the house, the car, fine clothes, the modern kitchen, upholstered furniture. These serve our comforts and needs, but they serve as well to symbolize the dominant values of modern America—values such as hard work, achievement, personal accomplishment, and the ability to reap monetary rewards.

Observers have said we are a nation of joiners, and studies indicate that no other culture has produced so many groups for so many specific purposes. At least one reason for this is that Americans are not placed in many groups by birth. Our affiliations are mostly self-made, by personal choice and predilection, according to ends we consider desirable. Lacking in culturally established affiliation, we form associations for everything from stamp-collecting to president-making, and we use these groups both for personal satisfactions and for the accomplishment of social purposes. Individual choice, freedom of action, and practical usefulness all characterize this aspect—like other aspects—of our culture.

Even the family falls into this category. Our family system de-emphasizes family ties. New and separate families are created with each marriage. The broader family tends to serve only such ceremonial occasions as Christmas and Thanksgiving. Our strongest family ties are with the spouse we have chosen and the children that we choose to have—for even birth has become an act of personal will on the part of the parents.

Our attitudes toward authority are ambivalent. We not only cherish our freedoms from restraint but also pass myriads of laws to apply specific restraints to specific situations. We decry authoritarianism but resent the non-conformist. Ours has been one of the most stable governmental systems in the modern world, but it is based upon the balance of powers—on checks and balances. So, too, we do not like the employer who is too bossy or the father who is too strict. Conformity is important; but it must lie in the will to conform rather than in the command.

Our American culture is built upon mobility. We are a people on the move, and have been since the first colonization of our shores. This mobility is not only geographical but also social. This means that status in our society is fluid—that a person not only can but should change his status if possible. Though we have no sharp class or status system, we are anxious about status in general. Indeed our very mobility tends to make us conscious of our status, even while it tends to undermine the clear definition of the proper role that a person of any particular status is expected to play.

In modern societies there are two worlds of art: the art of the artist and the art of popular taste. The anthropologists are more apt to be interested in the latter, for popular art tells us more about the people as a whole. The art of the artist emphasizes newness of technique and style and individuality of creation. And in these qualities it shows itself also a product of our dominant cultural motifs. The popular art of the movies, of calendars, and of the "hit parade" emphasize minor variation within great uniformity of style and technique. This art tends to be sentimental and to idealize the world. It deals with reality, but it does not treat realistically the conflicts of emotions or human motivations. American popular art appears to supply an escape from reality.

Religion in America is a matter of personal choice—a fact in itself indicative of our culture. But the different religions share many common elements, and in particular they emphasize the same kinds of virtue. Indeed, the very fact that religion makes explicit reference to moral conduct and gives supernatural sanction to behavior is a part of this unity. And each of the major philosophies emphasizes the dualism between good and evil and places the responsibility for good conduct upon the individual himself. From the anthropological point of view, these unities of religious attitude mark them off as alike—though to the members of each religion the unity may be lost in view of the detailed differences.

Such remarks can supply only a few elements in the American culture as seen by one observer of a vast and complex subject. We have purposely followed the order of scripts to suggest the kind of things that can be said about the American culture. Though America is a large area, though many streams of cultural influence have converged upon it, though it has regional variations and differences in social class, and though it is rapidly changing— even so, certain dominant unities do appear.

Some of these unities are the very product of differences and change. A certain unity emerges out of the fact of uncertainty, such as the strong sentiment in favor of progress and the feeling of need for conformity. The feeling for the importance of money as a basis for social position, for example, would appear to be the product of the absence of established and rigid class lines. The very strength of nationalism is in part a denial of the Old World heritage—loyalties from which millions of second-generation Americans have rebelled.

Of course, no statement can be made about America to which exceptions cannot be found. What applies to New York City is not likely to be equally appropriate to a Mississippi village. What applies to a penthouse is not likely to have the same force in a slum flat.

Perhaps it is possible to suggest a few motifs that run through the American culture. Certainly one is a belief in progress—that the future is better than the past, and that human beings are continually on the road toward improvement. This feeling is held for mankind in general, for America as a nation, and for each person in America. It is our duty—so we see it—to endeavor to improve ourselves. (Self-help books are among the most popular of our best-sellers.) Because the environment tends to give freedom of opportunity to all, failure is viewed as a fault and success as a virtue. For in our religion, in our language, and in our everyday thinking the person is viewed as the agent of action, and whatever happens is viewed as an accomplishment or as a failure of some individual or some group. We see this repeatedly in popular discussions of national life that focus attention upon the persons responsible—"Wall Street," union bosses, Hitler, Stalin—rather than upon situations. We treasure our freedom from restraints, and do not like to be tied to any one religion, community, or family—though we have strong loyalties to those we have chosen. Given this freedom to act, we "naturally" have only ourselves to blame for what we are.

Neither the history nor the culture of the other great nations of the world supports this system of ideas. The Chinese farmer, long tied to the land, lives within the narrow confines of his peasant community, surrounded by a network of family ties that bind him closely in every social interaction. He ekes out a difficult livelihood by the careful fulfillment of traditional techniques. He can hardly be expected to see the world in terms of his own mastery and his own personal action. In India, extreme poverty and the caste system are more apt to support a religious philosophy that elevates inner tranquillity to a prominent place. Russia, England, and France each has been subjected to historic and economic forces that give its national character distinctive traits.

Just as it is useful to know the attitudes and motives of another person when you have relations with him, so too it is important to understand the cultural attitudes and motives of those other great nations with which we are inevitably involved in international affairs. The cultural patterns of these other peoples will be expressed in their responses to international situations, and if we are to guide a course that leads to permanent peace, it must be through an understanding of these cultural orientations, and an adjustment of competing national interests.

>>>->>>

But to have sympathy for a foreign culture is not to deny the validity of our own. We must preserve and build upon our own way of life even as we learn to understand other cultural modes. Loyalty and a sense of commitment to the American culture are not impaired by recognizing the propriety of alternate modes; nor is international understanding bettered by a wavering sense of one's own cultural values. The ultimate need, then, is to recognize and to support the positive elements in our own culture while maintaining a sympathy and understanding for those of foreign lands.

APPENDIX

How This Book Came About

How This Book Came About

Many persons have had a hand in *Ways of Mankind*, both as radio drama and as book. The work is so much a product of collaboration that mere acknowledgments seem inadequate, and instead I have tried to show, in the paragraphs that follow, how various persons contributed to its development. Because the collaboration has seemed to many a rather unusual co-operation between the realm of scholarship and the worlds of art and entertainment, I have also tried to show how the scripts were brought into being.

Origin

The project began in a conference in July of 1950 at the University of Illinois. The National Association of Educational Broadcasters brought scholars from various fields together with persons devoted to improving the quality of educational radio in the United States. Anthropology was represented at this conference by Professor Robert Redfield, chairman of the Department of Anthropology of the University of Chicago. His day-long discussion of the possibilities of anthropology led to the inclusion of the subject by the NAEB when it subsequently sought funds for actual programming.

A committee of the NAEB undertook to explore the possibilities for financial support in developing educational radio. The members of this committee were George E. Probst, chairman (director of radio at the University of Chicago); Richard Hull (director of WOI–TV at Iowa State College, Ames); Harold B. McCarty (director of WHA at the University of Wisconsin, Madison);

Seymour Siegel (director of WNYC, New York City, and at that time president of the NAEB); and Parker Wheatley (director of WGBH–FM and WGBH–TV, Boston).

The committee held conferences with C. Scott Fletcher, president of the Fund for Adult Education (an independent organization established by the Ford Foundation). The Fund for Adult Education granted $300,000 to the Adult Education Committee of the National Association of Educational Broadcasters for experimentation in four fields, specifically including social anthropology. This committee administered the grant with the assistance of the Lowell Institute of Boston. Ralph Lowell, trustee of the Lowell Institute, provided generous co-operation and efficient handling of the fiscal administration, with the aid of Ruth Perkins, his assistant. William Harley, program manager of the University of Wisconsin radio station, was appointed co-ordinator for the several projects sponsored by the committee.

Meanwhile Professor Redfield had written a memorandum outlining the purpose of the series. He said: "I imagine a radio program in ten or twelve half-hours that would communicate some idea of both the universality of human nature and the variety of the forms which that human nature takes. The program should in effect say: Here we all are; so different, and yet so much the same! On the one hand it should suggest how differently men in separated parts of the world have developed their customs and institutions; on the other, and more important side, the series should show that all men have the same necessities to meet, the same material and spiritual wants to satisfy." Redfield recommended that an anthropologist be hired to take charge of the project, and suggested several names, including mine. When Harley called on me in August of 1951 as a result of Redfield's suggestion, the preparation of radio shows was far from my mind. I had never had any experience in radio nor endeavored to utilize the mass media for the uses of anthropology. The challenge was too great to reject.

The project was offered with what seemed— and very nearly proved to be—an adequate budget. I was hedged by no binding directives, but was rather given a broad mandate to prepare radio programs that would present materials in the field of social anthropology and that would be popular. No rules with respect to time, number of shows, or any other limitations were imposed upon me, and the letter of agreement carefully placed final decisions in my hands rather than in those of the radio personnel or of the committee. The maintenance of final authority in the hands of the scholar as distinct from the professional radio personnel still seems to me a crucial element in planning—though, in fact, the production of the *Ways of Mankind* series never involved any strife between scholarship and the medium of communication.

The NAEB committee strongly urged that I work with radio personnel in Toronto, rather than in Los Angeles where I live. Neil Morrison, the Canadian Broadcasting Corporation's Supervisor of Talks and Public Affairs, arranged an all-day conference one Sunday in September 1951. A group of writers, producers, and CBC radio officials— including the four writers whose scripts are represented here—met with Harley and myself. In the course of this stimulating meeting I was first awakened to radio's real potentialities, and immediately arranged to work with these people. When Andrew Allan

(who was at the time producing radio shows for the British Broadcasting Corporation) upon his return to Canada accepted the invitation to serve as producer, I agreed to production in Toronto. What was surprising was that this group agreed to work with such a newcomer and outsider as myself.

An office was established at the University of California, Los Angeles, and I took partial leave from my teaching responsibilities. The regents of the university placed various facilities at my disposal, and my colleagues in the department of anthropology and sociology were helpful in lightening my university burdens and in giving me moral and intellectual support. Ruth Oreck, a graduate of our department, served as my assistant for a year and a half and was of inestimable service.

A conference of anthropological colleagues helped to translate Redfield's broad directives into more specific plans. To this conference came five anthropologists: Ralph Beals and Harry Hoijer (University of California, Los Angeles), Edward P. Spicer (University of Arizona), David G. Mandelbaum (University of California, Berkeley), and E. Adamson Hoebel (University of Utah). Also participating were Walter Kingson, associate professor of Theater Arts at UCLA, and two writers, Millard Kaufman of Los Angeles and Len Peterson. The discussions of this conference led to a memorandum listing many separate program possibilities with detailed suggestions of intellectual content and some plans for presentation. The thirteen shows included in this volume developed out of this memorandum.

A board of anthropological consultants was appointed consisting of Redfield and Beals (already mentioned), Margaret Mead (American Museum of Natural History), Cora Du Bois (Institute of International Education), and A. L. Kroeber (University of California, Berkeley). Though for geographical reasons it was never possible to hold a meeting of this board, they set the intellectual content, reviewed plans, and gave invaluable advice on specific scripts.

The preparation of the programs—a work of close collaboration with the producer, the writers, and other artists—is described below. But I would like to mention here that the quality of the productions comes from the excellent personnel assembled in Toronto, and from the *esprit* that characterizes this group. Andrew Allan, as producer, was central to this *esprit*; but the actors, the sound technicians and engineers, and the assistant producer, Eugene S. Hallman, all gave more than their fair measure. As for my co-authors, the four men who wrote these thirteen scripts, I should like to express my appreciation of their work, and acknowledge my indebtedness to them for many new insights and for the pleasure of working with them.

Through her sound critical judgment and her enthusiastic support, my wife, Gale Goldschmidt, has contributed far more than she realized.

In the preparation of the book itself, I am indebted to Beverly Linnebach, who typed the manuscript, and of course to Arminta Neal, who had the difficult task of capturing in her illustrations both the spirit of the scripts and the quality of the aboriginal cultures. She was aided in preparing these illustrations by Frederick H. Douglas and Willema Cartwright.

Subject Matter

Anthropology is a broad, inclusive science. It involves both biological and social science, and is itself included among the humanities. The present series covers but a portion of the whole field. Some indication should be given here of the basis for selection.

Ways of Mankind deals with the division of anthropology known as *social anthropology*.

We are trying to arrive at generalizations about the nature of human society and the character of culture and its many components, based upon an examination of many different societies. Social anthropology is not concerned with the historical development of social behavior, though it recognizes the obvious fact that all cultures are a product of development through time. Nor is it concerned with the biology of man, though it recognizes that man's biology sets conditions for social life.

Those aspects are included in *other* fields of anthropology. *Physical anthropology* deals with the origin and development of the human species, and the variety of its present-day forms. *Archeology* deals with the origin and history of human cultures as pieced together from the remains of extinct human habitations. *Ethnology* not only describes the varieties of culture and their distribution over the earth but attempts to reconstruct the history and development of culture.

Even within our chosen division, we could not include every major aspect of social anthropology. The ways in which culture changes —by innovation, by borrowing, by the impact of one culture upon another—constitute an important problem which we did not examine. Many studies have been made of the effect of our own culture on primitive ones, usually called *acculturation*. Some evidence regarding the effects of such cultural impact may be seen in the script "Desert Soliloquy."

In recent years anthropologists have been particularly interested in the relation between the individual and his culture. Psychologists have come to recognize, for instance, that different cultures tend to produce different kinds of abnormal behavior, just as they define different kinds of behavior as normal. This subject is new, and its study is fraught with difficulties and theoretical uncertainties. Except in a most general way, such problems were not included.

Social anthropology was selected because of the conviction that it would prove most interesting and most useful to the general public. Professor Redfield's original suggestion was based upon the assumption that the modern world needs to understand human behavior in the way modern social science—particularly social anthropology—has come to understand it.

In preparing the scripts, we tried to emphasize ideas. In each case the script was written to dramatize certain principles rather than to describe a culture or indicate a set of customs. The focus on *idea* rather than on *content* seems to us rather an innovation in educational radio. Our reply to those who ask why we have no script on such-and-such a culture is that no script was done "about a culture"—but rather a culture was selected because, for one reason or another, it was found useful for illustrating the points we wanted to make. Other illustrations, of course, could have been chosen instead.

The Hopi do not have a monopoly on primitive education (see Chapter 4) nor the Yurok on ethics (see Chapter 8). To appreciate the range of solutions for any one problem, many scripts would be necessary. (Indeed, a second series of *Ways of Mankind* scripts has included six separate cultural solutions to the problem of adjudication of disputes.) The examples were chosen through a constellation of many factors, of which the most important were that the specific subject had been adequately studied for the particular culture, and that sufficient general knowledge about the culture was known to enable us to understand the subject in its cultural context. Had we selected other examples, the details and "story line" would have been different, but the basic lesson would have remained the same.

Primitive societies have been rather consistently used for our examples, rather than the major social systems of China, India, or modern America. There are several reasons for this. First, patterns of behavior usually emerge most clearly in the relatively simple and homogeneous societies of the primitive world. Second, the use of little-known cultures avoids preconception and prejudice on the part of the listener. Third, by giving a picture of primitive cultures we help to remove such popular ideas as may still exist that primitiveness means the same as stupidity, wantonness, cruelty, or lack of culture. Finally, by using primitive cultures we could show both the data of anthropology and the usefulness of the scientific understanding of cultures.

On Collaboration

Ways of Mankind has been a collaborative effort. In particular, it has been a collaboration between science and art; and since we feel it has been both successful and pleasant, it seems useful to present our mode of working together.

I should indicate that this process is not entirely easy to describe. For one thing, the important experiences are personal and subjective, and therefore difficult to express. Moreover, the creative process worked out differently in each case. For some subjects the authors had a wide and useful knowledge and could write with very little direction; for others I had to cover each point in detail. Of course all the writers had some acquaintance with anthropology and had those insights into human behavior that result from long experience with the writer's craft.

It was my task to select the subject and indicate what ideas were to be communicated. Often we had long discussions; at other times the subject might be quite familiar to the writer. We talked over specific materials that might illustrate points to be emphasized. Together we worked out a general format—occasionally after one or two false starts. Once the message, the format, and the selected bibliography had been determined, the writer took over. After the script was written, I edited and corrected it for details of interpretation. Many scripts stand now substantially unchanged from the first version submitted. When necessary, the scripts were reviewed by colleagues who have special knowledge of either the particular culture or the particular subject (as indicated below in the Notes on Production and Sources).

The producer was not usually involved with the story until it was finished, though he sometimes sat in on our preliminary story conferences. Allan and I agreed at the outset that no script would be produced unless it was acceptable to both of us, but I do not remember that we disagreed on the acceptability of a single script—though perhaps we differed considerably in our degree of enthusiasm. Once a script was accepted, full responsibility was Allan's. Indeed, though I was always present during production, my role was only to give minor suggestions and assure proper interpretations. Occasionally Allan would suggest that I explain some of the intellectual background or talk about the spirit of the culture, to help the actors in their interpretations.

Only in cutting the scripts was my role at all crucial. A radio show must, of course, be produced exactly to time, and there is almost always a little cutting to get the show to the correct length. Since both the intellectual and the dramatic values had to be preserved, it was necessary that Allan and I collaborate in this delicate (and often strangely creative) art of deletion. Theoretically I was to protect the anthropological interests and Allan the dramatic, but I believe we reversed our roles as often as not.

The commentaries at the close of the productions (which are deleted from the present versions of the scripts) were my own. I was much aided in preparing them by the writers and by Eugene S. Hallman, who was assistant producer for the series as well as author of one script. The idea for having such commentaries, on the other hand, emanated from the writers.

Some lessons emerged from our co-operation that are perhaps worth recording. The most important one is the fact that such collaboration can work, and that in the process the scholar learns much from the writer. This point seems worthy of emphasis since there is so much mutual disparagement between the scholar and the popular writer.

Successful co-operation between the scientist and the creative artist requires a deep and abiding respect by each for the other—both for the other's area of interest and for the specific competence of the other as individual practitioner. It was only after each was fully aware that the other had a crucial role to perform, and that he would perform it well, that production could be carried out. For in the process it was frequently necessary for one to give in to the requirements of the other, a process that is not always easy in creative activity. But this giving in could not be the abandonment of judgment, for each had on occasion to stand firm on the points that he recognized as essential to the undertaking. I believe the hardest chore I had to perform was the rejection of the first script I received, because it didn't make the points I needed. It would be fatuous to suggest that conflict of interest never arose; yet the conflict could always be built upon for achieving our mutual ends.

This mutual respect involved a respect for the aims of each. The final purpose of the shows was, of course, to communicate scientific knowledge to the general public. The intellectual content had to be respected at all costs. Content without communication was equally useless: we were not addressing anthropological colleagues. Appealing formats, the needs of the story line, forms of expression —all had to be kept in mind. I would conclude from our experience that the two needs are by no means in conflict, but rather that each is well served by the other. I feel that sometimes I improved the theatrical quality by eliminating false emphases—and I am certain that the writers frequently improved the more academic aspects by their superior use of language.

We avoided unnecessary precommitments as to format. Except that each show was to fit into the half-hour period, there were no established rules. For continuity, a discussion by myself closed each script. But these discussions varied from approximately thirty seconds to three minutes, and in one case were inserted through the script as running commentary. Other than that, the rule for format was as follows: the message determines the content and the content determines the format. The form the script took rested ultimately on the needs of the particular points that were to be made.

Let me offer an example. We wanted to communicate the idea of culture—a broad and abstract idea. The idea of culture had to be central to our story, but it had to be given specific content in terms of a particular culture. Three plans suggested themselves. The first was to take two infants born at the same time in different places and show how they became different adults as a result of divergent cultural conditioning. But this would have been too involved for the presentation of such a broad concept. (The idea was later used for the more specific subject of values.) The second was to take an anthropologist into the field and discover with him a particular culture. We found the technical apparatus of this approach intruding itself on the concept, diverting interest from the primary point to secondary ones. We finally decided that the best way to communicate the idea was to

examine a piece of behavior that is inexplicable when taken out of cultural context but clear and unequivocal within it. But what action? Theoretically, any action would do; but in fact there were certain dramatic requirements. It had to be an important and an arresting action. It should involve the whole gamut of cultural behavior, while itself remaining a simple and direct piece of behavior. It had to be exotic for our purposes, but should be neither quaint nor offensive to our own culturally established sensibilities. These considerations all suggested the Tlingit mode of retribution, a piece of ethnological data that had long interested me. This decision then led to the content, for the important elements of cultural context were dictated by the available data on Tlingit culture. Yet even here, we had further concern. For it was necessary to have the startling act performed at the outset, so that the listener would be less concerned with the outcome of the story than with the cultural causes that made the act explicable. In order to point up the concept of culture as the central dramatic element, a running commentary was introduced in this particular script. Thus the concept of culture took the center of the stage, rather than either Datgas' death or the specific character of Tlingit culture.

It was Allan who first formulated what seems to me another of our most important generalizations—that the appeal in the story should always lie in the essential drama of the intellectual point itself, that the interest and drama should never be mere sugar-coating for an intellectual pill difficult to swallow. The above example suggests how this point was implemented. It is a tribute to the ability of the writers that this difficult rule was never abrogated.

An anthropological colleague first warned of the danger of falling prey to the "Oh, how quaint" school of anthropology—the idea that strange cultures are made up of amusing customs. Modern anthropology does not view other cultures as quaint, however interesting they may be. To avoid this pitfall, two rules were developed: either the behavior of the people in distant cultures should be sufficiently developed to make clear their motivation, explicable in terms of their own cultural context; or the odd custom should be juxtaposed to a counterpart within the realm of our own cultural experience. Part of this rule is a rule of all literature, that the individual characters should always be given depth. No people are all good or all bad. The radio play is not a shadow play, but the presentation of real people in real—though culturally determined—conflict.

Music

Music played an important part which the printed form cannot adequately communicate. Radio is a medium using only the sense of sound. Music communicates mood and feeling and gives the purely auditory performance an extra dimension.

The music was composed and conducted by Lucio Agostini, long a close associate of the producer, Andrew Allan. Sometimes recordings of native music were used; but the composer did not himself try to reproduce native music. Where possible, he listened to native music, so that some of the spirit of their idiom could be captured. Music was used to communicate idea. In "When Greek Meets Greek," the contrast in values was indicated by the two musical themes—strength and stridency for Sparta, delicacy and sweetness for Athens. For "Stand-in for a Murderer," the music was at once dramatic and foreboding; for "Desert Soliloquy" it suggested both the desert atmosphere and a contemplative mood. For scripts in essay form—such as "A Word in Your Ear" and "But I Know What I Like"—the music served immediate cues and pointed up the discussion.

Absence of sound can also have its impact. In "The Case of the Sea-Lion Flippers," both the nature of the story and the quality of the culture suggested that music would be inappropriate; hence we used none.

Music served its most important function in "But I Know What I Like," where music was the direct subject of the message. The musical accompaniment to Dryden's "Song for Saint Cecilia's Day" is perhaps the most satisfactory part of the whole series, from the standpoint of sheer listening pleasure.

Notes on Production and Sources

The scripts here presented are based upon the ideas of anthropologists as well as the researches and writings of numerous scholars. Because readers may wish to examine further both the specific materials and the general ideas, and because proper credits are traditional both in scholarship and the theater, we offer a few notes on each play.

There are few modern works that summarize anthropology for the interested layman, though there are numerous good textbooks, and quite a few that treat with some special aspect of anthropology and sociology. But the popular general work is rare.

The best-known popular book is *Patterns of Culture*, by Ruth Benedict, reprinted in a paper-back edition. Originally written as a theoretical treatise, it is largely responsible for present-day ideas about culture as a patterned whole. It treats three cultures and discusses the character of cultural patterning. *Mirror for Man*, by Clyde Kluckhohn, makes a frank effort at popular but accurate presentation. *The Study of Man*, by Ralph Linton (from which we quoted at length earlier in this volume), is a textbook, and not so easily read as the others, but it is one of the more enduring statements about the nature of culture and society. Its point of view is closely reflected in the *Ways of Mankind* scripts.

In addition, more specialized works have found some public interest. Most popular are the works of Margaret Mead. Her studies of native culture—with particular reference to the manner in which the child is brought to live according to his own culture—have been reprinted in paper editions.

"Stand-in for a Murder," by Len Peterson

The concept of culture is a broad one, not easy to define, let alone to dramatize. We developed the idea of presenting an incomprehensible act at the outset and then letting its "rationality" in terms of cultural context emerge.

The legal point in the story is based upon the analysis of Tlingit law by Kalervo Oberg in a paper entitled "Crime and Punishment in Tlingit Society" (*American Anthropologist*, Vol. 36, 1934). The ethnographic detail was derived largely from the works of John R. Swanton, especially the volume entitled *Tlingit* (Bulletin of the Bureau of American Ethnology, Vol. 40, 1911) and *Tlingit Myths and Texts* (Vol. 39 of the same series).

Agostini's music for this script is martial and exciting. Drum rhythms were based upon some recorded music obtained from the Kwakiutl Indians (near neighbors of the Tlingit) and loaned by Ida Halpern of the University of British Columbia. The music does not make any pretense at being native, but rather sets the mood for the action.

The general concept of culture is best described and developed in the two general works by Ruth Benedict and Clyde Kluckhohn. Recently a compendium discussing the various meanings that the word has had among scholars was prepared by A. L. Kroeber and Clyde Kluckhohn in a monograph called *Culture, a Critical Review of Concepts and Definitions* (Papers of the Peabody Museum of American Archeology and Ethnology, Harvard University, Vol. 47).

"A Word in Your Ear," by Lister Sinclair

The use of two narrators to emphasize the contrast between that which seems natural to us and that which seems strange was used in three of our scripts. It was first developed by Sinclair for this one. It not only gives variety and movement, but also succeeds in capturing the element of contrast that we wanted to emphasize.

The best popular works on language as a cultural phenomenon are *The Gift of Tongues*, by Margaret Schlauch, and *Leave Your Language Alone*, by Robert A. Hall, Jr. Probably the best general work in the field of linguistics is *Language*, by Edward Sapir. A still more technical discussion of the relation between language and human thought is to be found in a series of essays entitled *Four Articles on Metalinguistics*, by Benjamin Lee Whorf; these articles, which came originally from technical journals, were reprinted by the Foreign Service Institute of the Department of State. The relation of the Navaho language to its culture is discussed by Clyde Kluckhohn and Dorothea Leighton in *The Navaho*. Harry Hoijer acted as special consultant for the script, helping to outline the materials in advance as well as checking its final form. Abraham Halpern, anthropologist with the Rand Corporation, also served as consultant for this program.

The music cues were composed by Agostini to carry the humor and feeling of the context. The single exception is the Navaho Night Way Chant, which was taken from the Ethnic Folk Library recordings.

The Navaho editorial was adapted from one that appeared in English in Adahooni-łigii, a Navaho-language monthly published at Window Rock, Arizona. The Navaho reading in the production was rendered by Ralph Roanhorse, a Navaho Indian, in the studios of the University of California, Los Angeles.

The Spanish proverb (p. 23) and the Persian proverb (p. 23) are from Brewer's *Readers Handbook*. The Lord's Prayers were taken from the Wicliff and the Anglo-Saxon Bibles, respectively. The examples of sexual difference in language, and words referring to the Siamese king, are from *The Golden Bough*, by Sir James Frazer. Dorothy Lee has studied elements of the Trobrian language, based on the extensive work of Bronislaw Malinowski among that people.

"Survival," by Eugene S. Hallman

We were more interested here in showing the nature of technological accomplishment than in describing a particular technology. The contrast between the Eskimo, Arvik, and an American engineer and doctor gave us a good opportunity to show how knowledge is universally used and built upon. We emphasized the intellectual principles rather than the specific technical devices. We wanted to avoid making men seem entirely rational; and therefore we included references to magic. Music seemed singularly out of place in the Arctic wastes, and so none was used. But the sound engineer was kept busy.

The bibliography on the Eskimo is massive. Perhaps the best works for this general field are: Franz Boas, *The Central Eskimo* (Vol. 6 of the Annual Reports of the Bureau of American Ethnology, 1888) and *The Eskimo of Baffinland and Hudson Bay* (Bulletin of the American Museum of Natural History, Vol. 15, 1901–1907); W. Thalbitzer, *The Ammassalik Eskimo;* Knute Rasmussen, *The People of the Polar North;* and Peter Freuchen, *Arctic Adventure* (New York, 1935).

Eugene S. Hallman was himself a meteorologist in the Arctic during World War II. He was also given personal advice regarding details by Dr. Edmund S. Carpenter, anthropologist at the University of Toronto and a student of Eskimo culture.

"Desert Soliloquy," by Len Peterson

Probably no other single tribe has been so much studied as the Hopi Indians. Because the Pueblo Indians (of which the Hopi are one variety) were used by Ruth Benedict in her *Patterns of Culture*, special attention has been given to the educational processes among these peoples. Indeed, one of the difficulties in preparing this script lay, not in inadequate information, but rather in disagreement among the specialists regarding details. We have tried to stay within the area of general agreement. The more important sources from our point of view were *The Hopi Way*, by Laura Thompson and Alice Joseph; *Old Oraibi, a Study of Hopi Indians of the Third Mesa*, by Mischa Titiev (Peabody Museum Papers); and *The Hopi Child*, by Wayne Dennis (monograph of the Virginia Institute for Research in Social Science).

The flashback technique was almost inevitable in this script form. The actor who played the part of Naquima used a slight accent—more Spanish than Hopi, I fear—to help set mood and place, but the other actors did not. The music by Agostini was not based upon Hopi music, but it gave the desert atmosphere and the feeling of reminiscence.

"When Greek Meets Greek," by Lister Sinclair

The essential problem in presenting the concept of values was to show two cultures that differed in values but were the same in general cultural conditions. For dramatic unity, they should be naturally in contact. It was also imperative that neither culture be too closely identified with ourselves, for we wanted each value system to be appreciated in its own right and not be subject to the natural prejudice that members of a particular culture would bring to bear. These criteria led to the elimination of many possible peoples, and ultimately suggested the Greeks, to whom we owe so much, yet who are so distant. We

are more Athenian than Spartan in modern America, and some profess to see an analogy between the conflict of these two cultures and modern international affairs. We ourselves were not concerned with this analogy, however accurate it might be; rather, we wished to present each set of values as seen by the members of each culture.

The modern world knows much more about Athens than Sparta. One can get a feeling of the contrast between the two cultures by reading the accounts of Lycurgus and Pericles in *Plutarch's Lives*. Thucydides also gives us a good picture of Greek culture. A general account of Greece is found in Ralph Turner's *The Great Traditions*, while Werner Jaeger's *Paideia: The Ideals of Greek Culture* gives a highly technical presentation of the Greek value systems.

The movement back and forth between Athens and Sparta dramatizes the contrast, while the growing-up process dramatizes the manner in which a youth is "looped within the circle of his culture." The music carried the contrast in two themes: delicate and pretty for Athens, strong and strident for Sparta. While the Athenian scenes sometimes were spoken to the accompaniment of music, the Spartan scenes never were—for it would have offended spartanism to accompany words with music.

"You Are Not Alone," by George Salverson

To show the universality of groups, it was important to dissociate ourselves from any single culture: hence our disembodied travelers. The bus trip gives both unity and familiarity to the scene, and the light handling of the subject serves both to offer a valuable contrast to the rather academic character of the message and to emphasize the everyday quality of the facts in the case. Some of the scenes were adapted directly from sociological and anthropological studies: the "juke joint" and the references to bowling came from William Foote Whyte's *Street Corner Society*, a study of an Italian slum community; the Tlingit scene from the same sources as the "Stand-in for a Murderer" script; and the battle scene from Samuel L. A. Marshall's *Men Against Fire* (Infantry Journal, 1947). A technical analysis of the nature and function of groups in social life has been written by George Homans in *The Human Group*.

"Home, Sweet Home," by Len Peterson

Though we often think of our family system as "natural," it really represents an extreme type, in that it focuses on the married couple and isolates them from the broader bonds of family relationships. The Chinese family offers a good contrast, the more dramatic because we have all had the Chinese family idealized for us. The contrast shows the variety of problems that face people in their more intimate social relationships. You may wonder why we had a Chinese-American rather than a Euro-American visit China. It was done to avoid the language barrier. For it is dramatically correct to show people who speak a foreign language—Tlingit Indians, say, or Greeks—speaking to each other in good English; but it is not correct to have people of two different languages speak to each other, unless we can be reasonably sure that they would know one another's language. This problem faced us in several scripts.

Chinese village life has been reported by a number of anthropologists, and the Chinese part of the script was adapted from *Taitou, a Chinese Village*, by Martin Yang, and from *Under the Ancestor's Shadow*, by Francis Hsu. These two books, both written by anthropologists on the basis of first-hand investigation by Chinese scholars of their native land, give an excellent picture of Chinese peasant life. The material on the American culture did not require the examination of published

material, but there are good discussions from the modern anthropological viewpoint in essays by Talcott Parsons and Ruth Benedict published in *The Family in Modern Society* (edited by Ruth Anshen). Margaret Mead has written two books dealing in large part with modern America: *And Keep Your Powder Dry* and *Male and Female*. These offer a provocative discussion of American family patterns.

Francis Hsu was consultant for the script. The characters gave the slightest hint of Chinese voice quality, rather than accent, and the music was based upon Chinese themes, though composed by Agostini and played on instruments of European type.

"The Case of the Sea-Lion Flippers," by Lister Sinclair

Ethics underlies all our behavior but comes to the surface only when disputes and conflicts arise. Hence, it was natural for us to find a legal case to present ethical problems. Our choice of the Yurok derived from the fact that I had worked with this culture, and was aware both of the interesting ethical system of the Yurok and of the nice illustration provided by this particular case reported in *Yurok Narratives*, by Robert Spott and A. L. Kroeber (University of California Publications in American Archaeology and Ethnology, Vol. 35).

In addition to this monograph, details on the culture of the Yurok and their neighbors are presented in A. L. Kroeber's *Handbook of the Indians of California* (Bulletin 78, Bureau of American Ethnology); in Pliny E. Goddard's *Hupa Life and Culture;* and in numerous other special articles and monographs. An essay by myself, "Ethics and the Structure of Society" (*American Anthropologist*, Vol. 53), deals, as the title implies, with some of the problems presented in the script.

The production is straightforward and requires relatively little annotation. Music was not used because the aridity of Yurok culture seemed to call for a relatively dry presentation. The idiom used by the narrators is that found in Yurok stories and carries the flavor of their expression. The weeping done by Layek's sister is a kind of keening, a ceremonialized weeping. The sweathouse is a structure resembling a storm cellar—a roofed-over pit—which is the living quarters of the men. The family life takes place in a larger house. The dentalia are tooth-shaped sea-snail shells imported from the coast of Oregon and used as money.

There are no general works on comparative ethics involving primitive people. Perhaps the nearest approach is *Primitive Man As Philosopher*, by Paul Radin.

"*Legend of the Long House*," by Lister Sinclair

No anthropologist can fail to think of the Iroquois when he discusses the political machinery among primitive peoples, because of the dramatic quality of their famous League. Furthermore, they present an analogy to modern problems as formulated in the United Nations, since the Iroquois League was an instrumentality of government and authority organized on the principle of protecting the sovereignty of the individual tribes. The legend form was dictated by the needs of presenting the concepts, and allowing for appropriate generalization. It freed the author from the needs of realism, which would have impaired communication of the idea. At the same time, the facts of ethnography and especially of social and political organization are correct in so far as we know them. Of course, had we been more concerned with the Iroquois than with the ideas, we would not have used this form.

The best general account of the Iroquois is still Lewis Henry Morgan's *League of the Ho-de-no-sau-nee or Iroquois* (two volumes, 1901). There are innumerable special references on the Iroquois.

"*All the World's a Stage*," by Lister Sinclair

In presenting the concept of status and role, we wanted to get away from particular cultures and move about freely from one place to another. We therefore re-introduced our two narrators, Here and There, to give examples from our own culture, as well as from those cultures on which anthropologists have reported.

The title comes from Shakespeare's "As You Like It." Winston Churchill explained the situation regarding Darlan (p. 142) in *Their Finest Hour* (*The Second World War*, Vol. 2), p. 229. The scene regarding Paul is directly quoted from Acts 22: 24–29. The Hindu example is from Doss, *The Essential Unity of All Religions*. The Chinese poetry is by Fu Hsüan. Both the West African and the Irish examples of kingship are reported by Frazer in *The Golden Bough*.

"*But I Know What I Like*," by Lister Sinclair

In this script the emphasis was upon the variety of art forms and the relation of art to social life and culture. We were not so much concerned with esthetics or musical taste. We had, of course, to emphasize the auditory arts—poetry and especially music. We found it advantageous to use our two narrators to present the variation in art forms.

I know of no comparative study of the relationship between art and social form broadly based on anthropological literature. There are a number of works dealing with primitive plastic art, such as Leonhard Adam's *Primitive Art* (Penguin Books). The study of primitive music has not as yet attracted many specialists, nor do I know of any general works to which reference can be made. There are, however, record albums of primitive and folk music.

For our script, the recording of a Greek shepherd playing an ancient clarinet-like pipe was taken from Ethnic Folkways Library. So, too, were the Arabian song, the Tahiti song, and the Navaho squaw dance. The Ethnic Folkways Library is perhaps the most comprehensive effort to make commercially available the music of all exotic lands. The royal Watusi drums were recorded by the Denis Roosevelt expedition and reproduced by Commodore Records, while the classical music of China came from Musicraft. The Library of Congress has a large collection of recorded primitive and folk music from American Indians and the peoples of American territories and possessions.

All of the other musical cues were composed by Agostini. Agostini's accompaniments for the two selections from Dryden, using the instruments that Dryden mentioned, render this portion of the program a particularly exciting experience. For the final selection, he adapted part of Händel's "Hallelujah" chorus, which brought the program to a fitting and exciting climax.

Specific reference to materials quoted are: John Evelyn's *Diary;* Brillat-Savarin's *The Anatomy of Taste;* Keats's "Ode on a Grecian Urn"; Robert Burns's "Auld Lang Syne"; the *Dialogues* of Confucius; Plato; and John Dryden's "Ode on St. Cecilia's Day."

"Sticks and Stones," by Len Peterson

We decided to illustrate religion with an extremely primitive culture for two reasons. First, we wanted to avoid those unwitting sacrileges and theological controversies which might have been involved in presenting briefly and popularly a major religion with many adherents. More important, by showing the theological involvement of an extremely primitive people, we would make it clear that religion is not the special sphere of literate man, but that the religious systems of primitive peoples are extremely complex and involved.

The Arunta were selected because they filled the criterion of primitiveness better, perhaps, than any other people in the world, and because they have been throughly studied. Sir Baldwin Spencer and F. J. Gillen have written a number of books on Australian Aborigines; the material for this script was taken from *The Arunta*. These men first visited the Arunta when the culture was still unaffected by Western civilization, and returned after the people had become detribalized. Thus they not only saw the activities of Arunta religious life, but also could ask the Arunta about them, after they had lost some of their sacredness.

The production was straightforward. An "anthropologist" (in this instance played by an actor) was narrator, to allow for explanation and freedom of action.

The music for this show did not actually come from the Arunta, whose culture was destroyed before means of field recording had been adequately developed. It was obtained from similar groups living to the northwest of the Arunta by Professor A. P. Elkin of the University of Sydney expedition. The "instrumentation" is extremely primitive: largely sticks and a "bull-roarer," a board shaped much like the blade of an airplane propellor and whirled about the head on a string.

"Museum of Man," by Lister Sinclair

The form of dramatic monologue was used because we wanted to present necessary social features and avoid a focus on any single set of cultural solutions. The Museum of Man is the world of human cultures, and it is through careful examination of the displays of this museum that the anthropologists and sociologists have derived their significant generalizations. Andrew Allan, the producer, performed as the guide for the radio presentation.

No music was composed for this show, and

sound effects were at a minimum. The narrator gave perspective by placing a sound baffle to one side of the microphone, and moving from one side to the other.

The music cues include "The Tibetan Lament for the Dead" and a Balinese gamelan orchestra, both taken from Ethnic Folkways Library recordings.

There is no general work that deals with the subject precisely as handled here, but the nearest approach is Linton's *The Study of Man*. The point of view is also considerably influenced by Talcott Parsons and by modern sociologists in general. The specific quotations are as follows: the poet (p. 180) is Wordsworth ("The Prelude"); the philosopher is Francis Bacon (*Advancement of Learning*); the lawmaker is Blackstone ("Introduction" to his *Commentaries*). On page 180 we quote from *Hamlet* and from Thomas Carlyle (*Sartor Resartus*). On page 182 we quote from Francis Bacon ("On Death") and on page 183 from Francis Quarles ("Esther"). Rhadamanthus is from Greek mythology. The Shakespearean quotations are from *Richard IV* and *As You Like it*.

INDEX